VICTORIA R.I.

A  BOOK

Also by Elizabeth Longford

JAMESON'S RAID
(writing as Elizabeth Pakenham)
WELLINGTON: THE YEARS OF THE SWORD
WELLINGTON: PILLAR OF STATE

VICTORIA R.I.

illustrated edition

ELIZABETH LONGFORD

Harper & Row, Publishers

New York, Evanston, San Francisco, London

This work is an abridgment of *Queen Victoria: Born to Succeed.*

CONTENTS

Acknowledgements 7

PART ONE

1 Born to Succeed 1815–19 11
2 'I Will be Good' 1819–30 17
3 Royal Progress 1830–34 22
4 'She Must be Coerced' 1835–37 29
5 Little Victory 1837 37
6 The Wonderful Year 1837–38 46
7 Disenchantment 1838–39 57
8 'Mama's Amiable Lady' 1839 62
9 Ladies of the Bedchamber 1839 67
10 'My Beloved Albert' 1839–40 76
11 The Blotting Paper 1840 86
12 'I am Going' 1841–42 92
13 A Safe Haven 1842–46 98
14 'Great Events make me Calm' 1846–48 107
15 The Devil's Son 1848–50 115
16 'Our Happy Home Life' 1846–51 120
17 'Every Age has its Advantages' 1852–54 132
18 The Unsatisfactory War 1854–56 137
19 Dinner à Trois 1855–59 145
20 Last Years of Marriage 1855–60 153
21 'He was My Life' 1861 159

PART TWO

22 Still December 1861–64 171
23 Brown Eminence The 1860s 178
24 Granite and Rock 1865–68 184
25 Head of all the Family 1865–69 197
26 The Royalty Question 1870–74 203
27 The Faery Queen 1874–78 209
28 'I had No Alternative' 1878–80 216
29 Among the Trumpets 1880–83 223
30 The Bitter Cry 1883–84 230
31 Gordon and the Tup-Tupping 1884–85 235
32 Home Rule 1885–86 242
33 The Jubilee Bonnet 1887–91 246
34 'Still Endure' 1892–95 253
35 The Labourer's Task 1892–1900 262
36 'Mother's Come Home' 1900–1901 273

Index 283

ACKNOWLEDGEMENTS

Photographs and illustrations were supplied by or are reproduced by kind permission of the following. The pictures on page 10, 12, 16, 19, 20, 26/1, 30, 32, 34, 38–9, 42–3, 84–5, 94–5, 110, 122, 133, 148–9, 151, 165, 170, 173/1, 173/2, 174, 174–5, 180, 199, 200, 240, 251 are reproduced by gracious permission of H.M. The Queen. Bettmann Archive: Inc., 106; British Museum: 15, 24, 49–1, 63, 72–3, 78, 90, 99, 105, 114, 179, 205, 210, 222, 248; Cambridge Folk Museum: 52; Cheltenham Ladies' College: 270; A. C. Cooper: 161, 219; Courtauld Institute: 271; Edinburgh Museum of Toys: 141; Giraudon: 77, 102; William Gordon Davis: 48/2; Guildhall Library: 270–1; Miss Hillyard: 160, 278–9; *Illustrated London News*: 249; Dorian Leigh Ltd: 202; Lewisham Local History Department: 195/1; J. Charrot Lodwidge: 124; London Museum: 91; Mansell Collection: 31, 54–5, 61, 79, 88, 104, 125, 140, 146, 154, 155, 185, 188–9, 207, 214, 218, 227, 263, 281; Mary Evans Picture Library: 26/2, 255; National Portrait Gallery: 44, 71, 108, 191, 198, 236, 272; H.M. Postmaster General: 48–9; Radio Times Hulton Picture Library: 260; Reuter: 212; Rowena Ross: 124–5, 130/1 and /2; Rugby School: 195/2; The Science Museum: 48/1, 186–7, 189; Victoria and Albert Museum: 175, 128–9, 130/3 and /4; The Wellcome Trustees: 134; John E. Wells: 256; Margaret Willes: 267.

The colour illustrations between pp 65 and 66 are from Dulwich College and the London Museum; between pp 80 and 81 from the Fishmongers Company and by gracious permission of H.M. The Queen; between pp 240 and 241 by gracious permission of H.M. The Queen; and between pp 256 and 257 the British Railways Board and the National Portrait Gallery. The endpaper drawing of The Great Exhibition is from the Victoria and Albert Museum.

PART ONE

I

Born to Succeed

1815–19

The circumstances of Queen Victoria's birth are strangely at variance with the legendary propriety of her long life and reign. A double crisis, in the British Monarchy and in the private fortunes of the man destined to be her father, must be held responsible. But for these two unedifying events, there would have been no Victoria to stamp a great age with the royal cypher. The nineteenth century would still have been great without her. It would not have been 'Victorian', as we understand it.

The man was Prince Edward, Duke of Kent, fourth son of King George III. In 1803 he had been retired from the army on a charge of disciplinary fanaticism amounting to brutality. Since then he had sunk into graver and graver debt, until finally in 1815, at the age of nearly forty-eight, he decided to recoup his fortunes by exiling himself in Brussels and living 'in retirement and *very much reduced*' for four years. His exile would be shared by a dear friend, 'Edward's French lady', the charming Julie, Mademoiselle de St Laurent, later created Comtesse de Montgenet. The details of Julie's origins and of her long and sedate partnership with Edward were to afford endless scope for gossip in the future, but when Prince Edward came home at the end of his four years it was with a different lady at his side.

In February 1816, not long after the Duke of Kent's arrival in Brussels, a young German Prince, Leopold of Saxe–Coburg, landed at Dover as the guest of the Duke's brother, the Prince Regent, and suitor for the hand of his only child, the Princess Charlotte of Wales. Within three months Prince Leopold and Princess Charlotte, a popular and handsome pair, were married. Some eighteen months later a shocked country heard the appalling news that the young Princess Charlotte had died in childbirth, her son still-born.

Before this disaster the young couple had urged the Duke of Kent to seek another solution to his personal problems. As all royal personages knew, there was one certain way of acquiring a substantial income from Parliament. This was to marry. And in the remote castle of Wald–Leiningen there was a suitable bride for the Duke of Kent: Prince Leopold's thirty-year-old widowed sister, Victoria of Saxe–Coburg, Princess of Leiningen. During the autumn of 1816, the Duke paid a flying visit of inspection, discreetly sandwiched between visits to numerous other small German courts. He was clearly taken with the handsome widow and her attractive children, Charles and Feodore. But for the moment both he and the Princess sought only their personal advantage. He needed an income and she

Opposite Queen Victoria painted by Landseer in 1839.

needed a husband, but neither was in a particular hurry, and she was loth to leave the comfortable independence of her widowhood.

Princess Charlotte's death changed all that. The Monarch, George III, had a little longer to live but illness had destroyed his mind. Of his fifteen children, twelve ageing Princes and Princesses still remained. They inspired the nation about as much as the procession of Banquo's descendants inspired Macbeth. All five Princesses were spinsters or childless. The seven Princes could not boast between them a single offspring who was not either a bastard or otherwise debarred from the throne.

Only three of the Princes were validly married. These three were George, the Prince Regent, Frederick, Duke of York (childless) and Ernest, Duke of Cumberland. The dead Princess's father, the Prince Regent, abhorred his wife and would never breed from her again. Ernest, Duke of Cumberland, had allied himself to a twice widowed German Princess who was rumoured to have murdered her previous husbands. He himself, with his horribly scarred face, looked like a murderer. Scandal-mongers said that he had cut his valet's throat as well as being vicious, incestuous, perverted, disgusting, tyrannical, reactionary and un-British. No one regretted the fact that their union, up to the death of Princess Charlotte, had not been blessed. All the same, it deepened the fear that King George III's huge family was heading for extinction.

In this crisis Parliament demanded an appropriate return from the four unmarried Royal Dukes who had for years been receiving steady, if inadequate, incomes from the public coffers. To the altar with them all.

Augustus, Duke of Sussex, let the call go unheeded. Nothing could tear this faithful Hanoverian from the Lady Cecilia Buggin who shared with him everything but a marriage certificate. William, Duke of Clarence, Adolphus, Duke of Cambridge, and Edward, Duke of Kent, were prepared to obey.

Edward's courtship was somewhat impaired by remorse at deserting Julie after so long and by the fear that he might in fact lose both Victoria and Julie at the same time. But in the end Julie behaved better than Edward deserved and removed herself with unobtrusive dignity to Paris. Edward's guilt remained and took the form of anxious letters and entreaties to his friends to visit his deserted mistress. Meanwhile, in the marriage stakes, Adolphus, Duke of Cambridge, had forced the pace. News reached Brussels that his brother, the youngest, had been accepted by Princess Augusta of Hesse-Cassel and would marry her without delay. The Duke of Kent snatched up his pen and on 10 January 1818 asked the Princess Victoria of Leiningen for a 'positive' answer. This time her scruples were overcome. She would hope to find compensation for her 'agreeable and independent' position in the Duke's love.

By the spring of 1818 letters were flying merrily from London in the Duke's neat, legible hand. He wrote in French but with lover-like ardour proposed a 'double plan' to learn each other's language, which would beyond everything increase their 'mutual attachment'. At length came the day of their formal betrothal: 27

13

May 1818. He despatched a little note to his 'Victoire', touchingly reminiscent of one his daughter was to send to her Albert on their wedding morning, twenty-two years later.

He brought his bride to Kew for the English marriage ceremony on 11 July 1818, where his elder brother William was simultaneously united to Princess Adelaide of Saxe-Meiningen. The service was printed with German alongside the English, even down to the operative words, *Ich will*. For Edward's 'double plan' was proceeding very slowly: 'Victoire' had become Victoria but that was about all. Nor was language the Kents' only problem. Edward had made light of his debts before his marriage and felt certain that Parliament would solve his problems. But his extra allowance was only a quarter of what he had confidently expected, so that the newly married couple were forced to pig it in Kensington Palace, until at last Edward gathered up his wife's manifold chattels – hats, mantles, shawls, furniture, lady-in-waiting, maids, dogs and bird-cages – and swept them off to cheaper Germany. The marriage for the succession already showed signs of fulfilling its purpose and the Duchess was pregnant.

The great matrimonial marathon of the four Royal Dukes was singularly meagre in its results. True, 1819 was a bumper year with four royal births. The Clarences and Cambridges led off in March. William, Duke of Clarence, was already the father of ten lusty illegitimate children. Two weakly girls who did not survive infancy followed by still-born twins were his total contribution to the succession. Adolphus, Duke of Cambridge, produced a son, George, in the marathon year and later two daughters. The second pair of 'succession babies' made their appearance in May, both doomed to be only children. The younger was another George, son of the Duke of Cumberland. He became the sad, blind King of Hanover and lost his throne. The Duke of Kent's daughter had arrived three days earlier and again it seemed that many brothers and sisters must follow her to reinforce the succession, for the Duchess was young and the Duke had never suffered from a day's illness. Eight months after presenting Princess Victoria to the nation he died.

It was from this low ebb, both physical and moral, that his daughter rescued the royal line, replenishing not only the nurseries of Windsor but also the thrones of Europe.

The Duke of Kent always intended to leave Germany before the Duchess gave birth. But she was nearing her time before he could borrow enough money to get her to England. Stuffed to the roof with humanity and belongings, their huge shabby coach was driven by the Duke himself to save the expense of a coachman. The 'unbelievably odd caravan', as an eye-witness called it, reached Dover in a gale on St George's Day, 23 April. And on 24 May 1819, the event which the Duke's arrangements had made somewhat precarious took place. The birds' chorus had begun and the scent of lilac and may was drifting up from the shrubberies of Kensington Palace when Princess Victoria gave her first gusty cry at a quarter past four in the morning. Any disappointment that it was not a boy must be forgotten. 'The English like Queens,' announced the baby's Coburg grandmother firmly.

Opposite After the death in November 1817 of Charlotte, Princess of Wales, three of King George III's ageing sons rushed to the altar to try and provide the country with a legitimate heir. This cartoon, published in April 1819, shows the Duke of Clarence (later William IV) and Adelaide of Saxe-Meiningen whose children would all die in infancy; on the right the Cumberlands and in the centre the Duke of Cambridge and Augusta Hesse with their son George; and to the right the Duke of Kent with his Duchess heavily pregnant with the child who would become Queen Victoria.

The new baby took her place in a cheerful family group which settled itself into the south-east wing of Kensington Palace. If her early upbringing was conscientious – she was fed by her own mother and was the first royal baby to be vaccinated against smallpox – it was also Germanic, and it was German, not English, which she first heard spoken. German lullabies hushed her to sleep. German voices broke into subdued raptures over the baby's cradle, voices such as those of the child's twelve-year-old half-sister, Princess Feodore and her governess, Fräulein Lehzen, who was to be the most important influence on Queen Victoria's early life, or the famous midwife, Fräulein Siebold. But Fräulein Siebold did not stay long. After a few weeks she returned to Germany for the confinement of the wife of the baby's maternal uncle, the Duke of Coburg. The child, Prince Albert, was born on 26 August, a date which was to become one of the most precious in Queen Victoria's calendar.

15

2
'I Will be Good'
1819–30

On 24 June 1819, the Cupola Room at Kensington Palace was prepared for the Princess Victoria's christening, a golden font in the centre. Over it hovered the traditional bad fairy. He was Victoria's 'wicked uncle', the Prince Regent. He had been invited to stand as the child's godfather and also to approve of her being christened Georgiana Charlotte Augusta Alexandrina Victoria. Alexander I, Tsar of Russia, had consented to be the other godfather: hence 'Alexandrina'. No answer whatever had been received from the Prince Regent until the evening before the ceremony, when a curt message at last reached the affronted parents,

that the name of Georgiana could not be used, – as He did not chuse to place His name before the Emperor of Russia's, – and He could not allow it to follow.

As for the other names, he would speak to the Duke about them at the christening. And so the Archbishop of Canterbury, baby in arms, stood waiting for the Prince Regent to pronounce the first name.

Determined to give pain, the Prince remained silent. At length he gruffly proposed 'Alexandrina'. Then he stopped. Again the Archbishop waited. One name was enough for the little intruder, thought the Prince Regent, but his brother prompted him with 'Charlotte'. At the mention of Charlotte the Prince Regent fiercely shook his head. They should not use the name of his dead child. Deeply wounded, the Duke nevertheless went on to propose 'Augusta'. No, certainly not. The Prince resented its suggestion of grandeur. What name? What name? 'Let her be called after her mother,' he thundered, glaring at the poor Duchess of Kent, whose elaborate curls and enormous hat shook with tempestuous sobs.

So dramatic a scene was not likely to escape the gossips, and in fact Princess Lieven, wife of the Russian ambassador who stood proxy for the Tsar, passed on one of several variants to the famous diarist, Charles Greville. Everyone agreed, however, that it was the Prince Regent's distinction to have settled on 'Victoria'. He had added rudely that the Tsar's name must always come first. Thus the child born fifth in succession to the throne of England was called for the first nine years of her life by the foreign diminutive 'Drina'. Baptized and vaccinated, baby Drina was now prepared to meet the world, the flesh and the devil.

The financial stringency of the Kents continued. It was only Edward's determination that the English Princess should be brought up in England that prevented another flight to Germany. As it was, Christmas was spent in Devon at the seaside

Opposite Victoria's 'wicked uncle', King George IV. Painting by Sir Thomas Lawrence.

town of Sidmouth which had the advantage of being both cheap and invigorating. Edward arranged that one of the breaks in their long journey should be at Salisbury. He toured the icy Cathedral and caught a bad cold. Having frequently boasted that he would outlive all his brothers, he felt no undue anxiety but settled his family into the small white house called Woolbrook Cottage and stalked outdoors to draw the sea breezes into his congested lungs. There was a moment when his baby daughter's life seemed to be in greater danger than her father's. A boy shooting sparrows in the road sent a shower of pellets against the Princess's windows, breaking the glass and tearing the sleeve of her nightgown. It was Victoria's first but by no means last experience of fire. She stood it as befitted a soldier's daughter, observed the Duke with pride.

Out on the sea-front the air was not doing him the good he expected. His cold grew worse, his breathing more difficult; he was forced to take to his bed. Suddenly it became obvious to all that the burly soldier with dyed brown hair and whiskers was not going to recover. He died of pneumonia on 23 January 1820. Six days later his father, George III, was released from a phantom existence. They were both buried by night in the family vault at Windsor, into which the Duke's enormous coffin, fitfully illuminated by smoky torches, was with difficulty manoeuvred after becoming jammed in the entrance.

How serious was the loss of a father? The Duke's legacy to his family consisted of a mountain of debt. Spendthrift jauntiness was so pronounced a characteristic of the House of Hanover that one is astonished at Queen Victoria's good fortune in inheriting neither this nor any other of her father's besetting sins. When people remarked that she resembled her royal father she would claim with a tightening of the lips to have inherited 'more from my dear Mother'. But she was always keen to hear tales of her unknown father and was to spend much of her life looking for father-figures. The first was her Uncle Leopold who came to the rescue with money after her father's death. Unfortunately the comfort he gave was counteracted by the man who poisoned the Princess's childhood, Sir John Conroy, Comptroller of the Duchess's household. She may well have noticed as she looked at portraits of the Duke of Kent that Sir John Conroy was not unlike His Royal Highness in appearance.

Queen Victoria often spoke of her dull, sad childhood, but there is a sparkle in many of the earlier, fragmentary pictures which have survived. While her 'Uncle King', as she called George IV, was steadily ridding himself of all his better qualities except good taste; while the London mob was howling at somebody's carriage wheels or breaking somebody else's windows; while Roman Catholics were clamouring for emancipation and Protestants for the freeing of African slaves, her earliest childhood passed serenely enough in the old, red brick Palace of Kensington, between Hyde Park and the small market gardens of Fulham.

One senses the determination of the adult in some of her early portraits, even though the very small chin sloped gently away. Her nose already had that slight downward curve which was to be so striking in later years. But she was still a child. Beechey painted her at three years old clinging round her Mama's neck, all curves

and curls, a cupid-bow mouth slightly opened in a smile, hair waving away from a centre parting, dimples everywhere. At seven the blue eyes were larger than ever, there were no curls and her hair was smooth and darker. Her tightly closed mouth was secretive. On her left shoulder she wore a miniature of 'Uncle King', which he had given her to mark one of the happiest days of her childhood.

It was in the summer of 1826. King George IV was living at Royal Lodge, Windsor, with his favourite, Lady Conyngham, her husband, the Lord Steward, and their children. To this strange family party were summoned the Duchess of Kent and her two daughters, Feodore and Victoria. For the first time Drina faced the preposterous, ageing figure of the King – swollen, gouty, bewigged, bedaubed –

as he roared out in coarse affection, 'Give me your little paw.' Out shot the child's hand, very tiny now and destined to become famous for its diminutive size even when it was older and plumper and covered with rings. Lady Conyngham brazenly pinned the King's miniature on Drina's chaste dress; then the little one was hauled on to the royal knee so that she might kiss the rouged cheek. Despite that dreadful kiss, the Princess could appreciate regal grandeur when she saw it: in later years she recalled not only her uncle's dissolute appearance but also his wonderful dignity and charm.

He, too, warmed to his small niece. Next day the King's superb phaeton overtook the Princess and her family out walking. 'Pop her in!' the King shouted, as his magnificent horses were brought to a slithering halt. Between huge 'Uncle King' and Aunt Mary of Gloucester a space was made for Drina and away they dashed – the child exhilarated beyond words by the brilliant liveries and whirlwind speed. Remembering it, she wrote afterwards with characteristic simplicity: 'I was greatly pleased.' She remembered also the terror on Mama's face as she vanished from sight, clutched by her aunt round the waist. Mama is afraid I will fall out, thought little Drina. In reality the Duchess feared the King intended to kidnap her.

Every day there was some new entertainment to please Drina: Tyrolese dancers creating a 'gay uproar' or a party in the conservatory with coloured lights, and music drifting in on the scented air. Princess Drina knew how to please. 'What would you like the band to play next?' asked her uncle. She replied at once in her clear, clipped voice: 'Oh, Uncle King, I should like them to play "God Save the King"!' Having seen the grease-paint cracked by smiles, Drina was quick to repeat her success. 'Tell me what you enjoyed most of your visit?' enquired His Majesty at the end. 'The drive with you,' said Drina, as truthful as she was clever.

This mixture of simplicity and sophistication, mischief and truthfulness runs through her childhood. And truthfulness went as so often with a hot temper. Drina did not care to sail under false colours and made sure that her mentors always knew the worst. At four years old she was already learning her letters off printed cards and finding it tedious to sit still so long. One morning as her tutor was about to begin her reading lesson he asked the Duchess if she had been good. 'Yes, she has been good this morning', the Duchess replied, 'but yesterday there was a little storm.' Drina chipped in. 'Two storms – one at dressing and one at washing.'

When Drina was five she passed out of the hands of her nurse Mrs Brock into those of Fräulein Lehzen. Louise Lehzen, created a German baroness in 1827, was the daughter of a Lutheran pastor in Coburg. Her family were socially unassuming. One of her sisters worked in England as a maid. Louise came in for her full share of the ridicule reserved for everything German. Germans were reputed to scratch their heads with their forks. Later on, malicious gossip fastened upon Princess Victoria's table manners: she picked her bones and did unmentionable things with her asparagus. Lehzen was constantly reminded that her passion for caraway seeds was vulgar.

The German governess had no gift for passing off this treatment lightly. Though she was kind-hearted and later popular with Queen Victoria's maids-of-honour, her talents did not lie in delicate human relations. She was highly strung and sub-

Baroness Lehzen, Victoria's German governess and constant companion in the difficult years of her childhood. Victoria wrote in her journal, 'She is the most affectionate, devoted, attached and *disinterested* friend I have, and I love her most *dearly*.'

ject to headaches, cramps and occasional migraines. Insensitive to the feelings of her mistress's friends as well as of her enemies, Lehzen responded fully to one thing only: the supposed needs of Victoria. Victoria for her part held her governess in awe but she adored her.

Lehzen's rule was strict but it was not all iron. It was she who laid the foundations in the Princess of a real interest in history. And it was due to her versatility that Princess Victoria acquired her famous collection of dolls. She and Lehzen dressed one hundred and thirty-two tiny wooden puppets, copying them from stars of the opera or Court. This silken, feathered, tinselled family with their high-flown names and empty wooden faces turned out to be a substitute for the brothers and sisters the Princess lacked. After her beloved half-sister Feodore's departure to be married, her childhood friends were grown-up people or dolls.

Education did little to fill the gap in Princess Victoria's life. She disliked learning and suffered from too few of what she called 'holly days'. In another sense there was too much holly, for a sprig was often pinned to the front of her dress to keep her chin up. Languages and music, especially singing and dancing, were her best subjects. Her gift for both was encouraged by her intense love of the opera and ballet. Under this stimulus Italian was added to her existing accomplishments in French and German. And it was through the opera, rather than formal education, that she saw into the world of art and poetry. In religion she was taught to avoid bigotry and to revere tolerance, as befitted the probable sovereign of many races holding different creeds. She inherited a simple piety from her Lutheran mother and governess which rarely failed her.

On 11 March 1830, after her teacher Mr Davys had gone home, Princess Victoria opened *Howlett's Tables* of the Kings and Queens of England, to begin her history lesson with Lehzen. She found to her surprise that an extra page had been slipped into the book. 'I never saw that before,' she exclaimed. 'No, Princess,' said Lehzen. 'It was not thought necessary that you should.' Victoria studied the genealogical table. So many possible heirs to the throne but each one with the date of death written after the name, until she came to the names of her two uncles, George and William, and then her own. She drew the deduction. 'I am nearer to the throne than I thought.' Then she burst into tears. After the 'little storm' had subsided, she pointed out to her dear Lehzen that whereas many children might boast of the splendour they would not realize the difficulties. Lifting up the forefinger of her right hand she spoke the famous words: 'I will be good.'

Some people have thought that Princess Victoria realized her destiny long before she was eleven. Walter Scott, having met her during the celebrations for her ninth birthday, came to the conclusion that though no servant was permitted to whisper in her ear, 'a little bird' had carried the truth into her heart. He was mistaken. The Princess knew no more than that her rank was high until the disclosure of March 1830. It was a traumatic turning-point in her life. She rightly guessed that the tensions at Kensington were about to increase. Her first storm of tears, often repeated when she thought of the future, testified to the shock.

3
Royal Progress
1830–34

By the spring of 1830 the exacting pleasures and pains of King George IV's life were drawing to a close. For Kensington Palace this meant unqualified relief and a burst of diplomatic activity. King George would be succeeded by his brother William whose health was uncertain. If King William died before Princess Victoria reached her majority at the age of eighteen, a Regency would be necessary. Both Prince Leopold of Coburg and Sir John Conroy had no doubt that the Duchess of Kent must be Regent.

How could Parliament be persuaded to choose her? Surely by proving that Princess Victoria's education under the Kensington system was not only in advance of girls of her age but also perfectly suited to her exalted destiny. With this in view, the Duchess described her system to the Bishops of London and Lincoln on 1 March 1830. She expressed herself aware that to give a child of Victoria's sex a liberal education invited criticism. The Duchess of Northumberland (Victoria's official governess), therefore, was present in the room during *all* lessons, and she herself during most. Deportment and dancing were taught by mistresses for reasons of delicacy. There was to be a clear distinction between the morals of Kensington and the morals of the Court.

When King George IV died on 26 June 1830 and Parliament debated the Regency Bill, the Duchess and Conroy reaped their reward. Notwithstanding scraps with both political parties – the Tory Duke of Wellington refused to have her created Dowager Princess of Wales and the Liberal Lord Grey called her 'a tiresome devil' – Parliament duly appointed her Regent in case of need, with an additional £10,000 a year at once for the Princess's education.

With this advance in status the Duchess's relations with the world should have improved. Thanks to Conroy, they did not do so. Unfortunately the one person who might have guided her prudently, Leopold of Saxe-Coburg, had recently become inaccessible.

For many years Princess Victoria's handsome Uncle Leopold had visited Kensington every Wednesday afternoon. He had become a hypochondriac under the strain of his grief, but none of his eccentricities – wig, 3-inch soles, feather boa – damaged his excellent judgement. He had made a study of statecraft in a spirit at once serious and faintly cynical which gave his advice a rare detachment. His advice to the Duchess, however, was defective in one respect. He himself had fallen out with the Royal Family after Princess Charlotte's death and so he took no immediate steps to improve their relations with his sister. By the time Princess Victoria was ten, his affair with an actress, Caroline Bauer, reached its zenith, alienating him from Kensington. In addition, he was tortured by the problem of whether to accept the throne of Greece. One of his weaknesses was an inability to make up his mind – he was known as *Monsieur Peu-à-Peu* – a failing which was not transmitted to his niece. When George IV was seen to be dying, Prince Leopold declined the Greek crown in order, it was said, to become Regent of England, through his sister. To Conroy's relief, this scheme also was rapidly superseded. After the European revolutions of July 1830, the Belgian people broke away from Holland and invited Leopold to become their first king. England did not see him again for over four years and Sir John Conroy stepped into his shoes as the Duchess of Kent's first counsellor.

The Comptroller of the Duchess of Kent's household, Sir John Conroy, was two months her senior. He was a man of extravagant ambitions, an intriguer, a vulgarian and a scamp. He had brains, and, like most villains, was not as black as he was painted. In his own fashion he was attached to those whom he disastrously misled and whose finances passed through his hands like water. Though he had a familiar manner with women highly unsuitable in one determined to weave his way among royal entanglements, he was not a Don Juan. In one respect a closer parallel would be with Sir John Falstaff, namely in Conroy's final rejection, with its authentic touch of outrageous pathos. As he lay dying, he fixed his gaze on William Fowler's portrait of little Drina, aged five, opposite his bed. If his daughter-in-law, Mrs Henry Conroy, is to be believed, he then sank back with a happy smile as if to say, 'Ah! there – I did my duty.'

Fowler painted Conroy himself in 1827 and admirably caught his subject's personality. The lips are curled, but not in a smile, and he wears a military uniform to which King William IV constantly said he was not entitled. Despite the thinning hair and strangely cleft chin, there is a *panache* about the whole which must have had its effect. Conroy, though overbearing, possessed a swashbuckling charm which won many admirers.

A career in the Army was young Conroy's first choice but having reached the rank of captain he abandoned it for the Duchess of Kent's service. Soon he saw a way of satisfying his greed and desire for power. By stoking up her fears of her English relations until they became obsessional, he hoped to create a complete rift between Kensington and the Court which would deliver the future Sovereign into his hands. The bogy was already there in Princess Victoria's Uncle Ernest, the Duke of Cumberland.

As we have seen, people would believe almost anything of the Duke of Cumberland. Conroy fed the trembling Duchess with every ugly rumour: that Cumberland was hatching a devilish plot to remove the only life which stood between himself and the throne; that he would weaken the little Princess's health with small doses of poison introduced by a bribed servant into her bread-and-milk, so that the public would become used to the idea of her being a sickly child; that at the critical moment Cumberland would get the King to have her kidnapped; that she would survive at Court for a few weeks in a decline, and then, to no one's surprise, perish.

Sir John Conroy, the Comptroller of the Duchess of Kent's household and the villain who poisoned Victoria's relations not only with the Court at Buckingham Palace but also with her mother at Kensington.

The 'Cumberland plot' culminated in a scandal which still lives while the rest is forgotten. Soon after Cumberland returned from Germany to England in 1829 a whisper began to circulate that the Duchess of Kent was too fond of her Comptroller. Who started it? Cumberland, came the pat answer from the Conroy circle; Cumberland started it in order to make the King remove Princess Victoria from the care of her 'immoral' mother. The plot, they said, was thwarted only by the intervention of the Duke of Wellington, followed by the King's death.

It is now generally believed that the 'Cumberland plot' was a myth, and later Queen Victoria was to reject fiercely every aspersion on her Uncle Ernest. Conroy, however, may have genuinely believed some of the rumours with which he terrified the Duchess. Others besides his dupes believed them. Baroness Lehzen recognized a need to guard Victoria every hour of the day and night. Though Lehzen did not sleep with her charge in the same room – this duty was performed by the Duchess – she sat in the Princess's bedroom each evening until the Duchess came to bed, to the detriment of her own health. Queen Adelaide also advised the Duchess never to leave her daughter. As for the Duchess of Kent, her credulity was painfully obvious. She did not allow Victoria to sleep alone until her daughter, having become Queen, insisted. She did not allow Victoria to walk downstairs without someone holding her hand, until that hand had been kissed in homage by her Ministers. The backstairs connecting the two floors of the Kents' apartments were narrow, dark and winding, with an oval skylight far above. Perhaps it is significant that Amy Robsart, whom legend disposed of by breaking her neck in a fall downstairs, occupied an important place among Princess Victoria's dolls.

The exploitation of this situation benefited no one but Sir John Conroy at the time; in the end it damaged him disastrously. Because it was he who cut off Princess Victoria from her 'Uncle King', who caused her life to be dull and over-protected and who made rude remarks about her royal relations, she began to hate him. He went out of his way to humiliate her, teasing her for looking like 'Silly Billy', the Duke of Gloucester, rather than her 'Uncle King' as Victoria herself fancied, and ridiculing her for saving up her pocket money in a manner unworthy of a princess. Did she also notice as a child that Conroy flirted with Mama and Aunt Sophia? The inference from her later comments on Conroy's 'behaviour' during this period is that she did. It would be surprising if one whose observation was as keen as her memory was retentive, missed anything of Conroy's technique for obtaining the mastery of Kensington.

The death of King George IV brought an end to the Cumberland bogy but not to the breach with Princess Victoria's royal relations. New divisions quickly developed to make her childhood more than ever restricted and sad. Attempts by William IV to encourage better relations between Windsor and Kensington were foiled by her mother on the grounds that Victoria, though she should remain on friendly terms with their Majesties, should have no association with the King's illegitimate children – the *bâtards* as they were called in the smart world. An even sterner rebuff occurred over the King's coronation. Seizing upon the question of precedence – always a fertile source of trouble – the Duchess and Conroy stopped the Princess from attending because she had been incorrectly assigned a place in the procession behind the Royal Dukes, instead of immediately after the King. The Princess watched the royal procession from Marlborough House in tears.

Conroy's ruthless campaign to isolate the Duchess of Kent and her daughter was felt in the Household at Kensington too. Baroness Späth, the Duchess's lady-in-waiting, was banished to Princess Feodore's Household in Germany. Both she and Lehzen had resented Conroy's airs, assumed after his elevation to the Hanoverian Guelphic order of Knighthood; he insisted on Lady Conroy taking precedence over the German baronesses and when Späth tried to put his daughter Victoire in her place, the axe fell. It was rumoured that Späth had remonstrated with the Duchess about 'familiarities' with Conroy, witnessed by Princess Victoria. Conroy also tried to get rid of Lehzen, but here he failed. That intelligent woman played her cards too well, allying herself firmly with the Court.

Victoria loved Baroness Späth; she doted on Baroness Lehzen. In this attempt to separate her from Lehzen is to be found a clue to the dramatic events which were to disturb the early years of her reign. The 'Bedchamber Plot' and the Flora Hastings scandal of 1839 were direct results of struggles which preceded them. Similarly, the strength and weakness of character which Queen Victoria was to show had taken shape during the hard years when she was manipulated by rival factions like one of her own puppets.

In 1832, when Princess Victoria was thirteen, her mother's Comptroller instituted a series of annual, semi-royal tours during which she was formally presented to the nation. Such publicity directed on a child could scarcely be justified and certainly not without the consent of the reigning Monarch. The Duchess's impresario, on the contrary, went out of his way to foster the idea of rival royalty. At Eaton Hall a jewelled crown held the bread at breakfast, and at Torquay a procession of girls carrying a crown in their midst met the Princess. Conroy exploited the emotions aroused by the year of the great Reform Bill. Citizens were encouraged to present loyal addresses containing references to the Duchess's support for the 'free people' of England – a tribute to the fact that Victoria's entourage was predominantly Whig, while William IV's was Tory. In theory Princess Victoria was being brought up non-party: she slept impartially at great Whig houses like Chatsworth, Woburn and Plas Newydd or Tory strongholds like Belvoir and Euston; but there was no doubt that the sympathies of Kensington lay on the opposite side to the King.

Victoria's half-brother and half-sister Charles and Feodore of Leningen, the children of her mother's first marriage. Charles and Feodore both made their adult homes in Germany and Victoria's relationship with Charles was affectionate but distant. Her devotion to Feodore never cooled.

Queen Victoria was indebted to these 'Royal Progresses', as the King sarcastically called them, for two things of inestimable value: her knowledge of the country and her talent as a diarist. A small notebook with mottled covers and leather back was presented to her. In an unformed, round hand she wrote:

This book, Mama gave me, that I might write the Journal of my journey to Wales in it. Victoria, Kensington Palace, July 31st.

The Journal, though often a burden, became a habit and a duty and gives us perhaps the most intimate view of the girl who was to become a great Queen. It has survived in the Windsor Archives, though some years have survived more than others, so to speak. For the years 1832–37 there exist all her original Journals in her own handwriting. For the years 1837–40 there exist all her original Journals but in typescript. From then until the end of her life the Journals have been copied out in an expurgated version by Princess Beatrice, who destroyed the originals on her mother's instructions.

The Princess's entry into her teens marked the beginning of a general tightening of the reins. Her tutor filled the whole morning with lessons, including more history and some natural philosophy. Her Governess, the Duchess of Northumberland, stated positively that her courses of reading went far beyond the Lucys and Harriets of her own age. The list gradually expanded to include Pope, Gray, Cowper, Goldsmith, 'parts of' Virgil in Latin and all Scott's poems. The last was the only item she really enjoyed.

She praised simplicity in all the arts, affecting to despise exaggeration of style or feeling. An actress who raged was described as '*outré*' – a sinister word in Princess Victoria's vocabulary. She sketched industriously, but only subjects of innocent charm: ships and trees, animals and ballet dancers, peasants, babies and cousins.

Humble life drew her increasingly. At Claremont she designated an encampment of gypsies 'the chief ornament of the Portsmouth Road'. She sent them blankets and soup, longing to have their children instructed. The contrast between their affection for one another and her own domestic strife shocked her, especially when her charitable efforts were met with frigid scepticism at home.

Washington Irving's book, *The Conquest of Granada*, set her wandering in imagination through the mysterious Orient – 'But these are all Phantom Castles', she added sadly, 'which I love to form!' The magnetism of the East continued to draw her whether she read about the Moors or admired the olive complexions of Indian and Persian visitors to Kensington Palace. The same spell was at work when she succumbed years later to the shining ringlets of Disraeli and the turbans of her Indian servants.

Princess Victoria's romantic susceptibilities seem to make nonsense of her own claim to abhor the *outré* and admire only simplicity. Her baroque tastes are also incompatible with the theory of some of her biographers that her nature was crystal clear, uncompromisingly sensible and utterly lacking in imagination. She is frequently denied the gift of introspection, though her Journals, after the age of sixteen, are by no means devoid of self-analysis. Victoria's character was in fact neither simple nor crystalline. Indeed, part of her fascination lies in her contradictions and inconsistencies – one way in which a rich nature presents itself to the spectator.

At the beginning of February 1832 the Duchess of Kent appointed additional ladies to her Household, among them Lady Flora Hastings, in order that Princess Victoria might be able to choose new friends from a wide but approved circle. There were other additions to Victoria's social life more congenial than the chance to have Lady Flora as a friend. She was brought downstairs by Lehzen, hand in hand, to meet increasing numbers of distinguished people, and knew by sight, when she came to the throne, such intimidating characters as Princess Lieven and Sir Robert Peel or that paragon, Lord Palmerston, 'so very agreeable, clever, amusing and gentlemanlike'.

Almost anything arranged by their Majesties delighted the Princess as much as it annoyed her mother. The King gave a juvenile ball at St James's Palace on her fourteenth birthday. The whole day was a touching mixture of childhood and adolescence. At one end of the scale Uncle Leopold sent her a serious letter recommending self-examination and a soul above trifles; at the other, she had a reunion with her old nurse, Mrs Brock. She opened the ball with her first cousin, George Cambridge, whom the King intended her eventually to marry, and rounded it off by 'one more quadrille with Lord Emlyn'. Madame Boudin, the Princess's dancing mistress, was present to see that no mistakes were made. 'I was *VERY* much amused.'

Even more amusing for the lonely girl were relations' visits to England. Her cousins Ernest and Alexander Württemberg came over in 1833 for the London season. Like Miranda in *The Tempest*, she drank in their astonishing masculinity and found them perfection – until another, more wonderful pair arrived three years later, Ferdinand and Augustus, and four months after them a pair more marvellous still, Albert and Ernest.

There was a moment when even Sir John Conroy redeemed himself in Victoria's eyes. He presented her mother on 14 January 1833 with a King Charles's spaniel called Dash. Three months later Princess Victoria had adopted '*DEAR SWEET LITTLE DASH*' and was dressing him up in scarlet jacket and blue trousers. She gave him for Christmas three india-rubber balls and two bits of gingerbread decorated with holly and candles. Dash showed his devotion by jumping into the sea and swimming after her yacht; when she was ill he spent 'his little life' in her room.

Animals became the Princess's companions after her dolls were put away. There was Mama's new parakeet which laughed and coughed, and the old canary, so tame that it came out of its cage to peck Dashy's fur. When her throat was too sore to go sightseeing on the Isle of Wight she found the strength to come down to the pier and see 'the dear horses' land.

The Duchess of Kent was not entirely satisfied with Victoria's development. On New Year's Eve 1834 she warned her that simplicity of character was all very well, but she should not overdo it or underestimate her station. Conroy cherished grandiose plans for 1835. It was a year which Queen Victoria was not to forget.

4
'She Must be Coerced'
1835–37

Princess Victoria's gift for predicting her future was never more apparent than on her sixteenth birthday. '...I feel that the 2 years to come till I attain my 18th,' she wrote on 24 May 1835, 'are the most important of any almost...' A wave of energy had swept over her at the beginning of this year. 'I *love* to be *employed*; I *hate* to be *idle*.' It was just as well, for during the following two years her battle against Conroy and the Kensington system was fought out.

The Princess's confirmation took place on 30 July 1835, at the Chapel Royal, St James's, and was attended by members of the Royal Family. The day opened with a homily from the Duchess of Kent: Victoria should behave with 'friendliness' to those around and always 'confide in me'. Friendliness to Conroy was too much to ask of the resolute young Princess, looking so deceptively meek in her white lace dress and rose-trimmed bonnet. Nevertheless she entered the Chapel with 'a firm determination' to become a true Christian. Immediately a shocking dispute broke out. The King counted her mother's retinue, found it too large and ordered her Comptroller out of the Chapel. For the poor Duchess, this was Victoria's christening all over again. For Victoria, it was a horror of embarrassment in no way alleviated by the Archbishop of Canterbury's formidable sermon. Misery, religious awe and July heat overwhelmed her. She returned to Kensington and cried bitterly. Her Journal, which the Duchess always read, recorded simply: 'I was very much affected indeed when we came home.'

September was passed in a grand tour of the North. Victoria implored her mother to cancel it. She *knew* it would make her ill and these 'Royal Progresses' only upset the King. But to no avail. After a week the Princess was wilting. She felt too sick to eat but, as on all other similar occasions during her childhood, her rigorous time-table remained unaltered. At last the ordeal was over.

Here is an end to our journey, I am happy to say. Though I liked some of the places very well, I was much tired by the long journeys & the great crowds we had to encounter. We cannot travel like other people, quietly & pleasantly, but we go through towns & crowds & when one arrives at any nobleman's seat, one must instantly dress for dinner & consequently I could never rest properly.

At the end of September the Kents moved to Ramsgate where they were joined by Princess Victoria's uncle, the King of the Belgians, and her new Aunt Louise, his wife, whom she was meeting for the first time. Victoria fell madly in love with both of them.

Princess Victoria aged
sixteen with her
spaniel, Dash.

She had not seen Uncle Leopold for four years. Of course there had been letters;
King Leopold would not ignore a niece who had written to him when she was nine:
'I am very angry with you, Uncle, for you have never written to me once since you
went, and that is a long while.' So many letters had passed between them – 'My
Dearest Uncle', 'My Dearest Love' – but a letter however full of wise advice was
not the same as meeting. 'What happiness was it for me,' she wrote on 29 September
1835, 'to throw myself in the arms of that *dearest* of Uncles, who has always been
to me like a father…'

Ten months before, Princess Victoria had sent her uncle 'a very clever sharp
little letter', as he called it, asking what a Queen *ought to be* – he had already used

the example of Queen Anne to show her what a Queen ought *not* to be. Now he would be able to answer this and many other questions. Leopold's Queen was a great success too. Aunt Louise, the favourite child of Louis Philippe, King of the French, quickly adopted her lonely niece and putting her arm through Victoria's told her to treat her as an elder sister. The sisterly bond was sealed by a raid on Aunt Louise's wardrobe. Chattering and laughing, Victoria tried on her aunt's Parisian clothes: brown silk, white moiré and a rose for the hair.

Two days before the beloved visitors were due to depart, Princess Victoria woke up feeling sick. Next morning she was no better, although Aunt Louise loaded her with presents – ribbons, bonnets, a *pélérine* and a fan. It turned out to be a severe attack of typhoid. Towards the middle of November she felt strong enough to draw herself in the mirror. Pinched cheeks, sharp chin – what a sad spectacle. The face in the mirror looked extraordinarily young but it had the anxious eyes of an old woman. After nearly five weeks of imprisonment she went downstairs. Lehzen had to rub her ice-cold feet at least once a day. She was still rubbing them in January. It was not till February that lessons were once more in full swing.

King Leopold of the Belgians, Victoria's uncle and first political mentor.

31

Sir John Conroy had not missed his opportunity to strike. He decided to confront the Princess, while still on her sick bed, with a fateful decision. Those large blue eyes staring out of the sunken face must be forced to look into the future. She would soon be Queen. She would need a private secretary. Who better equipped to fill this post than her mother's majordomo? Backed up by the deluded Duchess, Conroy applied every conceivable pressure to obtain a pledge in his favour, finally thrusting paper and pencil before the helpless invalid and commanding her to sign.

There was a fearful duel. Conroy had not banked on Princess Victoria's stubborn will. Backed up by her faithful Lehzen who never left her side, though lashed by Conroy's fury, she utterly refused to sign under duress. 'I resisted in spite of my illness,' she proudly told Lord Melbourne three years later. 'What a blessing!' exclaimed her doting Prime Minister.

This insight into Conroy's methods turned dislike into hate. Now it was that the iron entered her soul. If Sir John could not defeat her, worn down as she was by the tour and the ravages of typhoid, what chance had Ministers like Sir Robert Peel and Gladstone? Victoria was trained in a hard school. A sprig of holly had taught her to keep her chin up. At sixteen she knew how to say 'No'.

Self-portrait of Princess Victoria after having typhoid, 1835.

The year 1836 began well. It was delightful to return to Kensington Palace, to go for drives or to explore the spacious new suite which her mother's physician, Dr Clark, had insisted upon for the sake of Victoria's enfeebled health. Even more delightful was a fresh round of visits from her German cousins. Ferdinand and Augustus arrived in March, the former on his way to marry the young Queen of Portugal. Victoria found them very convenient as partners in the waltz and gallop, which etiquette forbade her to perform except with royalty. Then suddenly they were gone. 'No one can replace them', she wrote on 2 April. Six weeks later they had been replaced.

It was not without difficulty that King Leopold got his second pair of Coburg nephews to the shores of England. Ernest and Albert, sons of the Duchess of Kent's eldest brother, Duke Ernest of Saxe-Coburg-Gotha, were far from welcome at Court. Prince Ernest, nearly eighteen, mattered less, since he would succeed his father as Duke and settle in Coburg. But his brother Albert, seventeen on 26 August, three months after Victoria, was being groomed for her consort. Ever since Albert's birth, Victoria's Coburg relations, led by Prince Leopold, had come to the conclusion that a marriage between Victoria and Albert must be their aim. Albert would be another Leopold to Victoria's Charlotte, and the first ill-starred union of the Houses of Hanover and Coburg would be brilliantly resurrected in the next generation. The Duchess of Kent sent a personal invitation to her nephews on the occasion of Princess Victoria's seventeenth birthday.

King William, who had other ideas for his niece, was furious. First he tried forbidding the Saxe-Coburg family to land, a threat which drove his rival match-maker, King Leopold, into paroxysms of sarcasm. 'Now that slavery is abolished in the British Colonies,' he wrote to Victoria, 'I do not comprehend *why your lot alone should be to be kept a white little slavey in England*, for the pleasure of the Court...' William's high-handed action having finally been stopped by the Prime

Minister, he concentrated on catching his niece's fancy with rival suitors. His choice was singularly inept. Young Prince George of Cambridge did not interest Victoria at all; among her cousins she preferred blind Prince George of Cumberland, a match which Wellington is said to have favoured. The Duke of Brunswick, a Byronic desperado, might have stood a chance, but not Prince Alexander of Orange, the King's first choice. This youth was the second son of the Prince of Orange, who, strangely enough, had been rejected by Princess Charlotte. Victoria found him 'lumbering'.

The Coburg cousins arrived on an early afternoon in May 1836. That evening Princess Victoria's Journal gave Albert pride of place. Albert was as tall as Ernest but broader and extremely handsome. Like herself, Prince Albert had large blue eyes and hair 'about the same colour as mine' – a light brown. Ernest was altogether dark. Both were delightfully accomplished: they played well on the piano and appreciated prints, sitting on either side of her on the sofa; they drew well, 'particularly Albert'. They were both naturally clever, 'particularly Albert, who is the most reflective of the two'. Speaking with all the maturity of her sex, she praised both cousins for being so serious and yet 'so *very very* merry and gay and happy, like young people ought to be', but it was Albert who kept the breakfast table in a roar with his witty remarks and played so funnily with Dash.

The visit was not all roses. Princess Victoria knew that the King was in a rage, and strife with His Majesty always pained her. Prince Albert suffered tortures of sleepiness and for a time completely collapsed. Late hours were hitherto unknown to him and his little cousin's resolute attitude towards pleasure appalled him. He became unwell on the eve of her birthday and went to bed early. On the great day he was still very poorly. He took the floor at St James's Palace, turned pale as ashes, almost fainted and went straight home. Fortunately all was bliss during the last week and when, on 10 June, these dearest cousins departed, all was wretchedness. Victoria knew what was expected of her and particularly praised Albert to King Leopold. 'He possesses every quality that could be desired to make me perfectly happy.' Then, remembering his early beds and untouched breakfasts, she added: 'I have only now to beg you, my dearest Uncle, to take care of the health of one, now so *dear* to me...'

Once the cousins had departed it was not long before another round of hostilities between the Court and Kensington started. The Duchess of Kent began it by declining to attend Queen Adelaide's birthday. A few days later came the King's birthday, on 21 August, which could not be ignored. The King's temper had been rising for days and it seemed to many that there was bound to be trouble. Sure enough the King publicly insulted his sister-in-law at his birthday dinner in front of a hundred guests. The Duchess sat on his right, Princess Victoria opposite. King William rose to respond to the toast and at the end of a rambling speech suddenly pointed his finger at his terrified niece. He hoped that the royal authority would pass to 'that Young Lady' and not to 'the person now near me, who is surrounded by evil advisers' – a solution which he himself meant to promote by living another nine months until Princess Victoria came of age.

The Kensington 'system' had by now developed into something much wider than Princess Victoria's education. Her half-brother, Charles Leiningen, an admirer and supporter of Conroy, summed it up years later for the Prince Consort. There were three main aims – to win popularity for Victoria by cutting her off from the Court's morals and politics, to ensure a Regency for the Duchess and to secure the position of private secretary to the young queen for Conroy. Sir John had gambled everything on King William dying before Princess Victoria's eighteenth birthday. If the King survived he would throw in the sponge, consoling himself with the thought that Parliament would surely banish Lehzen, 'in disgrace and shame'. Leiningen strongly opposed this pusillanimity. In April he met King Leopold and urged him to intervene. Let him persuade his niece voluntarily to ask for a Regency, even if the King survived. Sir John, explained Leiningen, was indispensable; Victoria would be 'a young lady of 18' incapable of ruling England by herself.

King William IV soon quarrelled with the Duchess of Kent as heatedly as George IV had done and strongly resented the influence of her Saxe-Coburg relations on young Victoria. Painting by Sir Martin Archer-Shee, 1833.

34

It was King William, however, in no hurry to die, who was to force the pace. On 19 May he sent Princess Victoria a letter offering her three things: £10,000 a year of her own entirely free from her mother's control; an independent Privy Purse under Sir Benjamin Stephenson; and the right to appoint her own ladies. Each item was a blow in Sir John's vitals and he frantically set to work to thwart the King. For the moment he was successful. Princess Victoria was forced to sign a reply to the King, gratefully accepting the £10,000 but pleading her youth and inexperience as a reason for remaining 'in every respect as I am now'. The King, sure that Victoria had not written the letter, was enraged and refused to be soothed by a series of calming notes from Lord Melbourne, who was terrified lest the Tories should make capital out of Conroy's collision with the King.

Ironically, it was at this peak of Conroy's power that Princess Victoria at last celebrated her eighteenth birthday. Her formula for a happy day – 'I was *very much amused*' – was conspicuously absent from her Journal on 24 May 1837. It opened sombrely: 'Today is my 18th birthday! How old! and yet how far am I from being what I should be.'

During the few weeks that remained before the old King's death each side sought desperately for allies. First Baron Stockmar and then Lord Liverpool, a much-respected Tory and family friend, arrived at Kensington. Both were supporters of the Kensington 'system', but were somewhat out of touch with the way the situation had developed. Conroy saw them and emphasized the Princess's youth and frivolity to bolster his claim that she must have a private secretary. He even cast doubts on her mental stability. But Victoria herself was far more effective. Nothing would induce her to have Sir John Conroy as her private secretary or even Keeper of the Privy Purse. Did they not know what sort of man he was? It was out of the question. Both Stockmar and Lord Liverpool were convinced.

After her interview with Lord Liverpool, Princess Victoria remained for the next few days in her room, seeing no one but Lehzen, taking her meals alone. Conroy consulted one more friend, Mr Speaker Abercromby, who declared that, if Princess Victoria would not listen to reason, '*she must be coerced*'. Charles Leiningen, however, speaking hurriedly in German so that Sir John should not understand, begged his mother not to lock her up. Sir John afterwards confided to Leiningen that he abandoned coercion only because 'he did not credit the Duchess of Kent with enough strength for such a step'.

The news from Windsor was critical. The King was dying. Almost suffocated with asthma, he whispered on Waterloo Day his last earthly desire. 'This is the 18th of June; I should like to live to see the sun of Waterloo set.' The Duke of Wellington sent to his bedside the tricolour flag. 'Right, right...' he murmured to Lord Munster; 'Unfurl it and let me feel it... Glorious day...' At twelve minutes past two on the morning of 20 June his own sun set.

Archbishop Howley, accompanied by the Lord Chamberlain, Lord Conyngham, and the King's physician travelled straight from the royal deathbed to Kensington Palace, where the young Queen lay asleep in her mother's bedroom. Excited by the hour and the circumstances, they galloped the whole way, only to find the lodge gates shut and the porter snoring. It was about five o'clock. At last they were

At six o'clock in the morning of 20 June 1837 Victoria's mother 'awoke the dear Child with a kiss' and led her downstairs to be greeted by the Archbishop of Canterbury and the Lord Chamberlain for the first time as Queen of England.

admitted and their carriage rolled on up the drive to the Clock Court and the Palace door. Again there was delay. The Duchess would not admit Lord Conyngham to Princess Victoria's presence, saying that she was still asleep. It was only when he demanded to see 'the Queen' that at six o'clock she 'awoke the dear Child with a kiss' and led her through the anteroom to the King's Backstairs.

Together they descended the awkward flight hand in hand for the last time, the Duchess carrying a silver candlestick and Lehzen hastening behind with a bottle of smelling salts. A cotton dressing-gown covered Victoria's nightdress and her long, light hair streamed down her back. At the door of her sitting-room she parted from her mother and Lehzen, entering the apartment, as she noted in her Journal, '*alone*'. She saw her visitors fall on their knees; she heard Lord Conyngham's first explanatory phrases. When he reached the word 'Queen', she shot out her hand for him to kiss even more swiftly than she had given 'Uncle King' her 'little paw'. It was not merely the efficient performance of a well-rehearsed act. Victoria would have stretched out both hands if etiquette had allowed. After so much travail she was grasping the glorious future.

5
Little Victory

1837

Still in her dressing-gown and slippers, Queen Victoria laid her head on her mother's shoulder and wept briefly for the old King to whom she had been unable to say good-bye. 'I then went to my room and dressed.' In putting on her plain black dress that morning she marked the beginning of a new life as surely as a nun in the ceremony of Clothing.

'I am very young,' continued the entry in Queen Victoria's Journal, 'and perhaps in many, though not in all things, inexperienced, but I am sure, that very few have more real good will and more real desire to do what is fit and right than I have.' Her modest confidence was justified. All her life she was buoyed up not only by a sense of duty but also by the knowledge that she possessed it. As for her inexperience, it existed in regard to the joys of life rather than its trials.

The qualities which introspection had revealed to Queen Victoria about herself were still hidden from the public. What was she like? How would she behave? Nobody knew. Those who guessed, guessed wrong. From an invalid couch the poetess Elizabeth Barrett prettily misinterpreted the young Queen's first tears:

> *The Maiden wept;*
> *She wept to wear a crown!*

Another writer, Thomas Carlyle, was 'heartily sorry for the poor bairn' when he saw her driving in the Park. Though a 'sonsy lassie', her comeliness could not disguise her timidity. 'Little Victory' he called her, with gentle irony. William IV had gone out, in Disraeli's words, 'like an old lion'; they expected Victoria to come in like a lamb.

Within a few hours of the poor bairn's accession, a large gathering of Ministers formed a different opinion of their young Sovereign.

Queen Victoria had already seen Stockmar once and Melbourne twice and written three letters when she came downstairs into the Red Saloon at Kensington Palace for her first Council. The Council met at eleven. Notwithstanding the short notice, there was a record attendance of Privy Counsellors, all eager to see the unknown Queen. The hopes of a new reign were enhanced by the shortcomings of previous ones, for the throne of England had been successively occupied, in the words of Sir Sidney Lee, by 'an imbecile, a profligate and a buffoon'. It was hardly possible to visualize a greater change.

There was a momentary hush as the doors flew open and a small black figure

entered, in her own words, 'quite alone'. The Royal Dukes, Cumberland and Sussex, came forward to meet her and lead her to her throne, the bizarre trio resembling, it was said, Beauty and the Beasts or Bel and the Dragons. The Queen read her Declaration in the celebrated silver voice whose extreme clarity and precision always concealed any nervousness she might be feeling. Then came the swearing-in. Blushing up to the eyes, she received the humble obeisances of her uncles; she approached the Duke of Sussex instead of waiting for him to approach her, a kindness towards the infirm which she was to repeat with effect at her Coronation. Charles Greville, Clerk of the Council, described her as bewildered by the multitude who had to be sworn, but after the first blush not a sign of emotion

Wilkie's painting of Queen Victoria's first Privy Council where her dignity and composure created such a favourable impression. The Duke of Wellington declared he could not have desired her to perform her part better if she had been his own daughter.

clouded her bright smooth face. Occasionally she glanced enquiringly at Lord Melbourne for instructions, but when he and other great personages – Peel, Palmerston and Wellington, all of whom she knew – kissed her hand, not a word or a smile escaped her. All agreed that the royal hand was 'remarkably sweet and soft'.

After she had retired, the Red Saloon echoed to an astonished chorus of praise. It was her unexpected exhibition of agreeable opposites which struck them all. Sir Robert Peel marvelled at her modesty and firmness, others at her perfect self-possession combined with graceful diffidence. Wellington said that he could not have desired her to perform her part better if she had been his own daughter. Even the cynicism of Greville melted away. She was tiny, she was unpretentious; yet her good nature together with her youth 'inspire an excessive interest in all who approach her, and which I can't help feeling myself.'

Victoria's first day as Queen of England was a crowded one. Complete satisfaction of that craving for employment which she had discovered on her sixteenth birthday had come at last. After the Council she saw her Prime Minister, Lord Melbourne, twice more; also the Archbishop of Canterbury, the Home Secretary, the Master of the Horse and two of her relations. She wrote another letter and her Journal, saw Stockmar twice after dinner, appointed Dr Clark to be her physician and gave Baroness Lehzen the airy title of Lady Attendant on the Queen. It was safest to give the German confidante a post which did not officially exist. 'My *dear* Lehzen will *always* remain with me as my friend,' ran the last entry in the Journal for 20 June, 'but will take no situation about me, and I think she is right.' Just above this tender sentence Queen Victoria wrote with harsh brevity, 'Went down and said good night to Mama, etc.' This was the only mention of Mama, apart from her mother's having woken her up at six o'clock. When Queen Victoria wished her Mama good night, darkness descended on the Duchess of Kent for three mournful years.

The first letter, dashed off by the Queen at half-past eight on that busy morning, had been addressed to her 'Dearest, Most Beloved Uncle'. It gave King Leopold the news of William IV's death. King Leopold had wisely decided not to rush over the moment his niece ascended the throne. 'People might fancy I came to enslave you', he wrote. So, for the first fifteen months of her reign, he left Stockmar in England as his *alter ego*, contenting himself with sending advice. Much of it influenced the Queen as long as she lived.

King Leopold wrote that she could not cultivate too much discretion; those around her observed that her discretion was preternaturally great, almost unpleasing in so young a girl. Leopold advised her never to give an immediate answer to Ministers; Greville heard that she always said 'I will think it over', even to Melbourne. Leopold advocated strict business habits such as seeing Ministers between 11 am and 1.30 pm each day; the Queen always saw Lord Melbourne between those hours. Leopold urged her to form her own opinions on all questions and stick to them; her reign was not two months old before people noticed 'slight signs of a peremptory disposition' and 'a strong will of her own'. Leopold insisted that if people spoke to her uninvited on personal matters she should change the subject 'and make the individual feel that he has made a mistake'; no one could deliver more effectively than Queen Victoria the look that froze or the phrase that made men and women shrivel: 'We are not amused.'

Was it possible that the King was trying to guide the young Queen a shade too masterfully, even from a distance? If he could have seen her Journal for the first day of her reign, one word, five times repeated, would have caught his eye: '*alone* … & of COURSE *quite* ALONE… quite alone… & alone… alone'. Beginning with Lord Conyngham and his companions at 6 am, she saw all her visitors alone. Over Melbourne's first audience she was most explicit: 'At 9 came Lord Melbourne, whom I saw in my room, & of COURSE *quite* ALONE as I shall *always* do all my Ministers.' The repetition of the word was a sign of independence not of loneliness; for an essential part of Conroy's coercive policy – fortunately thwarted – was to insist on the Duchess of Kent being present at all the Queen's audiences. She might have added in her Journal that her bed was removed that same day from her mother's room. The experience of a lifetime was reversed. Her waking hours were deliciously sociable and for the first time she slept alone.

Baron Christian Frederick Stockmar, the man whom King Leopold sent to England in his stead, was fifty years old. He had begun his practice as a doctor during the Napoleonic Wars and credited himself with exceptional psychological insight – more than he in fact possessed, when it came to a young woman like Victoria. He employed this gift in directing the lives of rulers, his principles being three: honesty in giving unwelcome advice, courage in bearing periods of coldness from offended Majesty and self-control in refraining from saying afterwards, 'I told you so'. But Stockmar's sagacity tended to obscure the fact that he made mistakes. His interpretation of the British Constitution was one. Unfortunately he had studied this illusive organism in books, unaware that it resembled in no way the logical, synthetic Constitution of Belgium, which he himself had drawn up for King Leopold. His researches into what historians had written about an unwritten Constitution gave him many erroneous ideas regarding the British Monarchy which he was to pass on to Queen Victoria and Prince Albert. His greatest mistake was to describe the Monarch as a 'permanent Premier' and to warn Victoria against attempts by the cabinet to reduce her to a 'mere Mandarin figure'.

Stockmar, having arrived in England in 1837, was to flit for the next twenty years to and fro between Coburg and Windsor unheralded, but never unwanted. With his wizened features. small stature and shrunken legs, too chilly to be exposed in

Baron Stockmar, King Leopold's unofficial representative at the English Court and adviser to the young Queen: 'He combined the qualities of Puck and Merlin.'

Victoria riding with
Melbourne at Windsor.
Painting by Sir Francis
Grant.

Victoria's first Prime Minister, Lord Melbourne whose relationship with the young Queen is one of the romances of history.

Court hose to the rigours of Windsor Castle, he combined the qualities of Puck and Merlin. The mysterious descents of the Welsh wizard upon the Court of King Arthur were deemed to be no more essential to royal welfare than the little doctor's visits to the Court of Queen Victoria.

One event of that crowded first day must have given the young Queen great pleasure – the dismissal of Conroy. But his nuisance potential was by no means exhausted. The 'terms' which he demanded for retirement from the Duchess of Kent's service astounded Melbourne, familiar though he was with Conroy's ambitions. Nothing short of a pension of £3,000 a year, the Grand Cross of the Bath, a peerage and a seat on the Privy Council would satisfy the Duchess of Kent's majordomo. A Minister of the Crown would have been offered less. Nevertheless, anxiety to get rid of Conroy overcame Melbourne's disgust at his impudence, and in the autumn of 1837 he recommended the Queen to pay Conroy a pension of £3,000 and to confer on him a baronetcy. An Irish peerage was also promised, but when the first vacancy occurred Peel was Prime Minister and refused to recognize an undertaking given by his predecessor. Conroy 'sneeringly' kept telling Stockmar that he would not fulfil his part of the bargain until the Queen fulfilled hers. In Stockmar's words, he intrigued more and more violently against the Queen in a 'spirit of feminine revenge'. Melbourne would have done better to have got rid of Conroy at once for he was to cause real trouble later on. Anything for a quiet life was Melbourne's motto, however, and he hoped to secure Conroy's retirement at once while paying for it in instalments.

The three-year partnership between Queen Victoria and Lord Melbourne is one of the romances of history. If King Leopold was her second father, Melbourne was her third; but since her association with him began when she had ceased to be a child it was that much more intense than anything which had gone before. He was fifty-eight when he became Victoria's first Prime Minister. Although he had lost the dazzling looks of his youth he was still physically attractive, a fact on which the Queen often commented in her Journal. To her he was more than a father but less than a lover. In spite of the Duchess of Kent's disapproval of their relationship, in spite of malicious gossip that they were about to be married, no mud has stuck.

Melbourne's fatherly devotion was enriched in her eyes with the wisdom of a political genius, the detachment of a philosopher, the brilliance of a scholar, the fascination of a man of the world, the glamour of one who had come unscathed through two divorce suits in both of which he was co-respondent, and the melancholy appeal of a bitterly disappointed husband and father whose dead wife, Caroline Lamb, had been mad and whose son had died the year before, an epileptic. To Queen Victoria, Melbourne was the first vista outside the prison gates; to Melbourne, she was the blind he would teach to see, the dumb who would learn through him to speak.

The world which Melbourne introduced to the young Queen was sophisticated and adult, witty, sceptical and slightly absurd. But Victoria was never shocked at Melbourne's cynicism. She had made up her mind that he was '*good*' and felt no danger in indulging her own taste for the *outré* in company so respectable as that of the Prime Minister. She delighted in the Johnsonian epigrams with which he entertained her. Of wife-beating: 'Why, it is almost worthwhile for a woman to be beat, considering the exceeding pity she excites.' Of doctors: 'English physicians kill you, the French let you die.' Melbourne's carefree charm captivated her and through his affection and praise he was able to do much to give her self-confidence. He made her feel part of a family by telling her endless tales of George II, George III and all her uncles, amongst whom her father was 'the best of all'. He calmed her anxiety about her lack of inches, telling her that her height was no misfortune. And indeed the contrast between her short stature and her dignity only heightened the queenly effect.

Was Melbourne's cool approach to the world the best training for a young impressionable queen? Certainly it provided a new standard by which she might correct her inherited effusiveness. And Melbourne's views on the duties of a constitutional monarch, despite their seasoning of irony, were a very valuable corrective to those of her other unofficial private secretary, Baron Stockmar. Political education was Victoria's greatest need. Her sudden liberation from bondage, her own headstrong temperament and her inevitable contacts with the undemocratic ideas of Continental royalty, made her vulnerable to dangerous thoughts. With Lord Melbourne as Minister it was sheer pleasure for the Queen to accept the full rigour of the Constitution. But she paid a high price for this pleasure. For Melbourne was the first of a long line of advisers to assure Queen Victoria that things were better than they seemed. The bringer of bad news is never popular, and it has always needed courage to inform royalty that some of the people are starving. Queen Victoria's naturally warm sympathies, however, would have made her exceptionally responsive to the sad truth. Melbourne did not dry up the wells of her pity – that would have been impossible – but he did blunt her social conscience by starting the evil legend that all discontent was due to a handful of agitators. Particularly was this so in Ireland. When the Queen asked Melbourne what happened to the 'poor Irish' who were evicted by their landlords, Melbourne replied, 'They become *absorbed* somehow or other' – which made them all laugh amazingly. He added that 'they ate too much and there was not enough for them and you'. Under Melbourne's callous tuition she gradually came to believe that every rebellious Irishman was 'a low Irishman'.

Melbourne profoundly distrusted social change. Nothing could be changed for the better, he felt, whether it was the factory system, the Church of England or the ventilation of Buckingham Palace. Nothing that had stood the test of time should be abolished, not even the flogging of men, women and boys; only animals should be exempt since they did not know what it was for. As a politician, he was the head of a weak Whig government, holding Tory views himself and feeling no sympathy for the Radicals among his followers. Queen Victoria, therefore, became a rabid Whig with little comprehension of what Liberalism stood for. In more ways than one she would have fared better had she started with a liberal Tory like Peel. As it was, she rejoiced exceedingly when the Whigs won the first general election of her reign by 38 seats. There could, there *must* be no other adviser than the present one.

6

The Wonderful Year
1837–38

The Queen was proclaimed from an open window in St James's Palace on 21 June 1837. As the trumpets sounded, the names 'Alexandrina Victoria' floated over the crowds – but for the last time. By the Queen's express command, her first name was removed from all official papers and never used again. George IV's joke was over and little Drina had vanished for ever.

The delightful business of reigning had begun. She chose a Household considerably more economical than Queen Anne's (the last Queen Regnant) and with her interest in lovely women appointed the Duchess of Sutherland to be her Mistress of the Robes. This exquisite creature had a burning social conscience and later kept the Queen in touch, sometimes to the latter's annoyance, with the kind of causes which found no place in Melbourne's cynical world. Among the maids-of-honour, Queen Victoria preferred those who were merry. Melbourne took no pains to balance her Whig Household with a sprinkling of Tories, though his majority in Parliament was so slender. As a result the Queen most unwisely surrounded herself with Whig ladies. When criticism reached her ears she and Melbourne were much amused. By the end of July a little of the gilt was already beginning to flake from the Queen's image. The Tories resented having an exclusively Whig Queen and their disgruntlement was fed by reports of domestic wrangling inside Buckingham Palace, where the relationship between the Queen and her mother was getting worse and worse. Victoria made no attempt to facilitate communications with the Duchess; on the contrary, she was put away as far as possible. Soon she was forced to seek special permission to see her daughter and often got a note back saying, 'Busy', or a frigid letter drafted by Melbourne. Letters from the Duchess continued to arrive, pleading for a favour to Sir John Conroy or complaining that she had been given the wrong precedence in a procession, but Victoria, who was used to her mother's scenes from the days in Kensington, was not prepared to relent. All she did was to sever herself even more completely from the Duchess and her Household. Hitherto the Duchess had always accompanied her daughter at official functions for the sake of appearances, but by the end of the year the Queen went frequently without her. All this was in some contrast to her thoughtfulness towards Queen Adelaide, whom she addressed on the first day of her own reign as 'Queen' instead of 'Dowager Queen', allowing her to take away her favourite furniture from Windsor. No wonder that the Duchess of Kent should give her a copy of *King Lear* for her nineteenth birthday.

I prithee, daughter, do not make me mad:
I will not trouble thee, my child; farewell:
We'll no more meet, no more see one another:
But yet thou art my flesh, my blood, my daughter ...

In December, Parliament voted Queen Victoria a Civil List of £375,000 a year for her life, divided into £60,000 for her Privy Purse, £131,260 for Household salaries and £172,500 for Household expenses, £13,200 for the Royal Bounty and £8,040 unappropriated. The Queen also enjoyed the Crown revenues from the Duchies of Lancaster and Cornwall, amounting to about £27,000 each at the beginning of her reign and rising to over £60,000 each at the end; Cornwall, however, passed to the Prince of Wales in 1841.

Queen Victoria's state thus changed in the first four months of her reign from penury to affluence, from the necessity to borrow from Messrs Coutts the bankers, to the ability to pay off all her father's debts. She plunged at once into this filial enterprise, setting aside £50,000 for the purpose – the whole of her Privy Purse for one year, apart from £10,000. Affluence never tempted Queen Victoria from her ingrained carefulness. Seven years' training by Lehzen in strict accountancy were not to be wiped out by sixty-three years a wealthy queen.

The joys of this *annus mirabilis* at times took little Victoria's breath away: 'the pleasantest summer I *EVER* passed in *my life*, & I shall never forget this first summer of my Reign.' Her fascinated subjects watched with amazement the girlish figure slipping, as Greville put it, into her new role as if she had been ruling all her life. The pressure of business she found greatly to her taste:

June 24th ... I received so many communications from my Ministers, but I like it very much. July 1st ... I *delight* in this work.

In August, with the season over, she reluctantly left London – 'the *greatest* Metropolis in the *World*' – for Windsor, whose cawing rooks and striking clock made her feel melancholy. But soon, with her gay Court around her, Uncle Leopold and Aunt Louise staying for the first time under her own roof, and Lord Melbourne nearly always in attendance, Windsor began to look less gloomy. She 'ventured' to admit Dashy to her *tête-à-têtes* with the Prime Minister; he behaved very well, licking Lord Melbourne's hand. 'All dogs like me,' said the statesman.

The little Blue Closet where these audiences always took place became one of Queen Victoria's favourite rooms: it was so 'cosy' and 'cheerful'. The great Corridor, 550 feet long, was a fine place for a game of ball with visiting children or battledore and shuttlecock with her ladies, while in the evenings the Queen and her ladies sat round a large mahogany table, Victoria drawing, the others working, laughing and talking. When the gentlemen were present the pace would be accelerated to include spilikins, puzzles, draughts and games of 'German Tactics' at which the English Queen twice out-manoeuvred her Coburg uncle. Chess was so serious a pursuit that Lords Melbourne, Palmerston, Conyngham and Sir John Hobhouse hovered over Queen Victoria giving contradictory advice in an effort to checkmate Queen Louise. There being two queens on the chess-board and two at the table, instructions about 'the queen' became very confusing, particularly as

Queen Victoria was born
four years after George
Stephenson had built his
first steam locomotive and
by the time she came to the
throne in 1837 England was
in the throes of a railway
boom which rapidly
transformed the country's
transport system.

Above The opening of the
Canterbury and Whitstable
railway, 3 May 1830.

One of Thomas Cook's
earliest posters.

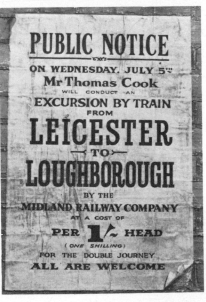

PUBLIC NOTICE

ON WEDNESDAY, JULY 5TH
Mr Thomas Cook
WILL CONDUCT AN
EXCURSION BY TRAIN
FROM
LEICESTER
~ TO ~
LOUGHBOROUGH
BY THE
MIDLAND RAILWAY COMPANY
AT A COST OF
PER 1/- HEAD
(ONE SHILLING)
FOR THE DOUBLE JOURNEY
ALL ARE WELCOME

Right from the start
the railways ran first,
second and third
class carriages.

'Late for the Mail!'
On the roads the horse
would still enjoy another
fifty years of unchallenged
monopoly.

Victoria, wearing a crimson velvet dress from Paris, was clearly the Red Queen. 'Between them all,' she wrote, 'I got quite beat, & Aunt Louise triumphed over my Council of Ministers!'

Better than all other recreations were the Queen's great cavalcades of up to thirty riders, galloping for miles without once pulling up. Her small stature did not show on horseback: she looked immensely seductive in a black velvet riding habit, top hat and veil, with her bright cheeks and eyes and fair hair. Her triumph as a horsewoman reached its peak when in August she reviewed her troops at Windsor wearing an adaptation of the Windsor uniform and the Garter ribbon, sitting 'Leopold' for two-and-a-half hours and then going out again for another hour-and-a-half's canter on 'Barbara'.

Suddenly it was autumn. The six weeks in the country had flown like six days – 'how quickly time passes when one is happy' – and now she was off to Brighton for her first visit to the Marine Pavilion where her 'Uncle King' had spent so many unedifying hours. Queen Victoria was not amused by the 'strange, odd Chinese looking thing'. But soon she was enjoying herself. Mr Creevey, the diarist, met her at the Pavilion and heard her loud uninhibited laughter. Like others, Creevey complained of her opening her mouth too wide when she laughed and showing not very pretty gums. She also gobbled her food. But her voice and expression were perfect. 'She blushes and laughs every instant in so natural a way as to disarm anybody.' The sight of 'the poor little thing' struggling to pull off a tight glove so that he might kiss her hand quite melted his heart.

Then it was back again to London for the season and another birthday and the Coronation.

The Coronation festivities, which included three State balls, two levées, a drawing-room and a State concert, opened with Queen Victoria's first State ball in May. It was talked of as the best ball ever to be given in London because, Melbourne said, the company was so select. Even in this rarified, aristocratic atmosphere, however, there was still no arm fit to encircle the Queen's waist in a waltz – she had to watch the waltzers dancing to Strauss's band from a dais among her aunts – so she danced quadrilles most beautifully until sunrise. 'It was a lovely ball,' she wrote in her Journal, 'so gay, so nice – I felt so happy & so merry; I had not danced for *so* long & was so glad to do so again!' Her only regret was that Lord Melbourne was prevented by indisposition from sharing her happiness.

What sort of person was emerging from Lord Melbourne's hands at the end of this first year? The boundaries between childhood and maturity had been crossed only in places. She had not yet developed her gift for demolishing an erring lady or gentleman with one look. Her adolescent timidity and kind-heartedness made the task of keeping her maids-of-honour in their place, especially the wild Miss Dillon who needed 'much managing', an uncongenial one. Melbourne urged her to 'start right' – either she or they must govern. The difficulty with the male members of her Household – most of them much older than herself – was even greater.

She was deeply conscious of her own faults. Starting with good, patient Lord

Melbourne, she feared she plagued those of whom she was fondest. Now and then she felt compunction even about the Duchess – 'I am sure I often plague my *Mother* (for that she *ever has* BEEN & is)' – but more often the growing strife with her mother brought out the side of her character which she herself called 'passionate' and which Melbourne called 'choleric'. They both meant the same thing – hot-tempered.

An uncontrollable temper was Queen Victoria's greatest conscious burden. Her obstinacy was a burden to others. She often spoke of herself as being, like King George IV, 'naturally very passionate'. Her words have been wrongly interpreted to mean hot-blooded in an exclusively erotic sense. Queen Victoria's passions were robust, but she was not in the least troubled with George IV's 'deadly sin' of lust. This limited interpretation of the word 'passionate' has led to another error: the legend that like the female spider she devoured her mate, Prince Albert, and a few years afterwards, insatiable as ever, took another more vigorous partner, John Brown, from the Highland glens.

Apart from Queen Victoria's temper, she was developing a possessiveness which sometimes inconvenienced Melbourne. She grudged every minute of his time spent with the famous Whig hostess, Lady Holland, now nearly seventy, who in turn questioned him suspiciously about what went on in Buckingham Palace. 'Lord Melbourne dines with Lady Holland tonight,' wrote the Queen on 15 February 1838; 'I WISH he dined with me!' Nevertheless she often asked Melbourne whether he was not bored spending so much time with her, to which he always replied with tears in his eyes, 'Oh! no!'

Hardworking, dutiful, conscientious; full of kindness and animal spirits; still shy and modest, wilful and excitable; capable of loyalty and affection so fierce that there was a danger of jealousy and partisanship – this was the nineteen-year-old girl who went to be crowned in Westminster Abbey on 28 June 1838.

London was awake most of the night before. For days there had been din of hammers, dust of scaffolding and bits falling on people's heads. The town was all mob, the Park all encampment. The enthusiasm had extended everywhere. One hundred and sixty more peers were coming to Victoria's coronation than had attended the last one; Parliament was making a splash, spending £200,000 compared with £50,000 on King William IV. The Queen, like her people, had slept badly. She was awakened at 4 o'clock by the guns in the Park and was kept awake by music and shouting until she rose at seven, 'feeling strong and well'. She took two bites at her breakfast, one before and one after dressing, and at 10 o'clock stepped into her State coach. Those inside the Abbey heard the salute of guns to show that she had started. The wind and rain which had chilled the crowds earlier had vanished. Glorious sunshine – 'Queen's weather' as it came to be called – flooded the route, warming thousands of cheering people, some of whom the Queen feared would be fatally crushed in the vast press. ' ... I really cannot say *how* proud I feel to be Queen of *such* a Nation,' she wrote in her Journal afterwards, needing no Uncle Leopold to teach her patriotism.

Wearing a diamond circlet, the Parliament Robes of crimson velvet furred with

A poster announcing some of the varied coronation celebrations to take place at Cambridge.

ermine, bordered with gold lace and fastened with a tasselled golden cord, Queen Victoria entered the Abbey attended by her eight train-bearers. She was 'gay as a lark', said one observer, 'like a girl on her birthday'. But when she saw the towering pillars hung with crimson and gold, the congregation ten thousand strong with the banks of peers and peeresses glowing and sparkling, she clasped her hands, drew in her breath and trembled, glad to throw herself down on the faldstool. The congregation in its turn was deeply moved by the poignant dignity of the childlike figure in the centre of the great nave, surrounded by a cloud of silver and white train-bearers like the vapours of dawn. Slim as a girl of twelve and no taller, she added something unique to the splendour of her Coronation.

The Sovereign took the oath to maintain 'the Protestant reformed religion as it is established by law' – an oath which Queen Victoria never forgot though she did not mention it in her Journal on that day – and was anointed with the holy oil. Leaving the altar she retired into St Edward's Chapel, 'a dark small place', as she called it, where she took off her Parliament Robes, putting on first a 'singular sort of little gown of linen trimmed with lace' and then the supertunica (which Melbourne afterwards said suited her best of all) woven of cloth of gold and silver embroidered with palms, roses, shamrocks and thistles, trimmed with gold pillow lace and lined with crimson silk, for the Crowning. Bare-headed she returned to the Abbey. The supreme moment had come. Seated in St Edward's Chair, she received the dalmatic robe, stiff with golden eagles, and the rest of the royal regalia. Then with a ray of sunshine falling on her head she was crowned by the Archbishop of Canterbury Queen of England. All the peers and peeresses put on their coronets, the silver trumpets sounded and the Archbishop presented the Queen to the people, turning her to the east, west, south and north. The pageant reached its zenith in a tumult of waving flags and scarves, of huzzas and cheers. The Duchess of Kent burst into tears.

After the Homage, the Queen descended from the throne, took off her royal crown 'very prettily' and humbly received the Sacrament. Throughout the hot summer afternoon the intricate medieval ceremony slowly unwound itself until at last the end came with the *Hallelujah Chorus*. The Queen in her Robes of State prepared to leave: 'the Procession being formed, I replaced my Crown (which I had taken off for a few minutes), took the Orb in my left hand and the Sceptre in my right, and thus *loaded*, proceeded through the Abbey – which resounded with cheers ... I shall ever remember this day as the *proudest* of my life!'

Queen Victoria was proud of her people but not of all those who played a conspicuous part in the ceremonies. The elaborate rehearsals of our own times did not find a place in her coronation, and there were numerous mistakes by the officiating clergy as well as much indecorous behaviour on the part of some of her more illustrious subjects. She was shocked to find that in St Edward's Chapel 'what was *called* an *Altar* was covered with sandwiches, bottles of wine, etc, etc'. Melbourne was so tired by carrying the enormously heavy Sword of State that he helped himself to a glass. According to Disraeli, who was among the Commons, Melbourne held the sword like a butcher, looking singularly uncouth with his robes under his feet and his coronet over his nose. Lord Ward, added this commentator, was seen

The Coronation of
Queen Victoria, 28 June
1838.

after the ceremony with robes disordered and coronet cock-eyed, drinking champagne out of a pewter pot. Any unusual incident provoked stormy applause. During the Homage, Lord Rolle, nearly ninety, caught his foot in his robes on the steps of the throne and rolled to the bottom. As he struggled to his feet and prepared again to make the perilous ascent, frantic cheering broke out; it became a perfect tornado when the Queen, anxiously whispering, 'May I not get up and meet him?' leaned down and saved him the risk of another roll. That it was Lord *Rolle* who took the toss delighted everybody. Foreigners were assured it was part of the *droit de seigneur* to demand a roll from this noble family in addition to their homage.

The Archbishop of Canterbury himself was not able to escape from the formidable list of errors which punctuated the Queen's *proudest* day. He crushed the ruby ring on to her fourth finger, not noticing that it had inadvertently been made to fit the fifth. She got it off again with great pain and only after bathing it in iced water. Later he tried to give her the orb after she had already got it, 'and he (as usual) was *so* confused and puzzled and knew nothing, and went away.' Any anxieties that the young Queen might have had, however, were soon quietened by the encouraging tears in Lord Melbourne's eyes and the smile 'of another most dear Being'. Baroness Lehzen was sitting just above the royal box and the enthroned Queen caught her eye. 'We exchanged smiles.' She did not exchange smiles with her mother who had made the last months hideous with grievances about her place in the procession.

At the end of five hours in the Abbey, Queen Victoria drove home in state. Some considered she looked 'white and tremulous'; Thomas Carlyle, peering towards the gilded coach, murmured:

Poor little Queen, she is at an age at which a girl can hardly be trusted to choose a bonnet for herself; yet a task is laid upon her from which an archangel might shrink.

Then the crowds dispersed and began to prepare themselves for fireworks in the Park – a display which one small child afterwards likened to the destruction of Sodom and Gomorrah.

Inside Buckingham Palace the Queen still had one duty to perform. An attendant standing at the foot of the stairs watched her gather her skirts and run up to her room to give Dash his bath.

7
Disenchantment
1838–39

Towards the end of 1838 word got around that the Queen was losing her girlish prettiness. Miss Martineau, the radical historian, said to be the ugliest woman in the world, was one of the first to declare that she began to look discontented; others pointed out that she was putting on weight. None of these strictures could equal the young Queen's increasing load of self-criticism. Many things combined to destroy her peace. At the centre of the trouble, exacerbating all the minor miseries, was the old, festering sore – her horror of Sir John Conroy. They still could not budge him. At one time there seemed a good chance of sending him abroad. Even the Duchess had suggested it, half admitting that she had been wrong in the past. But Melbourne thought it was all a plot to get 'J.C.' off abroad 'well endowed' and would do nothing unless the Duchess sent 'this man' away first. His advice served Queen Victoria ill. The dismissal of Sir John Conroy would have been cheap at any price. Had Melbourne seized the chance offered by the Duchess's evident wish for a reconciliation, the Flora Hastings affair would never have taken the disastrous form it did.

Melbourne did nothing to improve relations between the Queen and the Duchess either. Indeed he said that such situations between mothers and daughters were common, and summed up the Queen's mother as weak-minded and devoid of real feeling. The Queen in turn could not deny that her mother seemed to find something wrong in everything she did, from riding through the crowds in London, which she called 'highly improper', to overeating at luncheon. But criticism was by no means all on one side. The Queen was shocked to discover that the Duchess of Kent was £70,000 in debt despite Sir John's assurances of her solvency. And to cap it all, Conroy put it about that the Duchess's financial difficulties were due to her having paid off the debts left by her late husband, the Duke of Kent. Since Queen Victoria, unknown to her mother, was engaged in paying them off herself, this was a bit too much.

The growing rift between the Queen and her mother had split the Royal Family from top to bottom. Charles Leiningen changed to the Queen's side after the Coronation, while the Duchess of Cambridge and her children had been seduced into the ranks of the enemy. Queen Victoria's cousin, Augusta Cambridge, a girl of nearly her own age, was now seldom allowed to visit her alone for a chat. The Duchess of Kent was suspected of wishing to offer her daughter's hand in marriage to young Prince George of Cambridge. She requested Victoria to invite him to stay. After consideration, Melbourne advised against. Not surprisingly, when the Duchess of Cambridge caught sight of the Prime Minister going down a passage at Windsor, she exclaimed: '*Da geht mein grösster Feind*' – there goes my greatest enemy. 'Infamous woman' wrote the enraged Queen. She rounded off many bitter thoughts with the conclusion that she had had an unloved childhood: 'Ma. never was very fond of me.'

Such squabbles were repeated between the Queen's and the Duchess's ladies, the Palace rift cutting right through the two Households. The Duchess was even said to be jealous because one of her ladies, Lady Mary Stopford, did *not* quarrel with the Queen. The Queen's maids-of-honour found Baroness Lehzen a sympathetic, motherly figure, while they confessed themselves afraid to speak to 'Scotty', the Duchess's lady (Lady Flora Hastings), particularly as Sir John was so often in her room. Scotty 'plagued' Lehzen and annoyed the Queen. Such behaviour only served to increase the Queen's passion for Lehzen. She regularly referred to her now as her 'mother' or by the pet name of Daisy. 'Walked, with my ANGELIC, dearest Mother, *Lehzen,* who I do so love!'

Victoria's love for Daisy and the continued presence of Stockmar provided fuel for criticisms of 'foreign influence' which became so serious that Queen Victoria decided Stockmar must go. She believed that 'Ma.' invented stories against him which were circulated by 'J.C.' through the Duke of Sussex. There was the wicked story, for instance, that Stockmar was once discovered by the Duchess sitting in the Queen's room, 'with all the BOXES *open*!!' With his departure in the early autumn, zenophobia abated for a time, but the Queen was still liable to be attacked for patronizing foreign industry, decking out her manservants in gold lace made in France or herself following the French fashions. Increasing unemployment at home, particularly among the Spitalfields silk weavers, lent point to popular outcry. Melbourne refused to pay any attention, proclaiming that it was impossible to look well in English clothes – all English women dressed badly. 'Things don't fit well, nor stay on.'

This fanatical, closed society in which the Queen was now living, with its twin pillars of Melbourne and Lehzen, inevitably cut her off from other influences which might have let in fresh air.

King Leopold was the most important influence to disappear. Queen Victoria had only been on the throne a few months when the King of the Belgians noticed a new, sharp note in his niece's correspondence. The difficulty was political. As Queen of England, Victoria discovered that her Continental relations expected more of her than affectionate letters or occasional visits to Windsor. She was required to lend a helping hand whenever they were in trouble. King Leopold begged her in November 1837 to help her harassed sister-sovereigns in Spain and Portugal. Next June he himself was the suppliant. Would his beloved niece use her influence to win justice for the Belgian people in their territorial dispute with the Dutch over the Treaty of 1831, now reaching a climax? Only *great discretion* had prevented him from touching on his own affairs before. But in this emergency he counted on her kind Majesty *occasionally* telling good Lord Melbourne that she did *not* wish H.M. Government to take the *lead* in bringing about the *destruction* of her uncle's country.

Queen Victoria knew her constitutional duty. Without a moment's hesitation she turned over the King's letter to good Lord Melbourne, who, in his dual capacity of Prime Minister and private secretary prepared a rough draft in reply, leaving the final version to the Queen. In this, Queen Victoria conceded that the Treaty of 1831 was not very advantageous to the Belgians. But was it any more favourable to the Dutch? After some sententious remarks upon the sanctity of treaties, delivered with all the authority of an aunt to a nephew, she trusted that her dearest Uncle would at all times believe her to be 'his devoted and most affectionate Niece, Victoria R.' Leopold, stretching his famous sense of humour to the utmost, assured his 'dearest and most beloved Victoria' that her letter had given him '*great pleasure and satisfaction*'. It was a relief to find that he had not after all been put aside 'like a piece of furniture'.

Correspondence between uncle and niece continued but dearest Victoria was not to be drawn. She would tolerate no interference from abroad, not even from her *padre secondo*. In April 1839, she informed Lord Melbourne that whereas King Leopold's influence over her in the days had been great, it was now '*very small*'.

Politically, Queen Victoria's emancipation from King Leopold marked a step forward in her development. Psychologically, it drove her further back upon Lord Melbourne and was a regression towards her childhood pattern of the small tight circle, to which she clung ever more desperately but with a growing malaise.

The malaise took the form of worries about her health and appearance. She felt she was too fat. 'Was weighed and to my horror weigh 8 stone 13!!' Melbourne developed various techniques for reassuring the anxious Queen. He flattered her. 'The best figure for a woman was fine and full with a fine bust.' He assured her that all failings were due to her royal ancestry. No Hanoverian could flourish on a low diet and her tendency to plumpness came from her aunts. Playfully he told her that she had 'a good chance of getting very fat'.

But not even Melbourne's charm could overcome her worries, which manifested themselves in a kind of lethargy. She hated getting up in the morning, disliked washing and took her bath at night instead of before dinner in order to cut down on the dressing and undressing. She did not want to be brushed up, nor even to brush her own teeth. She would not walk because she got stones in her shoes or her feet swelled. She was worried, too, about her appearance. She feared she had inadequate eyebrows and intended to shave them to make them grow. In the winter her feet and hands were always cold, swollen and red. She covered her fingers with rings to improve their appearance and then found it extremely uncomfortable to wear gloves. Sometimes she tried to console herself with the thought that it was better not to be handsome; at others, with the fact that she still looked superb on a horse, but neither she nor Melbourne, who constantly praised her, could really overcome this new self-distrust.

Distrust of herself was fed by jealousies of others. Queen Victoria now admitted frankly that she could not bear her own Mistress of the Robes, the Duchess of Sutherland, to sit next to Lord M. at dinner because she monopolized him. Once she plucked up courage to tell Lord M. that she was jealous of his visits to Holland

House and later that her affection for him was greater than Lady Holland's. But these were situations with which the connoisseur of gallantry was well able to deal.

New Year's Eve 1838 found the Queen thoroughly out of sorts. Her besetting sins had increased during the past year in spite of unremitting efforts at reform. Her temper was shorter than ever; even poor dear Daisy came under its lash and in turn seemed to have caught the Queen's edginess. Lehzen admitted ruefully to having 'a Devil of a *temper*' and shouting at her maids just like Her Majesty, whose impatience with her dressers had become so extreme that she decided to employ only two maids instead of three: the tedious business actually got done quicker.

Tedium in the Queen's dressing-room was reflected in her Court. Charles Greville has left a biting tribute to its dullness. Invited to a dinner party at Buckingham Palace in January 1838, he found that the men, after only a quarter of an hour for coffee, were shepherded back into the drawing-room where they huddled round the door 'in the sort of half-shy, half-awkward way people do' until the Queen came up to talk to each. What Greville sarcastically called his 'deeply interesting' dialogue with H.M. proceeded as follows:

Queen: 'Have you been riding today, Mr Greville?'
Greville: 'No, Madam, I have not.'
Queen: 'It was a fine day.'
Greville: 'Yes, ma'am, a very fine day.'
Queen: 'It was rather cold though.'
Greville: 'It *was* rather cold, madam.'
Queen: 'Your sister, Lady Francis Egerton, rides I think, does not she?'
Greville: 'She does ride sometimes, madam.' (A pause when I took the lead though adhering to the same topic.)
Greville: 'Has your Majesty been riding today?'
Queen (with animation): 'O yes, a very long ride.'
Greville: 'Has your Majesty got a nice horse?'
Queen: 'O, a very nice horse.'

After this experience Greville said he evaded all further invitations to the Palace.

In vain Lord M. tried to cheer the Queen by saying that her Court was much more lively and intellectual than King George III's. By the end of 1838 she herself was in a mood to agree with every word Greville had written. Even Lehzen and Melbourne, her 'DEAREST *Mother*' and 'Father', were unable to shake her out of her growing distaste for Court life. At first Melbourne suggested that it was 'all stomach', though anxiety over public affairs no doubt contributed; but when the Queen persisted in decrying levées and drawing-rooms, Melbourne became alarmed. This rebelliousness must be countered. Kindly but firmly he told her that though the feeling was natural she must fight it. 'A queen's life is very laborious; it's a life of moments, hardly any leisure.' George III did himself harm by 'fidgeting for time'. This was a shrewd dig, for Victoria had often told Melbourne that she had a horror of madness. Even her handwriting had deteriorated; she left out words and sometimes wrote so indistinctly that the Prime Minister finally promised to send back all her notes he could not read.

In December the Queen was near to defeatism. 'I felt *how* unfit I was for my station,' she repeated, not for the first time. 'Never think that,' urged the Prime Minister. She must take courage, do her best and leave the rest to fate. At the beginning of January boredom absolutely engulfed her. She had taken to writing in her Journal the single word 'Dawdled'. Melbourne was away. She spent the evenings in the company of peers and peeresses whom she described in a manner that Greville himself could not have bettered as deaf, stupid, vulgar bores. Melbourne's absence made her think of the time when he might have to resign. His Government, she knew, was shaky, and the good, kind man had given her several hints of coming separation. In a gallant effort to train herself for independence she wrote out Melbourne's explanations of corn prices, eking out his 'lucid words' with a plentiful sprinkling of '&c. &c. &c.'

As Queen Victoria and Lehzen sat upstairs together one day talking in muted voices of the precarious future, they both dissolved into tears, the Queen's fears for the loss of Melbourne mingling with penitence for her wayward and peevish behaviour towards the faithful creature at her side. Into this gloomy atmosphere already laden with anxiety, guilt and remorse, broke the Flora Hastings affair, like a freak storm. No stroke could have been more cruel, no human being less prepared to meet it with calm judgement, than the despondent girl who occupied the throne.

One of Queen Victoria's drawing-rooms. Charles Greville mocked the tedium of her Court.

8

'Mama's Amiable Lady'
1839

The extraordinary affair of Lady Flora Hastings was tailor-made to arouse all Queen Victoria's prejudices. Lady Flora, still unmarried at thirty-two, was her mother's lady-in-waiting, a suspected spy of Sir John Conroy, an enemy of Lehzen and a member of one of the greatest Tory families in the land. Although hardly as plain and disagreeable as she was considered to be by the Queen and Melbourne, her qualities were not such as to disperse the unfair accusations that were to be made against her.

On 10 January 1839 Lady Flora Hastings came into waiting, having spent the Christmas holiday at her mother's home, Loudoun Castle, in Scotland. She and Sir John Conroy had shared a post-chaise on the return journey. The unfortunate woman had been ill ever since December, so on the very day she returned to Buckingham Palace she consulted the Duchess's physician, Sir James Clark, who was also the Queen's doctor, for derangement of the bowel, pain in the left side and a protuberance of the stomach.

Clark prescribed what he himself accurately described as 'very simple remedies' – a matter of twelve rhubarb and ipecacuanha pills ('one at bed-time') and a linament compounded of camphor, soap and opium. As one of his scornful colleagues pointed out afterwards, they could do neither good nor harm.

By the end of January the Palace was in a hubbub. The Queen and Lehzen had both noticed the change in the shape of Lady Flora's stomach, and had come to the conclusion that she was pregnant. Melbourne, too, had his suspicions, which were deepened after an interview with Lady Tavistock, one of the senior ladies-of-the-bedchamber who had gone to see him, probably on Lehzen's advice and certainly 'with her concurrence'. Not a word had been said to Lady Flora or to the Duchess. Relations were far too strained for such a communication.

Melbourne now sent for Clark. What was Clark's opinion of the patient whom he had been treating with rhubarb and camphor for over three weeks? Clark replied that things looked pretty bad morally but he could not be certain. It was agreed between them that the only policy was to wait and see. The fact of the Prime Minister's having conducted these two interviews seemed to give a validity to the ladies' suspicions which they had not before possessed. From this moment Queen Victoria firmly believed that 'Mama's *amiable* and *virtuous* Lady', as she called Lady Flora, was Conroy's mistress. On 2 February she decided for the first time 'to divulge' the truth in the pages of her Journal:

Lady Flora Hastings, the unfortunate lady-in-waiting whose illness and tragic death after an unnecessary Court scandal led to a sharp decline in Victoria's popularity.

We have no doubt that she is – to use plain words – *with child!!* Clark cannot deny the suspicion; the horrid cause of all this is the Monster & demon Incarnate, whose name I forbear to mention, but which is the 1st word of the 2nd line of this page.

The first word on the second line was 'J.C.'

The wait-and-see policy was an intolerable strain. Sir James Clark felt pretty certain that his patient's condition was due to pregnancy rather than disease. Nevertheless, he could not be quite sure until he had examined her. Having failed to make a satisfactory diagnosis over her dress, he suggested attempting one 'with her stays removed'. Lady Flora declined.

Matters now went forward more rapidly. Lady Portman, senior lady-of-the-bedchamber after Lady Tavistock, approached Sir James Clark with the request that he should inform Flora Hastings forthwith of the ladies' suspicions. It was Lehzen who, after much discussion, hit upon a delicate and discreet way in which Clark might convey this message to Lady Flora. He was to say to her, 'You must be secretly married.'

The interview took place. Clark dropped his bomb with the delicacy which

Lehzen had devised, and when his patient, 'lightly' according to one source, denied the charge, he roughly urged her to see a second physician. Lady Flora indignantly refused. Sir James afterwards confessed that this refusal finally convinced him of her guilt. In vain Lady Flora entreated him to look at her dresses. She had had them taken in, for the swelling about which she had consulted him was subsiding rather than increasing. In this Lady Flora was probably right, for during the course of her malady the swelling, due to pressure on the stomach from an enlarged liver, fluctuated considerably. This may also explain why the Duchess had not noticed her condition.

Meanwhile Lady Portman had been instructed to seek an interview with the Duchess. She broke the news of Lady Flora's predicament, adding that for the Queen's sake she was not to appear at Court again until her innocence had been proved. That evening, 16 February, the Queen wrote in her Journal that Lady Flora was 'of course' not at dinner: she herself had also 'seen Ma', who was 'horror-struck'.

Next day was a Sunday. Lady Flora changed her mind. She boldly and sensibly resolved to have her innocence medically established, despite the shocked protests of the Duchess who, said Lady Flora, treated her throughout with all the tenderness of a mother.

Sir Charles Clarke, a specialist in women's diseases, happened to be in the Palace at that moment. He went at once to Lady Flora accompanied by Sir James and Lady Portman.

From this ordeal Lady Flora emerged triumphant. 'I have the satisfaction of possessing a certificate,' she wrote to her uncle, Hamilton Fitzgerald, a fortnight later, 'signed by my accuser, Sir James Clark, and also by Sir Charles Clarke, stating, as strongly as any language can state it, that "there are no grounds for believing pregnancy does exist, or ever has existed".' She was a virgin.

When Lady Portman informed Her Majesty of this result the Queen at once realised the magnitude of her blunder. She sent Lady Portman to Lady Flora with a message of deep regret at what had happened and an offer to see her that very evening if she so wished. Her Majesty also hoped that Lady Flora would remain long enough in the Palace to convince everyone of the Queen's complete belief in her innocence. But soon the situation again deteriorated.

The two doctors were not as happy about their diagnosis as Lady Flora imagined. Sir Charles, especially, was so uneasy that Sir James suggested they should both see Melbourne. Melbourne told Queen Victoria the results of this interview and the Queen passed on the information to her mother in a somewhat chaotic note written in mixed German and English:

Sir C. Clarke had said that though she is a virgin still that it might be possible and one could not tell if such things could not happen. That there was an enlargement in the womb like a child.

While recovering from her shock, Lady Flora sent an account of the scandal to the head of her family, the thirty-year-old Marquess of Hastings. Her letter reached Lord Hastings on a bed of sickness. He rushed up to London with a high temp-

erature, breathing fire and slaughter. The danger from this quarter was reinforced by the Duchess of Kent's determination to champion her slandered friend with all the warmth of her nature. But, for the moment, the scandal did not break out into the open. The Duke of Wellington, who had come to possess for the Royal Family the moral authority of a father confessor, the wisdom of a judge and the experience of a family solicitor, persuaded both Lord Hastings and the Duchess to hush the whole thing up in the interests of the Queen, the public and 'the Young Lady herself'. For the moment they did so. Meanwhile the Queen appeared to have become reconciled with Lady Flora, expressing sorrow for the past and a wish that all should be forgotten. The curtain had fallen on the first part of the tragedy. There were few, however, who dared predict that it would not rise again.

Gossip, of which a steady trickle found its way into the press at the beginning of March, was mainly responsible for the new phase in the Flora Hastings affair. One question still had not been answered, and until it was, gossip would be busy fabricating a reply. Who had started the slander against Lady Flora?

While gossip fastened upon Lehzen, the public were suddenly confronted with information direct from the heart of the scandal. The letter written by Lady Flora Hastings to her uncle, Mr Hamilton Fitzgerald, was published by the latter in *The Examiner*. It astonished the world by its frankness. Sir James Clark, she wrote, had been talked over into a conviction that she was in the family way. She had no doubt who was the talker – 'a certain foreign lady' (meaning Lehzen). She had secured her certificate of innocence and the whole thing was a diabolical conspiracy of the Whig ladies to ruin first herself and then the Duchess.

Good bye, my dear Uncle, I blush to send you so revolting a letter, but I wish you to know the truth, the whole truth, and nothing but the truth – and you are welcome to tell it right and left.

Henceforth it was war to the death. Melbourne and the Palace party were viciously attacked in the Press, and Queen Victoria, who had formerly boasted that she did not care a straw what she read, could no longer bear to see the *Morning Post*, *Spectator* or *Age*.

Her thoughts were in a ferment. How could she live without Lord M.? And yet the Tories were resolved to tear him from her. On 22 March she heard that Melbourne's Government had been defeated in the Lords by five votes. There was still a chance that the Commons would give him a vote of confidence but the Queen was by now too much broken down to face the future with hope. Melbourne was the best friend she ever possessed:

But *I* am but a poor helpless girl, who clings to him for support & protection, – & the thought of ALL ALL my happiness being possibly at stake, so completely overcame me that I burst into tears and remained crying for some time.

The vote of confidence was in fact carried and her 'happiness', such as it was, returned for another few weeks.

There was one other person whose removal, if it could be accomplished, would put a permanent end to Queen Victoria's 'torments'. This was the Duchess of Kent.

On 17 April a significant conversation took place between Queen Victoria and Lord Melbourne. It opened with the customary: 'Said I felt so changed; – this year; that I did not enjoy pleasures so much: "Oh! you will, when they begin," he said, leaning towards me kindly.' (The season did not start until May.) Their talk then passed on as so often to the odious subject of Mama. It was impossible to live with her and yet impossible to live without her – as long as Queen Victoria was unmarried. Suddenly the solution she had hitherto refused to consider clamoured for recognition. The problem of Mama had a 'schocking alternative' – marriage.

Despite her predicament Queen Victoria was still extremely wary of the subject of marriage. Lord M. must understand that she only wanted to *discuss* it, not to *do* it. Nor did she want even to discuss it now. But one day perhaps he would notice a preoccupied look on her face; then he should ask her what was on her mind and she would tell him.

The very next day Lord M. saw the look. 'Now, ma'am, for this other matter,' he began.

'I felt terrified (foolishly) when it came to the point,' she wrote in her Journal; 'too silly of me to be frightened in talking to him.'

At last she plucked up courage to go into the 'schocking alternative': how Uncle Leopold and Uncle Ernest (Duke of Saxe-Coburg) were both pressing her to marry her cousin Albert but how she could decide nothing until she had seen Albert again: a visit was planned for the autumn.

The Queen's roundabout and inhibited approach to the whole subject seems to have convinced Melbourne that she did not really want to marry and this, added to his own doubts, led him at once to raise objections. The first obstacle was of course Mama. 'How would that be with the Duchess?' he asked, meaning, as Victoria went on to explain in her Journal, 'that if I was to make such a connection & then he was to go with Ma., that would be dreadful for me; I assured him he need have no fear *whatever* on that score ... '

Melbourne next argued that her Coburg cousins were unpopular abroad and hated by the Russians. 'The Duchess,' he added, 'is a good specimen of the Coburgs.' Queen Victoria burst out laughing but assured him that the men were better. 'I hope so,' said Lord M., joining in the merriment. The more Melbourne criticized the more Victoria warmed to her defence of Albert. By all she heard of him he would be just the person. Melbourne then fired his last shot. 'I don't think a foreigner would be popular,' he said, at the same time agreeing with the Queen that an Englishman would not do either. Marrying a subject, as she said, 'made one so much their equal' and created jealousies.

Consciously or unconsciously Melbourne had made marriage seem impossible. And indeed the more she thought about it the more the Queen was worried about the whole idea of marriage. Was there really any hurry to marry? It would be better to wait a few more years until her character had improved. So the marriage question was shelved. The present state, which the Queen found so dreadful, had to get worse before it got better.

66

9
Ladies of the Bedchamber
1839

When Queen Victoria and Melbourne had discussed the problems of marriage, he had given as his opinion that she would get her own way against any male colleague. But whereas he had visualized her outwitting a mere husband, it was the leading statesman of the day whom she defeated.

At the beginning of May the catastrophe which she had long dreaded, the resignation of Lord M., was at hand. A week after she had finally abandoned the 'schocking alternative' to life with Mama, her Journal spoke of 'new horrors' ahead. Melbourne's Government was in fatal difficulties over the Jamaica Bill.

At this period of her life the restless young Queen was compiling a formidable list of things which gave her the horrors; among them turtle soup, insects, 'cercléing' (going round the circle of her guests), Madame de Lieven, dying young and going blind. To these she now added the Tories, naïvely informing Lord M. that the British Royal Family ought always to be Whig. Yet here were the Jamaican settlers defying the Whig Government's reform laws on behalf of the sugar workers, and finding enough support in Parliament to bring the Government down. On 7 May Lord John Russell told a weeping Sovereign that Melbourne's Government must resign.

Melbourne arrived with a memorandum suggesting how 'the others' should be handled during the change-over. Her Majesty, he said, should first desire the Duke of Wellington to form an administration. If he declined in favour of Sir Robert Peel, the Queen should agree only on condition that Wellington also served in the Cabinet. Of her late Government, she should speak with praise and regret. Towards 'the others' she should show complete trust once they were in charge of her affairs; at the same time she must be very vigilant and watchful. The extreme confidence she reposed in himself (Lord M.) had perhaps got her into the habit of approving measures and appointments too easily.

One more point arose at the end of the memorandum. What about the Queen's Household? 'Your Majesty had better express your hope,' advised Melbourne, 'that none of your Majesty's Household, except those who are engaged in Politics, may be removed. I think you might ask him for that.' Melbourne was thus the first to put into the Queen's head the idea of retaining her Household intact, apart from those engaged in politics.

No doubt Melbourne had his reasons. The last thing he wanted was a contingent of Tory ladies let loose in the Palace, publicizing and criticizing his handling of the Flora Hastings affair. Apart from this natural concern, he knew Her Majesty was in no fit state for such an ordeal. Indeed, one of Queen Victoria's main reasons for clinging to Melbourne was her terror of facing the Flora Hastings affair alone. He besought her to be strong: 'You must try and be as collected as you can and act with great firmness and decision.'

The time had come for parting. It would be unwise for him to stay for dinner. With an infinitely kind look of pity and grief the Prime Minister kissed the Queen's hand and despite her entreaties to come back after dinner, said he had better remain at Holland House. She followed him to the door, tears running down her cheeks. As nothing would stop them, she spent the evening upstairs with no dinner.

All ALL my happiness gone! that happy peaceful life destroyed, that dearest kind Lord Melbourne no more my Minister!

Forgotten were her own storms, the peevishness, the discontent. She remembered only the infinite patience, stimulating frankness and warm humanity of her dear old friend. Melbourne came round next day, 8 May, for one last rehearsal before her audience with the Duke of Wellington. He cautioned her against showing too great a dislike for individual Tories. 'They'll not touch your ladies,' were his last words, to which the Queen replied sharply that they dared not; she'd never allow it.

Just before one o'clock the Queen left the dear Blue Closet where she always saw Lord M. and went to the Yellow Closet for her audience with the Duke. Wellington found Her Majesty gracious and civil but unaware of her constitutional obligations. Though she understood that Wellington's age, deafness and lack of contact with the House of Commons were reasons for his not accepting the Premiership, she did not at first see that he could not promise to be Foreign Secretary instead; this appointment, like all others, must be made by the new Prime Minister, Peel. Nor could Wellington make promises about her future Household.

The interview lasted twenty minutes. An hour or so later, the Queen allotted the same time to an audience with Peel. She hated every minute of it. The mannerisms of the Leader of the Opposition were not unknown to her, but everything she knew of Peel she disliked. It was not that she minded personal idiosyncrasies; after all, Lord M. had a 'peculiar walk' and laughed in loud hoots. Sir Robert's oddities, she felt, were not those of a gentleman: he reminded her of a dancing master, especially in the mincing way he shuffled his feet and pointed his toes. 'You must try to get over your dislike for Peel,' Melbourne had warned her before the interview; 'he's a close, stiff man.'

Worse than stiff, he was 'embarrassed and put out', as the Queen noticed when he arrived. The Duke's account to Peel of his own interview with the Queen was doubtless responsible for Peel's state, but it was unfortunate. His annoyance at once communicated itself to the Queen. In an effort to conceal her own embarrassment she became, as she boasted to Melbourne afterwards, 'very much collected, civil and high. . . .'

Nevertheless, the interview began moderately well. Three of the new Ministers now named by Peel were anathema to her: Lord Lyndhurst, for his championship of her mother, Aberdeen, for saying she was a baby in Melbourne's hands, Graham, for looking just like Conroy; but she accepted them after frankly expressing her dislike. She also hoped that Peel would not demand the dissolution of Parliament (the Whigs would have been defeated in a general election), but when he declined to be bound by a promise she accepted this too.

It was only when the Household appointments came up that there was tension. Peel explained that some changes in her Household were necessary to demonstrate her confidence in the new Government. The Queen then repeated the terms suggested by Melbourne: no changes except among the gentlemen of the Household who were also in Parliament. Peel replied that nothing should be done without her agreement. He made no comment on her terms.

Both sides felt hopeful. Sir Robert had not found the Queen too 'high' and was well satisfied with his reception. The Queen for her part felt sure that if she stood firm the whole situation would change. Melbourne, while urging her to be cautious, assured her that if she based her demand in regard to her Household on the rights accorded to previous sovereigns, he did not see how Sir Robert could refuse.

Sir Robert Peel was the most cautious of mankind. He began his second, fateful interview by again discussing the personnel of his Ministry – a subject on which the Queen had already promised to be quite fair. Having then tactfully, as he thought, offered her Lord Ashley, Melbourne's kinsman, as her Treasurer or Comptroller (in fact Queen Victoria disliked Ashley), he thought it safe to tackle the thorny question.

'Now, Ma'am, about the Ladies.'

The Queen put the sequel into her own words:

… I said I could *not* give up *any* of my Ladies, and never had imagined such a thing. He asked if I meant to retain *all*. '*All*,' I said. 'The Mistress of the Robes and the Ladies of the Bedchamber?' I replied, '*All*' –

Sir Robert was utterly taken aback. 'I never saw a man so frightened,' wrote Queen Victoria to Melbourne gleefully.

He explained that these ladies were married to Whig opponents of the Government.

They would not interfere in politics, countered the Queen, for she never talked politics with her ladies. Moreover, they had plenty of Tory relatives. She proceeded to enumerate Tories related to her bedchamber women and maids-of-honour.

He didn't mean *all* the lesser ladies, put in Peel; it was only the most prominent ladies who must be changed.

to which I replied *they* were of more consequence than the others, and that I could *not* consent and that it had never been done before. He said I was Queen Regnant, and that made the difference. 'Not here,' I said – and I maintained my right.

There was deadlock. The little creature glared at the tall, discomforted man. Even when Peel smiled, his smile was said to be like the silver fittings of a coffin; now he was just the coffin.

Further discussions with both Peel and Wellington did nothing to remove the deadlock. The Queen's obstinacy and cleverness were too much for the Tory leaders. Wellington attributed her ready arguments to Melbourne's coaching. But in fact Queen Victoria's gift for repartee was all her own, and apart from the argument based on precedent, she spontaneously dealt Peel her most telling blow. 'Was Sir Robert so weak that *even* the ladies must be of his opinion?'

Baffled, Sir Robert withdrew and after more consultations returned to inform Her Majesty dramatically that unless she surrendered *some* of her ladies, he could not go on. She coolly promised to give him her final decision that evening or next morning. Then, snatching up her pen she described the interview to Lord M., ordering him to stand by for action.

He was with her at half-past six and certainly seemed pleased, Victoria thought, with the day's work. 'Lord M. approved all & saw & said I could not do otherwise.' She herself had no doubts. For she believed that Peel's moves represented, not a serious desire to rule the country (for which she was prepared), but a plot to separate her from her ladies, with whom she had gone through so much. To the Tories, the Queen's stubbornness represented a plot to keep not her ladies but her lord; while Melbourne's support for the Queen was seen as a bid to climb back to political power through his Sovereign's infatuation. Both sides thus agreed on one aspect of the Bedchamber crisis. It was a plot.

For all his apparent approval of her stand, Melbourne was not sure that he could hold his party together. He called an emergency meeting that same evening where, after long debate, he was able to rally the waverers by reading aloud his letters from the Queen. 'It was impossible,' wrote one of those present, 'to abandon such a queen and such a woman.' On a wave of chivalry, Melbourne at last swept his colleagues in behind her. They even supplied her with a formula to send back to Peel: his proposal to remove her ladies was 'contrary to usage and repugnant to her feelings.'

The Queen was triumphant. In the teeth of the Tories and the Constitution she had won back the Whig Government. The catastrophe averted, she prepared to settle down again to life with Lord M.

The Bedchamber Plot is today far more interesting to the student of human nature than of politics. The battle of 1839 was the last to be fought on the issue of the Queen's ladies. In future Queen Victoria had to change only her Mistress of the Robes. Today the Queen is not expected to make any changes at all.

What caused the crisis? Part of the trouble was created by the personality of Peel himself. Later, when Prince Albert succeeded in interpreting Peel to the Queen, she came to see in him her greatest Prime Minister of all. But his gifts appealed at first sight to men rather than women, and his strained, gauche manner was partly responsible for the Bedchamber crisis. Queen Victoria interpreted it as a sign of double-dealing, and there was certainly much misunderstanding. Peel, for instance, had never asked for more than *some* changes in the Queen's ladies, as Victoria knew very well. But she had told Melbourne that *some* or *all* were the same, meaning that *some* was the thin end of the wedge. She was genuine in this belief. It must be remembered that it was in the atmosphere of hatred and suspicion generated by the Flora Hastings affair that the Bedchamber Plot grew. The Queen felt sure that Peel would sweep out every friend she possessed down to Baroness Lehzen

Sir Robert Peel, the Prime Minister whom Queen Victoria considered a distasteful successor to Melbourne. Even his smile was said to be 'like the silver fittings of a coffin'.

herself – the 'foreign lady' on whom the Tories blamed Lady Flora's purgatory.

This may well have been the intention of the Tory extremists, but not of Peel and Wellington who honestly wanted to make the changes on principle, with no thoughts of malice. And indeed both Melbourne and the Queen came later to regret their behaviour in the crisis. Sixty years afterwards Queen Victoria passed judgement on herself. 'Yes, I was very hot about it and so were my ladies,' she said to her private secretary, Sir Arthur Bigge, 'as I had been so brought up under Lord Melbourne; but I was *very* young, only 20, and never should have acted so again – Yes! it was a mistake.'

The 'mistake' knocked more paint off the Queen's battered image. Stockmar, who was abroad, did not help matters by suggesting that Queen Victoria, like her grandfather King George III, had gone mad. Though there was popular enthusiasm over her fight to keep her friends, Society became more hostile than ever. The Queen felt it deeply. She grew thinner – a slight compensation perhaps for her sufferings – and for weeks went on brooding over the old problems. Did the Tories eventually mean to take *all*? Had she damaged Melbourne's position? She

A cartoon of January 1838 satirizing Queen Victoria's preference for Melbourne and the Whigs against Wellington, leader of the Tories.

denounced everybody, including the faithful Duke of Wellington, and when Melbourne told her Peel was very hurt, she simply denied it. 'I felt thoroughly upset with my situation,' she wrote in her Journal on 14 May and a few days later she announced to Lord Melbourne that she was going to be ill. 'Oh! no, you won't,' said he. Melbourne was right. It was Flora Hastings who, at the end of the month, was desperately sick.

This first great political crisis of Queen Victoria's reign took place, fantastically, against the gayest possible background. The young Queen's stamina was remarkable. The week of crisis had been crowned by what might be called the Bedchamber Ball, where she celebrated her triumph by entertaining the Tsarevitch Alexander, Hereditary Grand Duke of Russia. During the following weeks she entertained the Russian Grand Duke with a theatre, two concerts, a reception and another ball. 'The Queen for ever! Bravo!' shouted the people as she drove through the streets to her parties. Her only complaint of weariness was made on the first day: 'Really all these Fètes in the midst of such very serious and anxious business are quite overwhelming.'

Several things had brought about this new pleasure-loving mood. Revulsion from the memory of her recent ordeal; another birthday, making her cling to her youth ('this day I *go out of my teens* & become 20!'); above all, Russian gaiety and the Russian Grand Duke. Quite deliberately she watched herself falling in love with him, calmly noted King Leopold's disapproval expressed in a crusty letter, and summed up her new feelings in a revealing remark made to Lord M.: 'I said all this excitement did me good.' When her towering dancing partner at last had to go, she confided to her Journal – 'I felt so sad to take leave of this dear amiable young man whom I really think (talking jokingly) I was a little in love with …'

The Grand Duke's sad leave-taking coincided with the news of another more welcome departure.

Ever since the Duke of Wellington's failure to hush up the Flora Hastings affair he had been working patiently to get rid of Conroy. At last, at the beginning of June he succeeded. Sir John resigned from the Duchess of Kent's Household and prepared to quit the country.

How did His Grace do it? asked the incredulous Greville. Partly by flattery: he sent Sir John a coveted invitation to a party on 18 May (Queen Victoria thought this 'shocking'), where J.C. had the satisfaction of cutting Lord M. dead. When Conroy finally told Wellington he had decided to go, the Duke warmly congratulated him:

I cannot but think that you are quite right in the Course which you have taken, and considering the sacrifices which you make, and that it is liable to misrepresentation it is an Honourable and a Manly course.

This letter the Duke ironically described to Lord Liverpool as a '*Pont d'Or*' over which Sir John might retire to the Continent.

Sir John's retirement cleared the way for reconciliation between the Queen and her mother but the process was to be extremely slow. Conroy and his family were to make demands of the Royal Family for years, and though his physical removal did of course do something to check the rumours of the Duchess being his mistress, the gossip and suspicions of the past remained in people's minds. As for the Duchess, Lehzen and the Queen agreed that she would be no better after Conroy had left: she was 'irredeemable'.

The Queen admitted in her Journal to feeling utterly callous about Mama. She told 'stories' to avoid going out with her, a drastic procedure which made the truthful Queen blush. Many years later mother and daughter were to become close again and when in 1861 the Duchess died, the Queen was overwhelmed with remorse by what she read in her mother's diaries.

This all lay far in the future and attempts by Wellington and others to bring mother and daughter together had little success, and were finally thwarted by a sudden worsening in the condition of Lady Flora Hastings. By June she was really ill and the general unpleasantness of the 'affair' was reawakened. The Queen and Melbourne were hissed at public functions but both retained their unsympathetic attitude to the unhappy woman's suffering. Melbourne apparently still believed that she was pregnant though he admitted that 'it would be very awkward if that woman was to die.'

As Lady Flora's end drew manifestly near, the Queen at last listened to her conscience and did all she could for 'this unfortunate Lady Flora', even visiting her on her sick bed despite her horror of death. The Queen's change of heart, worthy though it was, came too late to avoid another flare-up of public scandal. Lady Flora died on 5 July and the post-mortem, which she had desired and which her family agreed to have performed by anyone but Sir James Clark, showed that she had been suffering from a tumour on the liver for many months. Nevertheless, her friends went about saying that she had died from a broken heart and indicating who had broken it. Press attacks multiplied and the Queen thought it worthwhile to record in her Journal an occasion when she and Melbourne had ridden in Rotten Row 'without one hiss'. So calamitously had the young Queen become embedded in a decaying, partisan cause – Whiggery.

How far was Queen Victoria to blame for the most disastrous episode of her early reign? She certainly did not instigate the original enquiries into Lady Flora's condition. She told Melbourne after Lady Flora's death that she and Lehzen had never mentioned their suspicions to any one. But the fact remained that she was one of the first, if not the first, to entertain false suspicions. In future she promised not to judge by 'people's appearance'. When, as usual, she got stones in her shoes out walking and Melbourne said it was 'a penance', she did not disagree.

After Lady Flora's death the Queen dreamed more than once about the dead woman, and her *joie de vivre* vanished; perhaps the truest sign of her penitence. She and Lord M. talked about this and that, but the salt had lost its savour. Nothing seemed amusing, not even riding. It was high time for the twenty-year-old Queen to start life afresh.

10

'My Beloved Albert'
1839–40

Queen Victoria's need for a new life did not mean that she saw at once where to find it. Marriage was certainly not uppermost in her mind. Ten days after Lady Flora's death the Queen wrote to King Leopold warning him that the marriage with Albert was, for the time at any rate, off. It was possible, she admitted, that she might like him enough to marry him – 'all the reports of Albert are most favourable' – but then again, 'I might like him as a friend, and as a *cousin*, and as a *brother*, but no *more* ...' In any case there could be no decision for two or three years 'at the *very earliest*'.

King Leopold was diplomat enough to keep his head and refrain from pressing his niece about her feelings. He held her to one thing only – the visit of his nephews in the autumn. He had taken the precaution over a year ago of summoning Prince Albert to Brussels and telling him how the land lay. Prince Albert had agreed to wait, provided his cousin would marry him in the end; for if several years passed and she then refused him, what chance would he stand of winning an eligible wife? All the best princesses would long ago have been snapped up.

The Queen, while in no hurry to be snapped up, nevertheless had clear ideas about marriage and the sort of man she wanted as a marriage partner. At first the spell of Melbourne had led her to dream of a man older than herself. Later, her yearnings for young partners in the dance and young playmates in the Corridor made her forget the glamour of the old. But if it was a young husband she wanted, she would not marry to order. She found the idea of an arranged marriage repugnant. Her marriage must be a love-match and her partner must come up to her high standards of masculine beauty. For the Queen was very susceptible to beauty, and hailed it with an enthusiasm unexpected in one who set such store by sterling worth. Just before her marriage she frequently emphasized her admiration for male beauty, often discussing the handsome figure of one or other of her courtiers. Melbourne tried to damp down this ardour, perhaps because he feared no suitable consort would come up to the Queen's romantic ideals. He need not have worried.

As before, King Leopold cleverly set the stage for the arrival of Albert and Ernest by sending another batch of Coburg cousins ahead, to prepare the ground. They arrived in September and the visit was a great success. How different, how happy life was now, as the Queen forgot the misery of the past months and revelled in the renewal of warm Coburg family life. And how sad, alas, when they had to go. Queen Victoria was ready to sink under her grief: 'we were *so* intimate, *so* united,

Prince Albert by
Winterhalter.

76

Lithograph of Victoria's
proposal to Albert on
15 October 1839.

so happy!' But as soon as they were safely off the scene, King Leopold concluded arrangements for the visit of Albert and Ernest.

Queen Victoria would always remember 10 October 1839. It opened in the inappropriate way great days sometimes do. She awoke to find that a madman had broken some of her windows at Windsor. This was particularly disagreeable as she and Melbourne were both feeling unwell after eating pork the night before. She went out walking to get rid of her headache.

Suddenly she saw a page running towards her with a letter. It was from King Leopold to say that Albert and Ernest were arriving that very evening. She could hardly believe it, but at 7.30 pm she was at the top of the staircase ready to receive the cousins as they drove into the Quadrangle.

Prince Albert had spent September at the peaceful Rosenau, his happy birthplace, fortifying himself against the expected humiliations of Windsor. He set out with a letter of recommendation from King Leopold in his pocket and an ultimatum in his heart. As regards the engagement, Victoria must either make it or break it. He would not wait.

The crossing to Dover was appalling. He sailed in a paddle steamer which was hurled towards the cliffs, white as gravestones, on enormous seas. He was terribly sick and his 'cowardice' attracted unkind attention. He arrived at Windsor Castle without any baggage.

None of these misfortunes could disguise the Prince's triumphant good looks. As the pale young man in dark travelling clothes mounted the stone stairs, the Queen looked down upon an Albert she did not recognize. He had grown really tall, he had changed. Her heart suddenly leapt up like a flame for she knew that she was in love. That night she wrote in her Journal: 'It was with some emotion that I beheld Albert – who is *beautiful*.'

Next day when the Prince came to her room with letters from the other German cousins she observed his beauty in detail:

such beautiful blue eyes, an exquisite nose, & such a pretty mouth with delicate moustachios & slight but very slight whiskers: a beautiful figure, broad in the shoulders & fine waist.

Ernest's hollow white cheeks and striking black eyes got no mention in the Queen's Journal.

On the third day of the visit Melbourne praised Ernest's brains; Queen Victoria retorted that Albert was far cleverer, though at the moment for obvious reasons under a strain. She herself, she admitted, felt agitated by the whole business. 'Very naturally,' said Lord M., cautiously. Seeing Albert, she continued, had made her feel rather differently about marrying. Melbourne gave her another week to make up her mind. But the Queen's heart had galloped ahead of the old man's calculations.

Next day he found her mind made up; he therefore urged her to marry at once rather than wait. They laughed about the awkwardness of telling Albert – these things were usually done the other way round – and frowned over the awkwardness of telling Mama. In the short space of an hour they had planned all the next moves: the marriage in February after Parliament had met and granted the Prince an

Prince Albert's home in Coburg.

allowance; all the usual honours such as Field-Marshal and Royal Highness but not a peerage; secrecy for the present but people, including Mama, being allowed to guess by Victoria's marks of affection. Though Melbourne privately thought Prince Albert's character and capabilities inferior to his looks, he nobly supported the Queen's decision to marry him: 'a woman cannot stand alone for long, in whatever situation she is.' There were tears in his eyes and before they parted she took his hand and holding it thanked him for being '*so fatherly*'.

That night it was Albert who took the lead in showing affection. He still did not know his fate but as he and the Queen stood in the Corridor saying good night after the informal dancing which Victoria liked so much, he squeezed her hand in a way which she did not fail to notice.

After that handshake the night before, it did not seem so difficult to tell Albert the next day. On the morning of Tuesday, 15 October, Queen Victoria watched him charging up the hill after a hunt and at half-past twelve she sent for him to the Blue Closet. They both knew what was coming and only a few minutes passed before she asked him to marry her.

I said to him, that I thought he must be aware *why* I wished them to come here, – and that it would make me *too happy* if he would consent to what I wished (to marry me).

No more words were necessary. All the tensions were broken, the sleepless nights over, the whispering between Lehzen and Albert's valet finished. They fell into each other's arms, kissing again and again, while Albert poured out in German his longing to spend his life with her.

What sort of man was it who had thus so quickly overcome the young Queen's objections to marriage? Prince Albert had been permanently wounded by the loss of his mother in early childhood. The two little brothers, Ernest and Albert, had been shut up in their nursery with whooping-cough when their lovely young Mama, in tears, rode out of the courtyard and out of their lives for ever. It was a painful story. Tiny, sprightly, bubbling with spirits, Princess Louise had married at sixteen the much older Duke who neglected her shamefully while continuing to pursue his habitual debaucheries. After the birth of Prince Albert on 26 August 1819 she consoled herself elsewhere. Duke Ernest separated from her in 1824 and divorced her in 1826. She married again but fell ill and died seven years later. Albert treasured the memory of his lost mother, at first resenting all attempts to take her place. Thinking of his mother, he grew up wistfully chivalrous towards women and horrified by the masculine licentiousness which had driven her to her fate. Thinking of his father and brother, he was terrified by the immorality in womankind to which he attributed his male relatives' downfall. His ineptitude with women, due to his youthful experiences, presented Victoria with a problem as Queen (though not as wife) which she was not entirely successful in solving.

Despite his loss, Prince Albert's childhood, unlike Princess Victoria's, was at least outwardly free and happy. He was inseparable from his brother Ernest; he loved his severe, self-indulgent Papa, though given no cause to do so; he was devoted to his tutor, Herr Florschütz, who taught him the meaning of a verb by giving him a pinch; above all he adored his home, the Rosenau, a romantic little *Schloss* outside Coburg, hidden in the green heart of a German Forest, where in summer he could hear the sound of fountains through the open windows and in autumn the roaring of stags. The room in which he was born seemed part of the forest itself: green wallpaper with a trellis of convolvulus. He was enchanted by the simple pattern of country life: hunting, riding, gardening, arranging an Albert-Ernest museum in which were exhibited stuffed birds and shells and the insects which his cousin Victoria abhorred. He was an excellent shot but could not understand the fanatics who made sport into a business.

At Brussels and at Bonn University, where the brothers were sent to escape the depravity of Berlin, Prince Albert was happy and successful. He became master of the two most graceful sports, fencing and skating. His good-natured sense of fun came out in a talent for mimicry and practical jokes, all harmless and even popular in an entirely male society.

He studied under professors of international fame, becoming deeply impressed by the nature of scientific law: why should not human beings and governments learn to behave in the same reasonable way? This was totally unlike Queen Victoria; she never looked for laws in human behaviour, being thrown by events either into surprised ecstasy or equally surprised indignation. She had a shrewd idea, however, of how to deal with them once they had happened. And indeed Albert and Victoria

had little in common, except their love for music. In almost every other way the Prince was the Queen's complement. His Coburg grandmother had hailed him at birth as 'the pendant to the little cousin'. Except that Victoria was to hang on Albert rather than vice versa, the two young Coburgs did indeed complete each other like two pieces of Victorian jewellery.

Queen Victoria and Prince Albert at a fancy dress ball in 1842. Painting by Landseer.

For the first dreamlike days the lovers lived only for each other; they sang Albert's compositions, Albert scratched out the mistakes in Victoria's letters – 'he is such a *dear dear* invaluable Treasure!' – they exchanged rings and locks of hair, they held hands tightly while they danced, they flew into each other's arms the moment they were left alone, and as Ernest soon went down with jaundice, this happened more and more frequently. When there was no scratching out to be done in the Blue Closet he would blot the warrants as she signed them, whispering '*Vortrefflichste*' – incomparable one.

One day, when the Prince's visit was almost at an end, he asked to see her Journal. She showed him the '*15th* of October' – their engagement day. He read only a little before his own love, made stronger than ever by the poignant account of hers, choked him and there was no more Journal that evening. They played and sang together until it was time for dinner, followed by the last dance Queen Victoria would have 'as an *unmarried girl*' – a fact which grieved her not at all. On the last morning, 14 November, she kissed his cheek, 'fresh and pink like a rose', and then went away to cry and wait for his return.

After he had gone she apologized to Lord M. for being so tiresome and stupid these days. She could think of only one subject. Melbourne gave his stock answer, but with fatherly tenderness: 'Very natural.'

It was not long before politics caught up on the lovers. Melbourne had taken it for granted that the Tories would accept the Prince's precedence and his Protestantism without a murmur, and he confidently assumed that they would vote the usual £50,000 a year paid to a Consort. The Government was beaten by 104 votes, and Prince Albert's allowance reduced to £30,000. The Queen was frantic. Did this mean that the good, the beautiful, the learned Albert was worth so much less than Queen Anne's Consort, 'stupid old George of Denmark'?

Worse was to come. The Queen had set her heart on her treasure being created King Consort. Melbourne absolutely ruled this out, consoling her with the assurance that Prince Albert would receive the highest precedence without difficulty. Much to his surprise the combined opposition of the Royal Dukes and the Tory leaders meant that a Bill for Prince Albert's naturalization finally had to go through without any mention of his precedence. Thanks to Greville's constitutional researches, the Queen was later able to declare his precedence by royal prerogative. But not until after her marriage.

Further difficulties were to arise over the membership of the Prince's Household. Wishing to avoid the suspicion of party bias he at first suggested a balance between Whigs and Tories. Melbourne at once suspected that, being a German and therefore anti-Liberal, he would fill his Household with the enemy. The Prince's next solution seemed even worse. He would have a group of high-minded, non-political

81

Germans in the key posts. Melbourne was once again at the Queen's elbow, never letting her forget that foreigners were disliked in England. It was all very distressing for Prince Albert; did his wishes count for nothing?

So many setbacks made the Prince melancholy, if not sulky, and he returned to England fully expecting to find a hostile nation and a cool Queen. Once again the Channel was in a perfect fury, tossing the petrified Prince to and fro for five hours and finally drenching the crowds which had assembled to watch him disembark; but the warmth of his welcome at Dover, Canterbury and London belied his fears. As Lord Torrington, one of his escorts, kindly explained, the bad behaviour of Parliament did not reflect the feelings of the nation. By slow stages, to give him a chance to recover from his appalling sea-sickness, he arrived at the Palace on Saturday 8 February, still giddy but outwardly beautiful as ever.

The inmates of Buckingham Palace were in no better shape. The Duchess of Kent was nursing two grievances, one old and one new, and would not dine with the Queen. She wanted precedence over the Royal aunts 'just for the day' and she did not want to move into a separate establishment after the marriage. Melbourne dined but had a bad cough.

On 4 February, six days before the wedding, Queen Victoria had awakened with an atrocious cold. She felt too wretched to change for dinner and spent a miserable night. Next day she could not eat but dozed fitfully until 4 o'clock. Rumours spread through the Palace that she had caught the illness which they dreaded for her above all others – measles. Then the cloud lifted. Her natural buoyancy triumphed and she began to feel better. Having dined alone she went downstairs and stayed till half-past eleven.

After that things improved. She still had to rest a good deal but at least it wasn't measles. An enchanting letter arrived from the Prince with a book of caricatures. On 7 February Prince Albert's valet arrived with the Prince's charming greyhound Eos, while dearest Daisy departed for Windsor to see that all was ready for the honeymoon. Next day came the Prince himself. She never forgot her agitation over his arrival: her running down into the equerries' room to watch from their window for his carriage, hearing it at last and rushing to the door to receive him. Then a marvellous peace: 'seeing his *dear dear* face again put me at rest about everything.'

At length Queen Victoria was able to write in her Journal:

Monday, FEBRUARY 10 – the last time I slept alone. Got up at a $\frac{1}{4}$ to 9 – well, & having slept well; & breakfasted at $\frac{1}{2}$ p. 9 …

It was raining and knowing Prince Albert's temperament she sent him a reassuring little note:

Dearest, – … how are you today, and have you slept well? I have rested very well, and feel very comfortable today. What weather! I believe, however, the rain will cease. Send one word when you, my most dearly loved bridegroom, will be ready. Thy ever-faithful,
Victoria R.

The Queen drove the short distance from the Palace to the Chapel Royal, St James's, in a carriage with her mother and the Mistress of the Robes. She wore a

82

white satin dress trimmed with English Honiton lace, a diamond necklace, Prince Albert's present of a sapphire brooch, and a wreath of orange-blossom which she afterwards sketched in her Journal. She found her twelve immaculately fresh train-bearers, all in white like village maidens among the gold and jewels, waiting for her at the Chapel, having been securely locked in for ninety minutes. She had made the sketches for their dresses herself. Prince Albert was there, slim and tall in his uniform, Lord M. resplendent in a marvellous new coat which, he said, had been built like a 74-gun ship. He carried the Sword of State as he had done at the Coronation, but nobody said this time that he looked like a butcher. The familiar black skull-cap kept the eccentric head of Uncle Augustus warm. He sobbed throughout the ceremony while the Duke of Cambridge made loud, good-humoured comments. The trumpets sounded and the organ played as the Queen walked up the aisle, unusually pale but without a tear, contrary to the press reports. The singing she did not mention, possibly because the choir of the Chapel Royal always sang 'schockingly'.

At the end they were all received with loud applause, even Lord M. to his great satisfaction. The Queen kissed her aunt, Queen Adelaide, but only shook hands with her mother, a fact which sharp tongues remarked upon. She returned to the Palace alone with Prince Albert and sat with him 'from 10 m. to 2 till 20 m.p. 2' in her room, before attending an immense wedding breakfast. During that meticulously charted half-hour while they sat together on the sofa, she gave him his wedding ring and he said there must never be a secret which they did not share. 'There never was.' She then changed into a gown of white silk trimmed with swansdown and a bonnet with a brim so deep that the little face inside could hardly be seen.

At about 4 o'clock they set off for Windsor – 'I and Albert alone, which was SO delightful.' The sun suddenly broke through, and a joyful throng of well-wishers on horseback and in gigs galloped along beside them. Charles Greville sniffed because their chariot was neither new nor very smart; but the picture of this happy couple dashing off on their honeymoon with a rumbustious escort disputing every inch of the road is one that fascinates and astonishes a later age.

The Queen was utterly worn out by the experiences of the past week – outbursts of fury, an attack of fever, crowds and excitement, and at last that three hours of swaying rush through the winter evening. Arrived at Windsor, she and Albert explored the new suite of rooms together, running like children from one to the other, Albert perhaps a shade anxious to find that Lehzen's apartment was only separated from their own bedroom by the Queen's dressing-room. Then Victoria laid aside her swansdown and returned feeling like a dying swan herself, to find Albert playing the piano, wearing his Windsor coat. His embrace revived her for a moment but, when she tried to eat, a racking headache drove her to the sofa for the remainder of the evening:

but ill or not, I **NEVER NEVER** spent such an evening!!! My **DEAREST DEAREST DEAR** Albert sat on a footstool by my side, & his excessive love & affection gave me feelings of heavenly love & happiness, I never could have *hoped* to have felt before! – really how can I ever be thankful enough to have such a *Husband*!

The marriage of Queen
Victoria and Prince Albert
in the Chapel Royal,
St James's Palace.
Painting by George Hayter.

I I
The Blotting Paper
1840

To breakfast with that angelic being, romantically beautiful in open-necked Byronic shirt and black velvet jacket, was inexpressible joy. At noon the Queen took her husband's arm and they walked on the Terrace, alone but for Eos, the black greyhound with a silver streak whose name meant 'dawn'.

On the second morning of their Windsor honeymoon, try as they would to work at their two tables in the Queen's room, 'talk kept on breaking out'. The Queen told Lord Melbourne at the end of a week, with wondering enchantment: 'I never could have thought there was such happiness in store for me'. Rather wistfully he agreed that she would find marriage a great comfort: 'You find it already, do you not?'

Back at Buckingham Palace, solitary walks round the garden with the Prince were her great delight. When it grew dark they played duets on two pianos or read aloud: she professed to find Hallam's *Constitutional History* absorbing. State papers claimed her immediate attention but with what a difference; ' ... Albert helped me with the blotting paper when I signed.'

The pleasures of the dance reached their zenith. Like a tiny humming-bird in her blue satin gown from Paris sparkling with jewels, she flew on to the ballroom floor, rapturously gazing round at the new paint, gilding, mirrors and damask. Albert was a 'splendid dancer' and his performance on the dance floor was only equalled by his grace in the riding school. Round and round he dashed with his 'beautiful seat' and beautiful smile each time he passed his wife.

Needless to say life was not all roses. The Queen and Prince were determined that their Court should be strict and have a 'high' reputation, in contrast to the Courts of Queen Victoria's predecessors. In this ambition they were probably moving with the mood of the times, but not everyone found the new attitude pleasing. The Queen was criticized, rather unfairly, for her hard-heartedness and harshness over etiquette. In truth Queen Victoria was by nature unaffectedly kind and only insisted on etiquette from a sense of duty. More accurately the Prince was pronounced a prude. He was not immune to the impulses of the flesh, but was determined never to go in the way of temptation, for his childhood had taught him that sexual indulgence brought domestic disaster. As the Queen's husband he intended to teach the English people this lesson. Unfortunately the 'old Adam' seemed to lurk in the old aristocracy, and the Prince lacked the gift of reforming these raffish types with the light touch to which they might have responded.

Neither Queen Victoria nor Prince Albert at first suspected that their relations with one another would present any difficulties. But after the first few weeks of bliss there seemed to be some hidden longing which disturbed the Prince's happiness. He was irritable over trifles and every time she flew into one of her rages or sulked over some disagreement – for marriage had not changed her temperament – she would see by his sad, patient look that he was pining for something. She did not know what. Certainly not for women; when she introduced him to her ladies for the first time he found it very tiresome and could not remember which was which. Nor was it for male company. Prince Albert shared to the full the Queen's distaste for the English custom of remaining in the dining-room for port after the ladies had left. He deserted the 'stayers', as Queen Victoria called them, as soon as possible, preferring to sing duets with his wife. When the gentlemen joined them, he would play double chess alone while the Queen talked to her Prime Minister.

In May Prince Albert wrote to his friend Prince William of Löwenstein a sad letter: he was 'the husband, not the master of the house'. Queen Victoria's twenty-first birthday was celebrated soon afterwards and he presented her with a huge bronze inkstand. When would she think of advancing him beyond the blotting-paper stage to wielding the pen?

It seems strange, perhaps, that he did not immediately settle the matter with his wife. The ruthlessness with which he later cleaned up the Household and withstood shameful demands for money from Coburg, seems incompatible with his hesitancy in asserting his own rights. The answer is that Prince Albert's character combined timidity with drive. With the world he could be a masterful innovator; with his wife he was a Hamlet, always awaiting a better moment for doing the deed. They were both strong characters, warm and generous, but whereas Queen Victoria had a secret vein of iron, Prince Albert's hidden streak was of wax.

The Prince saw Lehzen as the main cause of his frustration. In this there was at least an element of truth. The Queen had accepted Lehzen's advice to follow the same plan with the Prince as she had adopted in Lehzen's own case. Jealousy on the part of the public, said Lehzen, had been avoided because she held no official position about the Queen. Let Albert do the same; let him be the invisible husband. The Queen was using the public's suspicions of the Prince to conceal from herself the dread of competition with her husband. This was really the root of the problem. The power of Lehzen, though still considerable, was not as great as the Prince thought. If he had dared he might have extruded Baroness Lehzen there and then. She was far too much of a muddler, and even too amiable, to conduct successfully a difficult campaign against a man much cleverer and more beloved than herself. Instead Prince Albert carried on a secret war of attrition against the Baroness which undermined his own happiness more than her power.

Meanwhile nature herself set in motion the events which were ultimately to solve the Prince's problem. Before March was out the husband in the house heard that he was to become a father. All the conflicting thoughts, including frank dismay, which come into women's minds at such a time were Queen Victoria's. All of them gave her husband fresh opportunities for capturing the citadel. His main task, however, was to restrain her exuberant energies rather than to exorcize her fears,

One of the many attempts to assassinate Queen Victoria. This one took place on Constitution Hill in 1840. The culprit, aged seventeen, was sent to a lunatic asylum for life.

despite the fact that it was only three months previously that she had described having children as 'the ONLY thing I *dread*.' He read to her, sang to her and kept her on her sofa. She gloried in her bounding health, refusing to sit down at levées and drawing-rooms and later battling against the autumn gales. 'I am so strong and active that I brave all that.' She was gratified but not surprised when she heard that the accoucheurs expected a very easy confinement.

The Queen's chief accoucheur, Dr Charles Locock, was taken aback by her frankness. 'She had not the slightest reserve,' he reported, '& was always ready to express Herself, in respect to Her present situation, in the very plainest terms possible.' When she asked Locock whether she would suffer pain he replied that 'pain was to be expected, but that he had no doubt that Her Majesty would bear it very well.' 'O yes,' said the Queen, 'I can bear pain as well as other people.' Prince Albert, on the contrary, told Locock 'he expected She would make a great *Rompos*.' The Prince was to prove wrong. There was to be no rumpus.

Two pistol shots suddenly swept Queen Victoria on to a new pinnacle of popularity and carried Prince Albert a stage further along his desired path.

At six o'clock on 10 June 1840 the Queen accompanied by the Prince was setting off for a drive in her low open carriage up Constitution Hill. Suddenly she heard an explosion and at the same time felt Albert's arms flung round her. 'My God! don't be alarmed!' She smiled at his excitement but next moment saw 'a little man on the footpath with his arms folded over his breast, a pistol in each hand ...' As he aimed at her and fired again she ducked. Then someone on the footpath seized him, her attendants closed in, the crowd shouted 'Kill him! Kill him!' and she sped on up the hill, coolly continuing her drive and at last returning home in the centre of a wildly enthusiastic escort formed by the ladies and gentlemen riding in the Park.

This was the first of many lunatic attempts on the Queen's life – two more were to follow in the summer of 1842. It set the pattern for her reaction to the others. She always showed courage though fearfully shaken, for the fact that her assailants' grievances were imaginary did not make their weapons any less real. In her heart she never believed that they were too mad to know what they were doing.

Prince Albert showed her the pistols 'which might have *finished me off*'. Suppose she were finished off like Princess Charlotte, whose death in childbirth not unnaturally preyed on her mind at this time? With all possible tact Melbourne approached the young expectant mother.

'There is a subject I must mention, which is of great importance, & one of great emergency; perhaps you may anticipate what I mean;' (which I answered I did not), 'it is about having a Bill for a Regency'.

She saw the point.

In July it was Prince Albert who was appointed Regent by Parliament in case of the Queen's death – one more step on the path from the blotting-paper to the pen. Later in the year, as her pregnancy advanced, the Queen found herself increasingly dependent on the Prince and more and more despatches were finding their way from her writing-table to his.

November arrived and with it the event which the Queen, like all expectant mothers, alternately hoped would come off quickly and be indefinitely postponed: 'an event which I cannot say I am quite looking forward to with pleasure.'

A daughter, the Princess Royal, was born three weeks prematurely – 'nothing ready' – to the Queen on 21 November 1840 at 2 pm, only Prince Albert, Dr Locock and Mrs Lilly the midwife being present.

Their first rush of disappointment at the failure to produce a son was the only blot on an otherwise perfect birth. The large concourse gathered in the next room heard Dr Locock's voice through the open door:

'Oh, Madam, it is a Princess.'

'Never mind,' came the Queen's clipped reply, 'the next will be a Prince.'

After her twelve-hour labour, during which she had 'suffered severely' but not felt 'at all nervous once it began', she found herself with no pain whatever and a good appetite. 'Dearest Albert hardly left me at all & was the greatest comfort and support.' Having swallowed a hasty, late luncheon, he dashed off to represent the Queen for the first time in Council, thus passing another milestone on his journey. The Queen insisted that his name should be inserted into the Liturgy: if the nation would not pay for him at least it should pray for him.

Relations with the little Princess Royal were at first affectionately remote. Twice a day the baby paid her mother a visit, one day carrying on her arm a little bag containing a lock of her own light brown hair. At six weeks old the Queen saw her bathed for the second time and found her 'much improved' despite the funny

A contemporary print portraying the scene in Queen Victoria's bedroom just after the birth of her first child, Vicky.

flannel washing-cap on her head. Until she was christened (Victoria Adelaide Mary Louise) the Queen simply referred to her as 'the Child'. After her christening she became Pussy or Pussette, the Queen discovering with surprise that Pussy was 'quite a little toy for us'. In toyland Pussy remained for many months. The Queen had neither time nor inclination to nurse her and a wet nurse had been obtained appropriately enough from Cowes. Mrs Southey, sister-in-law of the poet, was appointed Superintendent of the Nursery; unfortunately she introduced neither poetry nor efficiency into her kingdom.

There is a belief that Queen Victoria disliked children. This was not the case, but until a baby was six months old she certainly considered it 'froglike' and ugly. Nor was she one of those women who positively enjoy the huge, primeval paraphernalia of childbearing. This aspect of wedded life she called 'the shadow-side of marriage' or more often '*die Schattenseite*', since it was an indelicate subject which sounded better in a foreign language. Her first babies were born before anaesthetics were available, and though she was profoundly thankful to use chloroform later on she could never see a young girl entering on matrimony without a shuddering thought of the *Schattenseite*. Perhaps submerged memories of the Flora Hastings affair accounted for her almost Jansenist disgust for the things of the body, which combined strangely with her healthy Hanoverian nature.

King Leopold was given a characteristically sharp glimpse into his niece's mind on these matters after he had wished her joy of Pussy and of many more babies to follow.

I think, dearest Uncle, you cannot *really* wish me to be the 'mamma d'une *nombreuse* famille', … men never think, at least seldom think, what a hard task it is for us women to go through this *very often*.

Scarcely had Pussy been christened before the Queen was expecting another baby; 'I wish she could have waited a little longer,' wrote the Duchess of Kent in her diary. Queen Victoria, for her part, was furious.

The year ended symbolically with the disappearance of the Queen's closest childhood companion – Dash. He was buried under a marble effigy at Adelaide Cottage.

'The Child' had much to live up to. At four months old she was put into the arms of Queen Adelaide in the hope that she would show something of Dash's playfulness. 'I am sorry to say,' wrote her disappointed Mama, 'that the Child screamed & was naughty.'

The seventeenth-century cradle Queen Victoria used for her children.

12

'I am Going'

1841–42

Never had the Queen prayed so often or so fervently as she did around the beginning of 1841 to be cured of her faults and failings, her wilfulness, her impatience and her temper. At her Churching, at Christmas, on New Year's Eve and when taking the Sacrament in January, she made her customary humble petition for amendment. Never was it more needed, for the year 1841 offered her a chance to redeem the mistakes of 1839 and, incidentally, an unexampled opportunity for Prince Albert to become master in the house.

More and more frequently Lord Melbourne had to warn the Queen that the revenue was falling. He put it down to the introduction of penny postage, a curious crotchet which exposed his lack of flair for economics.

Queen Victoria realized that a falling revenue this time meant a falling government. The Whigs would have been out two years ago but for her savage twenty minutes with Peel. On 8 May 1841, with Melbourne's knowledge but unknown to the Queen, Prince Albert sent his private secretary, George Anson, to see Peel about the ladies. While Queen Victoria was in the tense, irritable first months of her new pregnancy it seemed better to present her with a *fait accompli*. At all costs a repetition of the 'Bedchamber' scenes which had occurred precisely two years ago must be avoided: such a catastrophe, all agreed, would mean the end of the Monarchy.

The Prince's courage as well as his kindness in by-passing the Queen were admirable, especially as she might well have expressed resentment when she found out. In fact she felt nothing but gratitude.

Peel proved as human this time as he had seemed harsh before, and if he still could not keep his feet still at the interviews, there was only Anson to see them. He exhibited the Victorian hallmark of genuine feeling – there were tears in his eyes. The party advantage which he would have gained from at long last forcing the Queen to give up her ladies, he chivalrously renounced. Instead it was agreed that the Queen should spontaneously announce three resignations: those of the Duchess of Sutherland, the Duchess of Bedford and Lady Normanby. When, by September, the Whigs were beaten at the polls and all the changes involved in a new Ministry had been smoothly accomplished, Prince Albert could congratulate himself on the success of his bold plan conceived in May.

The only real trouble was Melbourne himself. Alas, the old man could not rest away from his idol. The daily, hourly intimacy of the last three years had meant more to him than even he himself suspected. At the Queen's urgent request he continued corresponding with her, despite Stockmar's fulminations against so dangerous a practice. Though most of Melbourne's correspondence with the Queen was innocuous, he occasionally gave her advice on controversial matters which Peel would rightly have resented. She had reluctantly agreed, for example, to contribute to the Government's new tax levied on incomes. Melbourne warned her against throwing away her money and her prerogative, according to which she was constitutionally exempt from paying Income Tax. Melbourne's behaviour was unwise. After Prince Albert's death she again found it difficult to sever relations with a favourite Minister and to open them with someone she disliked, such as Gladstone. Her correspondence with Lord Salisbury in the 1880s, after his Ministry had fallen, was a case of carrying on what Melbourne had begun.

More typical of the shrewd and generous side of Melbourne's nature was the advice he left to the incoming Prime Minister on handling the Queen. Peel 'should write fully to Her Majesty, and *elementarily*, as Her Majesty always liked to have full knowledge upon everything which was going on'. There was genius in Melbourne's choice of the word *elementarily*, recognizing as it did the unique and awful simplicity of Queen Victoria's requirements. She wanted the whole truth – in one word. Melbourne's advice should have been pinned up for the use of all his successors at No. 10 Downing Street. It might have encouraged Palmerston to be a little fuller and Gladstone a little briefer in their communications.

Best of all Melbourne's services to the Queen was his recommendation to put herself henceforth under Prince Albert's guidance. Apart from the Prince's obvious fitness to be her adviser, it was easier for the old man to hand over his treasure to the husband than to his own rival, Peel. 'The prince understands everything so well,' he said, 'and has a clever able head.' The Queen was delighted, but did not as yet realize that the full warmth of Prince Albert's comfort would be felt only when Lehzen had left her side.

She found however that at last she could live without Lehzen. Dearest angelic 'Daisy', whom two years ago she had prayed not to survive, had been already left behind for one day on 14 June when the Prince visited Oxford to receive an honorary degree. 'Feeling a little low,' wrote the Queen in her Journal, plaintively remembering that she and Lehzen had never been parted since she was five. Lehzen wrote to her using as a letterhead the picture of a little golden engine with the words, 'I Am Coming' written underneath it. No little train, however, would bring Lehzen to join them, and Prince Albert hoped that before long her motto would have been changed to 'I Am Going'.

Later, on a politically unwise tour of great Whig houses during the elections, the parting was longer. Pussy, whose progress in the badly run nursery was not satisfactory, provided Lehzen with a face-saver: she remained behind to look after her.

The little Princess Royal was the innocent cause of Lehzen's eventual banishment. Prince Albert suspected that half the trouble in her nursery was due to Lehzen's interference. His suspicions were increased in the autumn and winter of 1841 when the child's health took a turn for the worse. The anxious young father

Landseer's painting of the
Queen and Prince Albert
with Vicky at Windsor was
described by Victoria as
'very cheerful and pleasing'.

attributed her failure to recover to the incompetence of Lehzen and Dr Clark. Finally his anxieties led to a violent quarrel with the Queen herself over the management of the child. When the Queen withdrew in floods of tears the row was continued, using Stockmar as a go-between. All Prince Albert's pent-up hatred of Lehzen poured out. He would die fighting rather than see his children and his marriage wrecked by the 'crazy, common, stupid intriguer' who had harmed his wife so much as a child and as a young Queen. Stockmar, who felt certain that Albert's tenderness for the Queen would overcome his present passion, decided to use the opportunity to force the issue. If such scenes recurred, he informed the Queen, he himself could not remain at Court.

The Queen was appalled by the chasm opening before her. She dashed off a propitiatory reply to Stockmar who, she said, would soon be thinking her as bad as poor Mama.

Albert must tell me what he dislikes, & I will set about to remedy it, but he must also *promise* to listen to & believe me; when (on the contrary) I am in a passion which I trust I am not very often in now, he must not believe the stupid things I say like being miserable I ever married & so forth which come when I am unwell.

When she reached the subject of Lehzen it was clear that her capitulation was at hand. All she wanted, she wrote, was to give Lehzen a quiet home under her roof, as a reward for past services which even Albert acknowledged.

The Prince handled Lehzen's departure just as he had handled the departure of the Bedchamber ladies – without at first consulting the Queen. When all was settled, he told her on 25 July that Lehzen wished to leave in two months' time for the sake of her health. Victoria was naturally upset though she felt it was 'for our & her best'. As the time approached Lehzen was gently detached. While the Queen and Prince were in Scotland she stayed behind with the children, again sending her little reports: dogs and babies behaving well, no more biting, and the Princess Royal warned not to pull tails.

Sir James Clark visited the Baroness on 27 September for the last time and found her covered in the dust of packing. She slipped away early in the morning of the 30th without saying good-bye to Queen Victoria, in order to spare her a scene. Nothing became Lehzen in her service to the Queen like the leaving of it. Queen Victoria was grateful for Lehzen's thoughtfulness but suffered notwithstanding. She dreamt that night that Lehzen had come back to say good-bye and awoke to the sad truth. 'It was very unpleasant.'

The rest of Lehzen's life was no less unselfish. She settled with a sister in Bückeburg and devoted her savings and pension of £800 a year to establishing her brother's children in careers. Photographs of Queen Victoria filled her house, but some of her habits became rather more advanced than her pupil would have approved. Eager to the last to know the latest gossip, she enticed local worthies into her sitting-room with a promise of Havana cigars. Queen Victoria corresponded regularly and saw her occasionally in Germany before her death in 1870 at the age of eighty-six.

The Prince's dislike of Lehzen was somewhat obsessional. With his passion for efficiency, he was maddened by what he considered Lehzen's frivolity and incompetence. Why, for instance, had she not immediately informed him when one of the courtiers fell idiotically in love with Her Majesty? The Baroness, used to madmen pursuing the young Queen, saw no reason to do so. There had been the Scotsman who came south at intervals to leer at her on the Terrace, and the Manchester businessman who climbed into the Castle grounds seeking a wife. Lehzen did not care a pin for such things.

In the end Lehzen became in Prince Albert's mind the scapegoat for Queen Victoria. All his dear wife's virtues were her own, all her vices Lehzen's. In particular he blamed the Baroness for what he considered to be defects in her education and her intellectual abilities. His animosity against Lehzen led him to exaggerate Queen Victoria's deficiencies. It was tempting to demolish the teacher by degrading her handiwork and Victoria was undoubtedly Lehzen's masterpiece. As Melbourne remarked to Anson in 1841, the world would have considered her accomplished had she been born an ordinary young lady instead of a queen.

Was she really so ill-equipped, even for a queen? Few girls in their early twenties could have equalled not only her experience but her ability to digest and use it. She read widely and could appreciate most of the books put into her hands. She had an excellent memory. Her own style was racy and often took a toss over grammar, but she had a genius for terse dialogue and could summarize a long argument with undeniable dexterity. And although she felt inferior to scholars, when she got on terms with them, as she did for instance with Macaulay, they found her charming and intelligent. Indeed once the Prince could see his wife without the shadow of Lehzen darkening her, he described her to his brother as 'the most perfect companion a man could wish for'.

Faults of character in the Queen concerned him even more than faults of intellect. In particular he feared the violent temper which Lehzen's upbringing had failed to cure, and which was a source of amused gossip. 'I suppose you saw the story of the Queen's giving a regular coup de Patte [smack] to one of her Maids of honour!' wrote Lady Longford to her sister-in-law, Mrs Stewart, in July 1840; 'if she goes on so, no one will envy Prince Albert the trouble of taming so violent a Lady!'

It is true that Lehzen had not inculcated self-control, but at least she taught Queen Victoria to recognize her weakness. In a later age, the Queen's childhood would have been held to excuse almost any pathological condition ranging from mild disturbance to delinquency. That Lehzen handed over to the nation a potentially great queen must be to her credit.

Nevertheless she had to go. It was only after Lehzen's ship, bound for Germany and loaded with the luggage of twenty years was launched at last, that Queen Victoria entered her own 'safe haven'.

13
A Safe Haven
1842–46

The day after Lehzen left, Queen Victoria re-read some of her old diaries. In marrying Prince Albert she had entered what she afterwards described as 'a safe haven'. In this spirit she chose Lehzen's departure as the moment to correct the entry of 1839 in which she had rhapsodized over her 'happiness' with Melbourne.

> 1st October. Wrote & looked over & corrected one of my old journals, which do not *now* awake very pleasant feelings. The life I led then was so artificial & superficial, & yet I thought I was happy. Thank God! I know now what *real* happiness means!

The end of her 'artificial' life with Melbourne seemed to tie up with the end of her emotional life with Lehzen. The act of re-writing this record was symbolic.

A domestic crusade organized by the Prince was already under way. Many of the evils at Court which he set out to remedy dated from the Queen's Accession. Courtiers had taken advantage of her youth. They would dine at her expense even when not in waiting, while people who had nothing to do with the Palace would order carriages by forging the names of ladies-in-waiting. Some of the older ladies were once caught smuggling and the young maids-of-honour needed much managing. They had a fine time in the Queen's service: Lehzen spoilt them, they had comfortable rooms, pianos, sheets like silk, lots of hot tubs and only one serious restriction; they were forbidden to walk on the Slopes at Windsor alone for fear of being assaulted.

The royal residence, despite high expenditure, were abominably run. Service was erratic. Guests wandered about looking in vain for their bedrooms or for the way downstairs. Comfort and hygiene were scarcely considered even when alterations were undertaken. The construction of a new lavatory was begun at Buckingham Palace immediately over the Queen's bedroom, the waste being connected to a nearby rainwater pipe which discharged itself on to leads in front of her dressing-room window. Worst of all was the cold. As an unmarried girl the Queen had taken a brash pride in telling shivering Ministers that she did not mind cold, but now she complained with the rest. On one very icy day she could not get her sitting-room temperature above 55 degrees Fahrenheit. Next morning she lost her voice.

Prince Albert reduced the evil to a simple formula: lack of a single authority in control. His prize example of muddle concerned the laying of a fire. Why was there no heat in the morning-room? Because the fire was laid by the Lord Steward but

Opposite The Queen and Prince saw more of their children than many other Victorian parents.

TO THE
QUEEN'S PRIVATE APARTMENTS

THE QUEEN AND PRINCE ALBERT AT HOME.

was lighted by the Lord Chamberlain; until the two could be co-ordinated there would be no fire. The Department of Woods and Forests cleaned the outside and the Lord Chamberlain the inside of the windows. Both sides were never clean at once so that Queen Victoria, whose first pleasure on waking was to observe the state of the weather, often had to depend on guesswork.

Into every corner went the Prince's broom, sweeping out among others a man-servant who enjoyed the perquisite of collecting each morning hundreds of candles which had never been lighted. The Prince has therefore gone down to history as a saver of candle-ends. His manoeuvres against the venal and incompetent persons who served Her Majesty required a tact which this zealous young German did not possess. In any case it would have been impossible to dismantle a spoils system without making enemies.

There was a clean sweep in the nursery. Lady Lyttleton, an old-fashioned Whig lady who adored Prince Albert, was installed as nursery governess. Now there was no more friction and it was pure joy for the Queen to visit the nursery. Her only regret was that at Buckingham Palace the nursery wing was 'literally a mile off', so that she could not drop in as often as she wished, to see Albert dragging the children round the room in a basket.

Prince Albert reformed the nursery just in time, for it was soon filled to overflowing. Albert Edward, Prince of Wales, was born on 9 November 1841, eleven and half months after his sister. There was great gladness over 'the Boy', as Queen Victoria called the Prince of Wales in her Journal. (It was only after the birth of his sister, Princess Alice, that he began to get a name – 'Bertie', while about the same time 'Pussy' disappeared and was replaced by 'Vicky'.) The children filled up much of their parents' day. The Queen sketched Pussy tearing round the bath-tub trying to get in – a naked cherub beside a huge tank on wheels – and wrote her Journal with Pussy on her lap. Prince Albert played his organ while dancing a baby on each knee.

It was not long before the Queen was pregnant once again. On 25 April 1843 a second daughter arrived, Princess Alice. The Prince was too busy now to spend much time with his wife afterwards; she therefore became bored with lying-in and returned quickly to normal. Normality included frequent fights between the two eldest children, but Alice and Prince Alfred ('Affie') who arrived on 6 August 1844 were no trouble.

Surveying the four children under four, Prince Albert resolved to bring up each one 'for its position': Bertie for King of England, Affie for Duke of Coburg in case Ernest had no heir, baby Alice to carry on some royal line. And the Princess Royal? At Prince Alfred's Christening her position was mapped out. The heir to the King of Prussia was invited to be one of Affie's godfathers. He had a son of twelve. Vicky was nearly four. Her position was to be the most interesting of all. She would rule Prussia.

While Prince Albert planned the future, Queen Victoria threw herself into being a good mother. At last she had begun to feel, what to her was the acme of desire, safe. The domestic daisy-chain of pleasant, small events was strung out across the peaceful months. In the spring they would play skittles in the Palace garden, coming back to cowslip tea and the family albums; in summer she would take the children into the kitchen garden to gorge themselves with fruit.

All the Queen's past discontents were melting away. She was happy everywhere. When the time came to leave Buckingham Palace for one of the other royal residences she felt regret – 'I have been so happy there' – but had to add, 'but *where* am I not happy *now*?' Albert, however, suffered from staying too long in London and for his sake she gradually trained herself to prefer the country.

The family was growing apace. Princess Helena (Lenchen) was born in 1846. But there was little privacy for family life. On Sunday afternoons at Windsor the little Queen would march bravely into a wall of humanity who stood grinning and staring until the last moment, when they slowly backed away. The problem was the same wherever she went. There was only one solution: a holiday home of their own right away in the country.

The subject was much discussed during the summer of 1842, when the Queen and Prince paid their first visit to Scotland, and in 1843 when they cruised along the South Coast and stayed with the French royal family at Château d'Eu, the first visit to be made by an English monarch since Henry VIII met Francis I on the Field of the Cloth of Gold. She was transported by the gaiety and elegance, but most of all by finding herself at ease 'in a family circle of persons of my own rank, with whom I could be on terms of equality & familiarity'. The portly King Louis Philippe paid a return visit to Windsor the following year and the phrase '*Entente Cordiale*' was coined.

Home again from her sea trip, the Queen felt 'pent up'. Now her thoughts and those of Albert turned firmly to the idea of a place of their own. By December their thoughts, guided by Sir Robert Peel, had fastened upon the Isle of Wight and secret plans were afoot to buy Osborne.

In the autumn of 1844 the Queen and Prince once more visited Scotland and this time stayed at Blair Atholl. The Queen soon ran out of glowing adjectives. 'I can only say that the scenery is lovely, grand, romantic, & a great peace and wildness pervades all, which is sublime.' Many of the patterns for their future life in the Highlands were laid down: Queen Victoria reading aloud from Sir Walter Scott; Prince Albert stalking deer and never losing his temper even when every shot missed; Pussette frightened at Papa saying he would call a roaring stag into the castle; old red-haired Peter Frazer, Lord Glenlyon's head keeper, nursing his master through a serious illness – 'one sees so much of that kind of attachment in the Highlands,' observed the Queen; Albert noting resemblances to Thuringia in every mountain and lake; Victoria saying good-bye to the 'dear dear *Highlands*' and watching with infinite despondency her life and the countryside steadily becoming flatter and flatter as she travelled south.

Her despondency soon vanished. The rest of the year was to be far from flat. First there was the return visit of King Louis Philippe, and then in October the first holiday at Osborne. The Queen found it exactly what she wanted – snug, complete, an excellent place for the children. Sir James Clark came to vet it for the

air. They were back in their 'dear little Home' next spring, the Princess Royal in raptures over the shells and Prince Albert over the scope for improvements. They planned to buy up the surrounding estates. 'Our possessions will be immense,' wrote the Queen with mingled awe and complacency. Soon they were to replace the 'dear little Home' by a splendid mansion.

In the autumn of 1845 the Queen visited Germany for the first time in her life and saw the Rosenau, Prince Albert's birthplace. The experience was profoundly emotional.

If I were not who I am – *this* would have been my real home, but I shall always consider it my *2nd* one.

A strange feeling took possession of her that she had lived there before, an indication that her rejected Kensington childhood was banished at last.

Contrary to the Queen's expectations she found Peel's Ministry an integral part of her safe haven. With her instinct to look on the bright side of people, she was

King Louis-Philippe's arrival at Windsor, 1844. Queen Victoria found it delightful to be with 'persons of my own rank with whom I could be on terms of equality and familiarity'.

102

soon remarking that despite his 'pompous' manner he had a good voice. As Peel gradually unfroze he talked 'very interestingly' about contemporary politics, vividly describing how Cobden attacked him and the Corn Laws in the Commons, 'twisting his black hair through his fingers'; or telling her that the rising Radical, Mr Roebuck, was a new Robespierre – very dangerous and bold. She admired the refusal of Peel, the cotton spinner's son, to accept honours, agreeing with Lord Aberdeen that it showed 'a proud humility'. Above all, she was deeply moved by his appreciation of Albert.

It was due to Peel that from 1842 onwards Prince Albert attended the Ministers' audiences with Her Majesty. In time the Prince was reading despatches to the Queen instead of her reading extracts to him, and when she expressed an opinion to Ministers she spoke of 'we' not 'I'.

The Queen rapidly developed interest in social affairs, now that she was guided by Peel and the Prince. She found it natural to help individuals or groups wherever possible but misunderstood their frantic efforts to help themselves. She could assist the unemployed silk weavers of Spitalfields by organizing a magnificent *bal costumé* or send money to the families of two sailors who had died at a Spithead review, but with the Chartists, for instance, she felt no sympathy. Workmen who demanded the vote and secret ballot, she believed, had been misled by professional agitators and the 'criminals and refuse of London'.

In the middle of 1844 economic affairs suddenly caused one of those political upheavals which the Queen so much dreaded. 'Why are the Tories like walnuts? Because they are troublesome to *peel*,' was a conundrum which had been going the rounds since 1842. Now it was not amusing. Distress was still acute, despite several years of buoyant revenue, and cheaper food brought about by the repeal of the duties on commodities like sugar and corn was the insistent demand of the Anti-Corn Law League. Peel, elected to defeat Melbourne's very mild instalment of Free Trade, had become converted by events to the Opposition's creed. In June he proposed to reduce the sugar taxes but was defeated. Only a later vote of confidence saved him from resigning.

Throughout the crisis Queen Victoria had despaired. To lose Sir Robert, so safe, so noble-minded – if anything a bit too much so – was unthinkable. How different from Disraeli who, at the head of the ultra-Tories, was attacking Peel in the unprincipled, disgraceful manner one would expect from a man of such bad, bitter character. The Queen tried to drown her future idol in a sea of raging adjectives. Disraeli was reckless, unsafe. . . . 'Oh! for a little true, *disinterested patriotism.*'

Next summer the heavens opened and rained away the last of peace and plenty. Peel warned her that a potato famine in Ireland would almost certainly mean a violent clash over the Corn Laws. For a moment he led her to hope that the reports of famine were exaggerated; the peasants might be able to grind their putrid potatoes into meal. By the end of November she learnt that the reports had shown a fearful optimism. Peel must reform the Corn Laws.

In December, while the Royal Family were peacefully at Osborne, a tornado swept Parliament and the blow fell. Sir Robert Peel announced his resignation to the

'I'm afraid you're not strong enough for the place, John.' A cartoon of 1845 satirizing Lord John Russell's failure to form a government to take over from Peel.

Queen on the 6th, for neither Lord Stanley nor the Duke of Buccleugh would support him on Corn Law reform. The Queen could not speak for tears. Good Sir Robert was even safer than Lord M., she wept: the fact that she had taken him so unwillingly and now was so upset to lose him, *proved* his great worth.

Next day she awoke as if to a bad dream. Peel drafted a letter for her to send to Lord John Russell, offering him the Premiership. The prospect of Lord Palmerston instead of Lord Aberdeen as Foreign Secretary was appalling. There would be 'horror' in Paris over the change, she wrote in her Journal, and relations with the French were already none too good. She and the Prince between them, said Lord Aberdeen encouragingly, must keep Palmerston straight. One grain of comfort lay in the fact that Russell's Ministry, if he succeeded in forming one, could only exist with Peel's support.

On 19 December came 'astounding' news. Russell had failed. 'Our excitement & suspense great,' scribbled the Queen. The excitement in Parliament was unparalleled. Next day she was celebrating her miraculous escape. In Disraeli's famous words, Russell handed back with courtesy the poisoned chalice to Sir Robert. Peel promised to 'stand by the Queen', and the Duke of Wellington forced the peers to stand by Peel.

The Queen and Prince realized that their unexpected reprieve from the Whigs might be short-lived. They supported Peel with intensified ardour. In January 1846 the Queen reported the sinister fact that Peel's speech announcing his programme for repeal of the Corn Laws was cheered by the Opposition, while his own Conservative ranks remained silent. More sinister in the eyes of the Conservatives was Prince Albert's appearance in the House of Commons, showing royal bias in favour of Free Trade. Such was the outcry among Protectionists that the Prince was forced to make his first appearance his last at a Parliamentary debate. The Queen was beside herself: it was too bad to be criticized by 'gentlemen who did nothing but hunt all day, drunk Claret or Port Wine in the evening, & never studied or read about any of these questions'. As for Lord Stanley who led the Westminster hunting men in their profligate view-halloo, she agreed with the *Spectator* that he ought to be sent back to Eton.

At the beginning of June, safely delivered of a fifth child, Queen Victoria turned again to the unsatisfactory state of politics. Fortunately her nerves were better after this confinement than ever before: Albert had been with her every moment

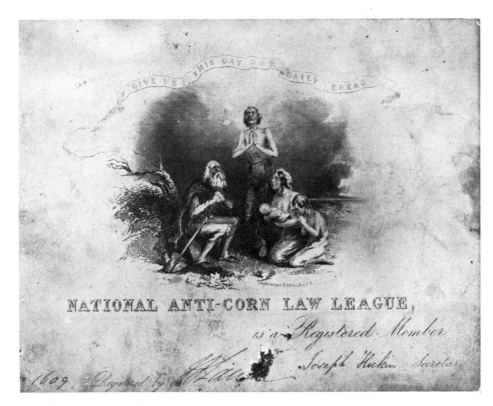

The Anti-Corn Law League pressed for repeal of the duties on corn and hence cheaper food for the poor. It was Peel's conversion to this cause against the Protectionist views of the Tory party that led to his downfall in 1846.

holding her hand and fanning her. 'I feel quiet & prepared for whatever may come.'

On 26 June the end came. Simultaneously with the passage of repeal through the House of Lords, Peel's Ministry was paradoxically defeated in the Commons on a measure for Irish coercion.

Queen Victoria controlled her feelings. Though she 'hated' the Whigs for their 'indecorous' place-hunting, and felt aggrieved that the crisis had developed when her lying-in was scarcely over, she was now training herself to take politics as they came. From inside her safe haven she looked forward to a time when the defeat of a Prime Minister would cause her scarcely more alarm than the departure of Mrs Lilly, her monthly nurse. Perhaps one day Westminster would run as smoothly as her nursery. Until then, life would continue to offer precious hours of peaceful seclusion.

Really when one is so happy & blessed in one's home life, as I am, Politics (provided my country is safe) must take only a 2nd. place.

Provided the country is safe... Queen Victoria had reached the conclusion that she and the Prince could contribute to the safety of the country in two distinct ways, over the heads of whatever governments were in power. In foreign politics, encouraged by Stockmar and Lord Aberdeen, they intended henceforward to assume special responsibilities. In domestic affairs, their happy family life would keep the country morally safe.

Perhaps it was as well that politics no longer came first with her. For whereas her domestic contribution was unassailable (except by 'the fashionables' as she contemptuously called Prince Albert's enemies), her right to control foreign affairs, now in the hands of Lord Palmerston, was soon to be sharply challenged.

The Irish potato famine of 1845–6. Scene at the gate of a workhouse. In deference to Irish feelings Queen Victoria rationed the Palace bread.

14
'Great Events make me Calm'
1846–48

As an unmarried girl Queen Victoria had been well aware of Lord Palmerston's darts, both those which charmed and those which hurt. The one-time student of Edinburgh University, nicknamed 'Cupid' for obvious reasons, was a man of fifty-three, still handsome, when Queen Victoria came to the throne. As her Foreign Secretary she found him an agreeable member of 'our pleasant little *cercle*' and at the end of her first three months as Queen wrote: 'I hope & trust I may spend many such *summers* with the *same friends*'.

Palmerston like Melbourne possessed the loud yaffling laugh of the self-confident Whig; he had much better manners than Melbourne, an equally good but more robust temper and a jolly taste in waistcoats and women. With women, as Greville remarked, he was always enterprising and audacious. He had been Secretary-at-War and a Tory from 1809–28 and then as Whig Foreign Secretary in 1830 had set up a throne for Princess Victoria's uncle, King Leopold, in Belgium. In Portugal and Spain he supported her two little royal 'sisters', Maria and Isabella, as constitutional queens. His mixture of Whig and Tory qualities should have made him permanently acceptable to the Queen.

Soon he was to develop a pattern of behaviour far from acceptable to either the Queen or Prince Albert. In 1840, in Egypt, he gave a first demonstration of his famous 'gunboat diplomacy'. Why could he not 'ménager' our French rivals in Egypt, she asked Melbourne, instead of sending gunboats and threatening to chuck Mehemet Ali into the Nile? His attitude to the Press, on the other hand, was too friendly: he encouraged them to put in tendentious articles. Lastly he juggled with the despatches. From Melbourne she extracted the admission that Palmerston delayed sending despatches which he did not like.

The man in fact was far from 'safe', the quality above all others which Queen Victoria and Prince Albert sought in statesmen. And yet – they could not deny that he was often right. He did the right thing in the wrong way.

If Palmerston was not 'safe', the trouble with Lord John Russell was that he was too 'little'. To begin with he was small in size, a terrier to Peel's great Dane, impudence to his dignity; so diminutive that when he married the widow of Lord Ribblesdale he was called 'the widow's mite'. Because he was a party man the Queen thought Lord John 'little' in politics, too, despite the fact that he had introduced the great Reform Bill of 1832. You only had to think of the Russells, to know what it meant to be a Whig. In Lord John she studied her first true specimen. Abroad, Whigs were unmoved by the divinity of kings but were devoted

to constitutional governments. At home, Whigs upheld the class structure in their own splendid palaces while intermittently extending the blessings of the Constitution to the lower orders.

Russell's Government of 1846, with Palmerston again as Foreign Secretary, was scarcely installed before Queen Victoria felt that there were going to be renewed troubles. Her contemplated Irish visit was hanging fire. At first the reports were conflicting. Lord Heytesbury informed her that the material condition of Ireland was excellent and only the moral state very bad, while Lord John Russell took a gloomy view. At the beginning of August he still thought there were arguments for Her Majesty visiting the afflicted island, but by the middle of the month he considered the potato famine so shocking that the royal tour must be postponed. Queen Victoria had been anxious to get it over; among other things she did not like her subjects speculating as to whether she *dared* go.

A feeling of intense pity for suffering humanity swept over Queen Victoria for the first time when she read about the Irish famine. Up till then she had worried over individual cases – gypsies, performing dwarfs or the widows of workmen accidentally flung from the scaffolding while carrying out improvements to her palaces. Now the state of Ireland filled her with that generalized 'social' indignation which is at the root of reform. For once those around her did not minimize the disaster.

Talked of the extreme distress in Ireland & the fear that the Landowners would try & turn the intended employment for the poor into an improvement of their own properties at the public expense.

The sufferings of the peasants were 'really too terrible to think of' and burials took place to save expense without clergy or coffins – an aspect of their misery which particularly appalled the Queen.

... & in the midst of all this, the Landlords appropriate the people's corn! after all we have done to supply the needy with food! God alone can bring help, for no human means seem able!

The Queen soon found that the starving Irish were turning to 'human means' for salvation of which she could not approve. What she called the 'insubordination of the poor' began to loom larger in her mind than the 'mismanagement among the higher classes', though in deference to Irish feelings she rationed the Palace bread to one pound per head. Towards the end of 1847 she greeted the murder of yet another Irish landlord with shocked despair. 'Really they are a terrible people.' When the Year of Revolutions dawned the Queen was more preoccupied with Continental eruptions than with Smith O'Brien, 'Young Ireland', and the other demonstrations of that terrible people's feelings, at least when they took place in their own country. She just found time to jot down 'risings in all directions', fires on the hills, bugles calling all night and poor Lady Waterford not allowed even into her garden for fear of being seized as a hostage.

It was not till August 1849 that a royal visit to Ireland was at last considered safe. In view of the continuing distress it was not to be an expensive State tour.

Opposite Henry Temple, 3rd Viscount Palmerston, the Foreign Secretary whose independent 'gunboat diplomacy' so much annoyed Victoria and Albert.

She first set foot on Irish soil at Cove (now Cobh), in order to give the people the 'satisfaction', as she put it, of changing its name to Queenstown. (They had the satisfaction of changing it back again some seventy years later.) She stuck to the safety of her yacht except for a brief disembarkation at Cork, whence she proceeded by sea to Kingstown, marvelling at the beauty of the women, their rags ('they never mend anything') and their extraordinary manner of expressing loyalty by shrieking. Her warm heart flowed out to these tatterdemalion crowds and only three things in Ireland drew down mild displeasure: the muggy climate, a 'poor little dove' carrying an olive branch which was plumped into her lap, and the two thousand ladies and gentlemen who presented themselves at a levée in Phoenix Park: some were awkward, others ridiculous, all in a dreadful state of perspiration having been packed into a stifling waiting-room – 'not quite pleasant for my *hand*!'

The Queen adored Phoenix Park and if Lord John's scheme for abolishing the Lord Lieutenancy had come off, would have liked to stay there for her proposed biennial visits instead of at the gloomy Castle. Everything that she could do personally to make her Irish visit a success, she did, even to standing up waving her handkerchief on the paddle-box of her yacht and ordering the Royal Standard to be lowered in response to the cheering crowds as she sailed away. Perhaps if she had followed up this visit as Lord John proposed, its good effects might have been more lasting. As it was, 'the idyll had been charming, but it brought no result.' There were too many Irish rebels behind the cheering crowds who wanted to see the Royal Standard not only lowered but rolled up and taken away.

Such sentiments were not peculiar to the Irish, as the Queen well knew. For the year before she had learned much about rebellion. The Year of Revolutions was indeed an experience that she would never forget. As usual the Queen made an excellent job of describing in her Journal the extraordinary things that happened. She learnt that the dreadful tocsin in Paris had sounded at midnight on 23 February 1848 and was thought by the poor dear French royal family to be 'only' a local rising. When the King discovered his mistake he promptly abdicated, forbidding the National Guard to fire on the mob. '*J'ai vu assez de sang*', he moaned over and over again, as his family hurried him across the dark Tuileries gardens, having escaped from the back of the Palace just as the mob rushed the front. Queen Victoria afterwards strongly criticized the old King's collapse and refusal to show fight.

On the 27th some of the 'heartstricken' French family began to trickle in, but not her darling Coburg cousin, Victoire Nemours, or the Duke of Montpensier, who had got separated from the rest and were 'God knows where!' On 3 March a letter arrived from Newhaven from the French King beginning 'Madame' instead of 'Ma Soeur', and signed simply and humbly 'Louis Philippe'. The old King had been smuggled across the Channel by a commando-type British Consul at Le Havre who decided to disguise him as his own uncle, 'Mr Smith', for which purpose he was clean shaved, stripped of his wig and equipped with goggles and a cap. Victoire Nemours turned up also, having lost all her clothes to the Paris mob. They were now being worn, remarked the Queen with what sounded like horrified relish, by 'the worst women!'

Winterhalter's famous painting of Victoria and Albert with their five eldest children.

'Victoria the Guardian Angel!' A German caricature of the Queen giving asylum to the monarchs of Europe following the revolutions of 1848.

Prince Albert, looking desperately careworn, organized clothes and other necessities for the travellers, while Queen Victoria tried in vain to dispel her husband's gloom. Things might not be so bad as they seemed.

They became worse. 'It seems as if the whole face of Europe were changing,' wrote the Queen as the revolutionary tornado threatened a great Empire like Austria, kingdoms like Hanover, Bavaria, Naples and Prussia, countless small Duchies like Schleswig, Holstein, Leiningen and even little Coburg and Gotha. Three countries stood firm: Queen Victoria's England, King Leopold's Belgium and the Tsar's monstrous despotism in the East.

As if to point the contrast between normality at home and chaos abroad, Queen Victoria on 18 March 1848 produced her sixth child, Princess Louise. The baby, the largest since Prince Alfred, was a fine child with very white skin but the Queen, no doubt tense with every kind of anxiety, had an unusually bad time.

On 3 April the Queen's confinement ended and she breakfasted once again 'in our dear old way with my dear Albert'. Suddenly came news well calculated to spoil Queen Victoria's and Prince Albert's first breakfast together: a gigantic Chartist meeting was planned in London for the 10th – only a week ahead. Frantically worried, the Prince strode out for a calming walk round the Palace gardens, perhaps soon to be invaded by a mob of 'the worst women' who would deal with Victoria's wardrobe as their French sisters had dealt with Victoire's. He returned in somewhat better shape only to find the Queen shivering with nerves and weeping uncontrollably. What would happen to her and the children, she sobbed, and to that little fortnight-old baby?

The Prince forgot his own torments in the business of soothing his distracted wife whose physical weakness entrapped her into recriminations against her best beloved. He was soon able to tell her that her Ministers advised the whole Royal Family to flee to Osborne – of course in a deliberate and orderly manner – two days before the Chartist meeting was to take place. The Queen's tears began to flow less wildly, and she managed to gasp out her willingness to accept anything as long as she and Albert were *together*. By the next day, 4 April, her efforts to regain self-command had succeeded so completely that she found herself penning to King Leopold a notable boast:

> ... I never was calmer & quieter & less nervous. *Great* events make me quiet and calm; it is only trifles that irritate my nerves.

Like many an honest apologia it was only half true.

In cold rain the royal party left London on the 8th, Queen Victoria stretched on a couch in the train. Having arrived safely at Osborne her mood characteristically changed. She suddenly felt out of everything. The intense peace 'bewildered' her. Those shady ilexes and primrose paths led away from an experience which, though '*most sad*', had been '*eventful*' and '*ever memorable*'; 'the contrast seems rather trying. Our coming here has made a break which is, at 1st., almost painful to me.'

Good tidings came through on 10 April. Nothing about the Chartist meeting turned out to have been monstrous except its failure. The number of demonstrators who gathered at Kennington Common for the march on the Houses of Parliament – 23,000 instead of half a million – was derisory; a pale and trembling Feargus O'Connor, who was to have led them, shook the hand of the Chief Commissioner of Police with fervent gratitude when informed that no march would be permitted, and with equal thankfulness allowed the police to hail for him and his lieutenants three cabs. In these vehicles petition and petitioners trotted harmlessly to Westminster, where the Chartist demands were tamely presented and left to lie on some eternal table, until in the whirligig of history they were dusted down and granted to the Chartists' heirs.

The Year of Revolutions was one of the few years during this domestically happy period to which the Queen and Prince said good-bye without regret, glad to get out of it with whole skins. There was no disguising that she had been badly shaken by the Chartists. The Prince of Prussia, a temporary refugee in England, saw the Chartists face to face and told her that they were the genuine revolutionary article, 'horrid-looking people'. Yet their very odiousness impressed the Queen as never before with the devotion of her people as a whole. 'High & low, Lords & Shop-keepers,' she wrote, set an example of firmness and loyalty which would benefit other less favoured countries.

The Queen was to experience this devotion again in 1849 and 1850 when two more attacks were made on her. The first, by an Irishman with an unloaded pistol, was similar to the attacks of the early 1840s. But the second was more serious in that it involved real physical battery. The assailant, a retired cavalry officer, struck the Queen on the head with his cane while she was driving in the park. Although not too much damage was done, the assault underlined the exposed nature of her position and that of her fellow sovereigns, as the Year of Revolutions itself had done.

Not unnaturally the result of such experiences was to reinforce the reactionary side of the Queen's nature. 'I maintain that Revolutions are always bad for the country,' asserted Her Majesty to Lord John Russell in August 1848, 'and the cause of untold misery to the people.'

Obedience to the laws & to the Sovereign, is obedience to a higher Power, divinely instituted for the good of the *people*, not of the Sovereign, who has equally duties & obligations.

We do not know what thoughts occurred to the pugnacious little Whig as he listened to this Victorian version of the divine right of kings.

Peel's police force, created in 1829, appearing quite relaxed while watching a Chartist demonstration.

15
The Devil's Son
1848–50

Theoretical arguments about revolution between the Queen and her Prime Minister were as nothing to their practical differences over one acute and growing problem – the Foreign Secretary. The uneasy relationship, sometimes inflamed, which had existed between Queen Victoria and Palmerston since he returned to foreign affairs in 1846, came to a head in the Year of Revolutions.

Both Lord Palmerston and Prince Albert explained to her in April 1848 the prickly Schleswig-Holstein question. Their accounts by no means tallied. The Prince earnestly desired that a new, liberal, united Germany, emergent from the revolutionary upheavals, should eventually control the two Duchies, while Palmerston supported Denmark's claim to them. Palmerston was bent on using the revived *entente cordiale* with republican France to free Italy from Austria by a concerted heave, but Prince Albert saw this as tearing to pieces an empire like Victoria's own. The Queen not unnaturally listened to her husband on subjects which after all, as a European himself, he must know more about than Palmerston. Every trick of the Foreign Secretary, or '*bock*' (blunder) as Albert preferred to call it, was used to frustrate the Court: delay in sending them drafts until after the despatches themselves had been mailed; bland ignoring of alterations agreed upon between them; the sending of a rude despatch, of course not vetted by the Court, to the Spanish Government in the summer telling them how to behave. The affronted Spaniards showed that they knew how to behave at least in regard to Palmerston: they sent the British Ambassador packing.

By mid-September the Court, entrenched for the first time at Balmoral, had hatched a plot to banish Palmerston to Ireland as Lord Lieutenant. The idea had a certain craftiness, for Palmerston, with Irish estates of his own, was not likely to regard the Irish rebels quite so sympathetically as he did those in Europe. In disclosing this plan to Russell, the Queen let fall the ominous remark that she might soon be unable 'to put up with Lord Palmerston any longer, which might be very disagreeable and awkward'.

Not only would it be 'awkward', it would also be unconstitutional. The Sovereign had no more right to dismiss her Minister for failure to consult her than the Minister had to treat her with this discourtesy. Constitutionally, both sides were sailing near the wind, Palmerston with unruffled good humour, the Court in a frenzy. Queen Victoria told her doctor that whenever she had to read one of Palmerston's despatches before dinner, it made her bilious.

Meanwhile in Europe Palmerston continued his rake's progress. His Italian despatches, the Queen declared when she saw them, were 'unworthy of a gentleman'. In January of the new year, 1849, *The Times* revealed that he had secretly supplied a British contractor with arms out of the Royal Ordnance for Sicilian rebels, thus enabling them to carry on their fight against their local tyrant King 'Bomba', without openly infringing Britain's neutrality. A typical Palmerstonian *bock*. Queen Victoria was thrown into transports of rage. England *must* apologize to the King. It was too monstrous.

Nothing but Prince Albert's increasing help and attentiveness made the Queen's position endurable. But even such a combination as '*I* and Albert' was no match for 'Pam', as Palmerston was affectionately called. Next year he was at it again. The notorious Don Pacifico case, described by the Queen as 'a most disagreeable business', was causing her deep anxiety at the beginning of 1850. At first she put down Palmerston's behaviour to 'mere love of mischief'. A Portuguese Jewish merchant, Don David Pacifico, born at Gibraltar and therefore a British subject, had had his house in Athens burnt down by a Greek Orthodox mob. King Otho of Greece and his Government rejected Don Pacifico's immoderate bill for damages and Palmerston intervened on Pacifico's behalf. Eager to thwart Palmerston France mediated between Greece and Britain, but two days after a compromise settlement had been reached in London, Palmerston's ever ready gunboats seized all King Otho's ships in the Piraeus and triumphantly vindicated Don Pacifico's claim. Never was a gentleman more misnamed. England stood on the brink of war. France recalled her ambassador and Russia joined in the general howl of hate. Quite coolly, as if nothing had happened, Palmerston gave Queen Victoria the shocking news. 'The levity of the man is really inconceivable!'

In the House of Commons on 25 June 1850, Lord Palmerston faced his critics. Radicals and Tories, among them Sir Robert Peel making the last speech of his life, challenged the Foreign Secretary to justify the Don Pacifico gunboats. In a 'most brilliant speech of 4 hours & $\frac{1}{2}$ without stopping for one moment even to drink a little water', as the Queen generously recorded in her Journal next day, the Foreign Secretary consummated a triumph of oratory with an appeal to national pride as telling as any in history:

... as the Roman in days of old held himself free from indignity when he could say *Civis Romanus Sum*, so also a British subject, in whatever land he may be, shall feel confident that the watchful eye and the strong arm of England will protect him against injustice and wrong.

Not without reason Palmerston felt confident that the strong arm of England would protect him also. He won his vote of confidence by a majority of 46 and the Queen was back where she had started, except that her Foreign Secretary's most colossal *bock* of all had made him more powerful and idolized than ever.

The Court was desperate. How could they get rid of him? It was Stockmar who eventually came to the rescue, as he had done on so many previous occasions. He had prepared a memorandum describing in emphatic language the minimum which the Sovereign expected of her Foreign Minister: to state distinctly what he intended and not to alter arbitrarily an agreed measure – otherwise she would exercise her constitutional right of dismissing that Minister. Prince Albert sent this document to the Prime Minister, drafted, of course, to look like a letter from Queen Victoria. Lord John showed it privately to Palmerston and on 15 August the Foreign Secretary appeared before Prince Albert. Primed no doubt by his anxious wife and harassed chief, Palmerston played his part to perfection. Instead of presenting the usual bland smile he was shaking all over, his eyes filled with tears. The softhearted Prince saw a broken man. 'What have I done?' stammered Palmerston. If he had given even the smallest hint of disrespect to Her Majesty he would never again show his face in Society. In regard to future despatches, His Majesty's command should be obeyed.

Palmerston was obedient for less than a month. The occasion of his next *bock* was the unwise visit to England of General Haynau, an Austrian responsible for putting down Italian and Hungarian nationalists with exceptional brutality. The indignant Radical Press published a cartoon of General 'Hyaena' flogging a woman. His lank figure, bushy brows, far-flung mustachios and deep-set, carnivorous eyes were thus imprinted on the public mind. When he visited Barclay's Brewery incognito he was at once recognized; one man tried to shave him on the spot, another dropped a bale of straw on his head; having fought his way into the street he was hauled along by his mustachios until, darting into a neighbouring house, he escaped at last filthy and bedraggled by river.

The Queen was horrified at this slur on British hospitality, but horror turned to anger when she learned that her own Foreign Secretary had nullified an official apology to the Austrians by including in it an attack on their illiberal régime. The Queen demanded the instant recall of the draft. Palmerston refused, offering to resign; but when a peremptory letter from Lord John Russell crossed his, he caved in and the draft was corrected. Yet as sometimes happened, the Queen was gradually coming round to Palmerston's view though not to his person. The assault on General Haynau, she was glad to have discovered, was unpremeditated and due in part to his own bad character.

In the autumn of 1851, Palmerston returned to his tricks. The great Hungarian patriot, Kossuth, who had failed heroically to free his country from Austrian oppression, came to visit England. Queen Victoria deprecated the 'stupid Kossuth fever' which immediately broke out among enthusiastic Liberals and Radicals; in Manchester Kossuth's welcome was more tumultuous than that accorded to Her Majesty in person. Kossuth and O'Connell, she felt, were on a par; how could we hold down Ireland and blame Austria for doing the same thing to Hungary? Suddenly she heard to her consternation that the Foreign Minister himself intended to receive Kossuth. Lord John Russell protested. Palmerston rudely replied that he would not be dictated to as to whom he saw in his own house. The Queen informed Russell that if Palmerston persisted she would dismiss him.

This looked like Palmerston's resignation at last. Not a bit of it. As so often when cornered, he surrendered. 'Oh! wonders,' wrote the Queen sarcastically on 1 November, 'Lord Palmerston yielded to the general will ... He lowers himself more and more.' Moreover, by yielding now, he would be able to bob up again, as indeed he did a week or so later, when he received a Radical deputation from

Finsbury congratulating him on his support for Kossuth, and violently attacking the Tsar Nicholas and the Emperor Francis Joseph. Greville considered this 'courting' of the Radicals the worst thing Palmerston had ever done. Worse was to come and speedily.

A dramatic *coup* in France tempted him to thrust his neck into the noose, as Prince Albert put it. The new 'submarine telegraph' had been working for only eight weeks when it brought the Queen extraordinary tidings. Prince Louis Napoleon, nephew of Napoleon I, who had been elected President of the French Republic soon after King Louis Philippe's exile, proclaimed himself on 2 December 1851, Napoleon III, Emperor of France. The agreed policy of the British Government, supported by the Queen, was to remain 'entirely passive' towards Napoleon III. What was her horror when it transpired that the rascally Foreign Secretary had thrown neutrality and passivity to the winds and assured the French ambassador of his cordial support for the new Emperor.

Palmerston had gone too far. The Prime Minister informed him that his want of 'decorum and prudence' unfitted him to remain at the Foreign Office and sealed his fate by reading to the House the Queen's famous letter of August 1850. When the House heard that Palmerston 'had been ungentlemanly towards his Queen', his case was lost.

But even now Palmerston had a few tricks to play. When Russell offered him the Lord Lieutenancy of Ireland he replied that since presumably 'decorum and prudence' were required in Ireland also, he could not be guilty of their lack. And when the Queen invited him to Windsor to hand over the Seals he never turned up, keeping Her Majesty waiting for ninety minutes. The Queen, though exceedingly cross, was inwardly relieved, since she had dreaded the interview, and looked forward with pleasure to better relations with the new Foreign Secretary, Lord Granville, a friend of the Court.

The explanation of the extraordinary relationship between the Queen and her Foreign Secretary lies partly in Palmerston's personality and reputation. 'Cupid's' early amatory exploits, for instance, did not endear him to a Court which was becoming puritanical. But there was also a basic clash of principle between the remedies proposed by Palmerston and the Court for revolutionary Europe. This was the 'neuralgic point' in their relations. It was a question of Sovereigns or Chambers, as the Queen noted in her Journal in 1846. The Prince believed that liberal institutions, where they were desirable, must be left to develop organically without foreign intervention. Palmerston thought that a salvo of despatches and even cannon balls would hasten their growth.

The clash was intensified by the fact that so many threatened thrones were German and often occupied by German relations of the Queen. Victoria was not only a queen but a cousin. She had a double fellow-feeling with the victims of Palmerston's spleen. To an extent which today would be impossible, his behaviour humiliated her personally. Not only did all her fellow Sovereigns lay their complaints at her feet – a situation with which Palmerston brusquely dealt by saying that she must confine her international correspondence to gossip about family affairs – but she herself felt bound to answer to the world for his misdeeds. She did not see that the development of ministerial responsibility gave the Crown its chance to enter an age of innocence. 'And I have to bear it all', remained a sad refrain, as we shall see, which the Queen had it in her power to drop.

In some ways it is remarkable that the unprecedented clash of Sovereign and Foreign Minister never exploded into irretrievable national disaster. The reason must be that the brinkmanship of the four major actors was deliberately geared to something less than catastrophe. The Prince knew that total war with Palmerston would topple the Crown: one must be *grob* (rough) with Palmerston, he wrote to King Leopold, but not *pfiffig* (tricky). Palmerston repeatedly allowed his bluff to be called. Lord John Russell kept up the disagreeable job of mediation for over four years, something of an achievement. No doubt Russell's duty was not to act as umpire but to captain his own Cabinet, whose united policy the Queen would then have to accept. His failure to control his team, particularly Palmerston, gave the Queen an unhealthy interest in Cabinet splits which caused much trouble during the later years of her reign. Palmerston's opponents in the Cabinet were tempted to use her as a joker in the pack, while she in turn exploited their discontent. Nevertheless, Lord John's mediation prevented complete disaster.

Finally the Queen herself, despite all, recognized Palmerston's abilities. Without Prince Albert's influence it is even possible that the martial music of '*Civis Romanus sum*' might have piped her in spirit aboard Palmerston's gunboats.

As it was she felt closer to the Prussian's opinion of her Foreign Secretary:

> '*Hat her Teufel einen Sohn*
> *Er ist sicher Palmerston.*'

> If the devil had a son
> Surely he'd be Palmerston.

16

'Our Happy Home Life'
1846–51

Improvements in the royal residences was one of the subjects to which the Queen could turn when politics became too provoking. The most ambitious project of these years was the rebuilding of Osborne. The Queen was afterwards to regret the lost charms of old Osborne – 'the character of that little house is gone' – but accepted the fact that they had outgrown it.

More than once during her lifetime she fled from the pompous and grand to the 'cosy' and 'snug' (two favourite words) only to be forced back again by the exigencies of children, Court and visiting notables into recreating precisely those large-scale surroundings which she had tried to escape. Indomitably she would then begin again planning smaller and smaller Chinese boxes within the all too spacious framework of her overgrown retreat.

The large new Osborne had its compensations. Standing together on the flat Italianate roof, the Queen and Prince could now direct the landscaping of their park. The Queen would watch her great ships glide out from Portsmouth and Spithead as she sat on the little sandy beach in a semicircular beach-hut designed for her by the Prince, with a mosaic floor and domed ceiling of blue, gold and pink. On hot days a loud grating sound would break the stillness of the woods. It was the Queen's bathing-machine running down a sloping pier to the shore. Having donned voluminous bathing apparel by the dim light from two frosted-glass windows high up under its eaves, Her Majesty would step out on to a closely curtained verandah and, descending five wooden steps, drop into the sea. It was only after the waves had taken over the concealing duty of the curtains that the machine could be removed.

This exhilarating operation first took place on 30 July 1847:

Drove down to the beach with my maid & went into the bathing machine, where I undressed & bathed in the sea (for the first time in my life), a very nice bathing woman attending me. I thought it delightful till I put my head under the water, when I thought I should be stifled.

In future the Queen sponged her face on shore before her dip and then, head erect, 'plunged about' in the ocean.

The Royal Avenue, a double line of cedars and ilexes, heavy as the mahogany furniture inside Osborne House, led up to the main entrance. The arcaded House Wing, a loggia, terraced gardens and two campaniles – the Clock Tower and Flag Tower – completed the Prince's vision of an Italian villa. Once inside, one could see why the Queen called Osborne her 'little Paradise'. Compared with Windsor

Opposite Osborne House, Queen Victoria's holiday home on the Isle of Wight.

or Buckingham Palace the ceilings were low and the rooms so small that for large receptions a marquee had to be erected on the lawn. The Horn Room, dedicated entirely to the antlers which composed every item of its furniture, was as cosy as even the Queen could wish. The Queen's small Audience Room was made smaller by a huge though frolicsome chandelier brought from Germany, its green glass leaves and pink glass convolvulus flowers recalling the wallpaper of the Rosenau bedroom in which Prince Albert had been born. Upstairs, each room, bright with chintz and bric-à-brac, had a view to the sea. The Prince's narrow bathroom with its plain lidded tub and shower came first in the royal suite. His study followed, austerely utilitarian; a knee-hole desk, a backless stool, a stand for walking-sticks; but dotted about everywhere like luminous white pebbles on a dark shore, small statuettes and busts, among them, on little crimson cushions, the marble hands and feet of his children.

Next came the Queen's sitting-room, its twin writing-tables standing side by side, hers nearest the beech-log fire. Next door, in the centre of her dressing-table, stood a folding book-rest. Her bathroom greatly outshone the Prince's in size and equipment, especially the fathomless bath standing in a curtained alcove. Last came the homely royal bedroom, all chintz and mahogany, a colossal wardrobe extending from wall to wall, its furthest door delicately disguising the entrance to what Queen Victoria used to call the 'little room'. Over the bedhead on the right-hand side hung Prince Albert's watch case. It hangs there today.

Throughout Osborne House the entwined initials V and A still speak of that idyllic Victorian union – everywhere, that is, except over the smoking-room door where there is a single letter A.

In September 1848 the Queen made her first visit to Balmoral, 'a pretty little Castle in the old Scotch style.' The Queen had bought a print of the 'little Castle' in Aberdeen and made a copy in her Journal of its four picturesque towers, granite walls, slit windows and high-pitched roof. On the very first afternoon she and Prince Albert climbed to the cairn opposite their new home and gazed around at a landscape which at once reminded the Prince of his beloved Thuringia. (When down-to-earth Duke Ernest came to stay he pointed out that the hills round Balmoral bore no resemblance to the towering Thuringian crags; it was just Albert's nostalgic fancy.)

Life in the Highlands was deliciously informal. They would go on what the Queen called 'a $\frac{1}{2}$ shooting expedition', the family setting out on ponies and Prince Albert breaking away for a short time to stalk deer or shoot ptarmigan while the Queen sketched or chatted with the ghillies. 'I like talking to the people here, they are so simple & straightforward, & I like their curious Highland English.' Grant, the handsome head ghillie, was so 'faithful'; when he and good sturdy Macdonald dragged her pony up the rocky tracks she felt so 'safe'.

Each year Queen Victoria became a little more Scottish. From the beginning the Royal Family were all dressed in 'Highland things', economically passed down from child to child, irrespective of sex. Soon there were lessons in Scottish dancing, whilst the Prince bought a Gaelic dictionary as big as himself. The Queen learnt to stalk, to eat bannock and dry the Prince of Wales's scarlet socks by her tenants'

'A tableau of the seasons' acted by the royal children. *Left to right:* Princess Alice, Prince Arthur, Princess Royal, Princess Helena, Princess Louise, Prince Alfred, Prince of Wales.

A nineteenth-century
photograph of Balmoral
Castle.

The Prince of Wales and
Prince Alfred in
Highland Dress.

A caricature of the Queen's love of all things Scottish.

peat fires. As a good landlord she took a great interest in her tenants, visiting their cottages and giving them presents such as the new petticoats taken on one occasion to Mrs Grant and Mrs McDougal. 'For me?' exclaimed the latter in amazement when a smiling little woman popped into her 'placie' and pressed a roll of stuff into her old hand. 'The Lord bless ye.' But perhaps the Queen's greatest interest was in her Highland servants. On her second holiday the name of J. Brown was added to 'faithful' Grant and good sturdy Macdonald in the list of those Highlanders who had taken most care of her.

Here in the Highlands she was able to indulge her fancy for the 'cosy' and 'snug' to her heart's delight. About five miles from the Castle were two granite huts or 'shiels' used by ghillies, perched side by side above Loch Muick. Allt-na-Guibhs-aich – 'the burn of the fir trees' – became the Queen's favourite and humblest retreat. She had the two huts joined together by a short covered passage and lived in one while her servants inhabited the other, 'the washing & cooking & everything going on in a line with one's own dwelling'. How cosy to have no iron curtain between the workaday world and royalty.

These were the nearest to cloudless years in Queen Victoria's life. Anxiety over the Prince's health was only intermittent; the joy of his companionship was interrupted neither by the Queen's friends as in the early days nor by his own later preoccupations. All the fun which Victoria had missed as a child she now had with her children: games of blind man's buff and fox-and-geese; quadrilles with the seven-year-old Prince of Wales as her partner and strolls on summer evenings helping him to catch moths. When a new baby was born the Queen, like every good mother, would have all the rest of the family into her room that same day. To see 'our tribe' trailing after their father on a walk gave her acute pleasure, and so did the sight of Prince Albert riding with the Princess Royal – 'quite the grande dame' – or with 'his Boy', the Prince of Wales.

Prince Albert and Stockmar, with their usual zeal, had devised a plan for the 'Boy's' education. But though Albert's industry and the young Prince's amiable character seemed to guarantee success, his parents were disappointed in his progress. On his ninth birthday his mother noted that lessons were a complete failure, though 'there is much good in him'. A new tutor was engaged but still there was little improvement. Bertie failed to shine and was compared very unfavourably with his elder sister Vicky.

Notwithstanding these disappointments the Queen was immensely proud of her 'blooming family' and spared herself no effort on their behalf. In the shimmering heat of August 1850 she walked the half-mile down towards the sea at Osborne where garden plots had been laid out for the children, helping them to use their initialled tools: P.o.W., Pss.R., Pss.A., P.A., Pss.H., Pss.L. Prince Arthur had arrived that May so there would soon be another miniature barrow, trolley, spade and fork to keep her busy. Prince Albert's health still caused her some tremors. Even the dry soil of Balmoral did not prevent him from catching a chill every autumn. As for herself, she faced her thirty-first birthday and the turn of the century with 'such perfect health' that it was 'a blessing to us *both*'.

Two deaths in the midst of these happy years indicate how Prince Albert had changed the Queen's attitude to the world. Melbourne died in November 1848, but her incomparable old friend had been dead to her long before a succession of fits carried him off. His memory was cherished, certainly, but not as ardently as might have been expected. Melbourne's crime had been to allow her to make the fatal mistake of postponing her marriage to Prince Albert. How different was her reaction to the death of Peel after a riding accident in 1850. It was he, not Melbourne, who was mourned as if she had lost a father. For, by the time of Peel's death, the Queen had come to honour every aspect of his character. His background linked him to the manufacturing classes whom Prince Albert chiefly cultivated, and separated him from the 'fashionables' and 'fox-hunters' who chiefly hunted Albert. As keenly as the Queen herself, Peel promoted the Prince's cause. Above all Peel represented to Queen Victoria the embodiment of firm leadership and the negation of party politics.

Some months before Sir Robert's death, Prince Albert inaugurated a great project which was to separate him still further from the 'fashionables'. In early 1850 he presided over the first meeting of the Commissioners of the Exhibition, 'to take place in 51'. The Queen soon came to share his enthusiasm. 'I *do* feel proud at the thought of what my beloved Albert's great mind has conceived.' The troubles into which the Prince ran almost at once greatly strengthened the Queen's ardour and awakened her fiercely protective feelings. Although the Prince often addressed her in letters as 'Dear Child', their intricate relationship included maternal feelings on her side also.

Prince Albert's lofty conception was for a festival of work and peace housed under domes of glass designed by the creator of Chatsworth conservatory – Joseph Paxton. Here the nations of the world would exhibit their swords beaten into ploughshares – if possible into mechanical ploughshares – by the new industrial processes. All history points, said Prince Albert at the Mansion House, to the unity of mankind. At the Crystal Palace he intended to achieve on a world-wide scale that 'reciprocity' which Palmerston prevented in Europe. 'Paxton vobiscum', giggled the 'fashionables'. At home, inspiration would flow from the liberated minds of a thousand independent, self-reliant creators. If Samuel Smiles was the publicist of the mid-Victorian creed of 'self-help', the Prince was its impresario and Joseph Paxton himself, in Professor Asa Briggs's words, its epitome.

The Prince's dream was attacked from all sides. The Protectionists saw it as an advertisement for Free Trade. The riders in Rotten Row objected to the site in Hyde Park. The foreign exhibitors were denounced as a source of plague, political agitation and crime. And abroad the despots regarded Prince Albert's adopted country, the haven of refugees, as a training ground for regicides, radicals and constitutionalists. It was with much misgiving that the Prussian Crown Prince and his family eventually came to the Exhibition and not a single crowned head trusted itself under Prince Albert's glass roof; a passport to England was too obviously a passport to eternity.

But nothing could deter Albert from the fulfilment of his dream. At last on 1 May 1851 the Queen, her family, a few bold Royalties and thousands of exultant

The Great Exhibition of 1851 was organized by Prince Albert and was the finest monument to his patronage of art, science and industry.
The opening of the Exhibition, 1 May.

THE ARTIST IN THE LONDON STREETS.
GOING TO THE EXHIBITION.—A MORNING SKETCH.
(*Great Expectations.*)

THE ARTIST IN THE LONDON STREETS.
COMING FROM THE EXHIBITION.—AN EVENING SKETCH.
(*Les Misérables.*)

Two chairs with plaques of Victoria and Albert which were made for the Exhibition.

season-ticket holders made their way to the opening. Dressed in pink and silver, wearing her Garter ribbon and the Koh-i-Noor diamond, a small crown and two feathers on her head, she drove in an open carriage to the Exhibition and then processed up the central aisle, past the flashing fountain to the royal dais, with a blue and gold canopy above her and a vast elm tree behind. One after another the organs burst into music as she passed; in the vast spaces she could hardly hear them. Floods of emotion swept over her: it seemed like her Coronation over again except that the continuous cheering made it 'more touching, for in a church naturally all is silent'. Afterwards she cut out an article from *The Times* likening it to the concourse of all peoples on the Day of Judgement and confessed to having felt more truly devotional than at any Church service.

Queen Victoria visited the Crystal Palace almost daily from its opening until she went to Osborne towards the end of July, getting up early, arriving before 10 am and systematically working her way through every section. The French courts she found beautiful beyond description, the American machinery 'inventive' but 'not entertaining' (later the 'cotton machines' from Bradford and Oldham won her unstinted applause); only the Prussian and Russian sectors were contemptibly thin. Among individual items she selected for special notice the Indian pearls, the Sheffield bowie knives made exclusively for America, the Chubb locks, the electric telegraph and a machine for making fifty million medals a week.

Particularly desirous was she of sharing her thrilling experience with the humblest of her subjects. John Grant, head ghillie at Balmoral, was brought to London.

It was quite a pleasure to see his honest, weather beaten face again, as quiet, demure, & plain spoken as usual, in spite of all the wonders & novelties around him.

The Exhibition closed on 15 October, fittingly, as Queen Victoria felt, for it was the twelfth anniversary of her engagement. Two long-term blessings seemed to flow from it. The visit of the Prussian Royalties which had begun under a cloud ended with the Queen gaining a close new friend in Crown Princess Augusta of Prussia, and the Princess Royal an admirer in her son, Prince Frederick William. Young Fritz, aged twenty-two, though not handsome according to Queen Victoria, had fine blue eyes and was both amiable and liberal-minded. He intended, she noted with approval, to resist the 'old traditionary doctrine' of the Junkers when he joined his regiment at Potsdam. He escorted 'our children' all over the Exhibition and there was no doubt which of 'our children' inspired these attentions. Queen Victoria and Princess Augusta, closeted together in delicious intimacy, discussed their children's future union.

Beyond all other blessings was the vindication of Prince Albert. In transports of relief and delight the Queen poured out her full heart to King Leopold:

It was the *happiest, proudest* day in my life, and I can think of nothing else. Albert's dearest name is immortalised with this *great* conception, *his* own, and my *own* dear country *showed* she was *worthy* of it.

The Great Exhibition marked the half-way point in Queen Victoria's married life. The happiest and proudest year of her life also turned out to be the slippery summit of her husband's career and the climax of early Victorian England.

17
'Every Age has its Advantages' *1852–54*

The Queen looked forward to halcyon days with Lord Granville at the Foreign Office: 'he keeps me regularly informed of everything,' she wrote happily in her Journal at the beginning of 1852, 'which Lord Palmerston had long ceased to do.'

Among the information supplied by Granville was an ominous detail from France: Napoleon III was restoring the imperial eagles to the flags and uniforms of the French army. Queen Victoria wrote it off as 'rather nonsense' but fears of French aggression soon swept over the country. Lord John Russell proposed to deal with Napoleon's hordes simply by strengthening the local militia. Palmerston saw the chance to revenge himself. Nothing short of a national militia would do, he argued. Parliament agreed with him and Lord John Russell's Government fell within two months of Palmerston's own removal. 'I have had my tit-for-tat,' remarked the jocular ex-Foreign Secretary.

To the Queen, though she secretly sympathized with Palmerston's tough attitude on defence, a change of government with its attendant alarms and excursions always meant a period of anxiety. How she longed for an end to party confusion and instead of 'this sorry Cabinet', a strong government.

She commanded Lord Derby (formerly Stanley) as leader of the Conservatives to form a government, hoping against hope that he would not succeed – '& yet I am wrong,' she admitted, for Derby, besides being a constitutional necessity, might soon be supplanted by a better team, provided he survived long enough to prove 'his incapacity to rule'.

The Derby Ministry did indeed prove weak and short-lived, but Derby himself rose in Queen Victoria's opinion. She was soon able to write that he '*is* a Prime Minister'; most attentive, fluent and clear. Even Disraeli, the new Chancellor of the Exchequer, awakened the Queen's cautious interest by his 'curious notes' on Parliamentary debates. She copied one or two of them into her Journal. 'They are just like his novels,' she commented; 'highly-coloured . . .' But she was amused. At the beginning of April 1852 she had the satisfaction of amazing 'the world' by inviting Mr and Mrs Disraeli to dinner.

She is very vulgar, not so much in her appearance, as in her way of speaking, & *he* is most singular, – thoroughly Jewish looking, a livid complexion, dark eyes & eyebrows & black ringlets. The expression is disagreeable, but I did not find him so to talk to. He has a very bland manner, & his language is very flowery.

When Queen Victoria later walked into 'Dizzy's' parlour she had her eyes open.

Death was to strike again in 1852, this time to remove one of the great father-figures in her life. On 14 September 1852 the Duke of Wellington died at the age of eighty-three, up to the last an arresting figure as he rode between Apsley House and the Horse Guards in his snowy white trousers and tight blue frockcoat, acknowledging like a king the respectful salutes of passers-by. The Queen was much shaken by his death, so soon after those of Melbourne and Peel.

It was not long before the need for his fatherly wisdom was felt. Scarcely a month after the Duke's magnificent State funeral, Lord Derby's Government was defeated by 19 votes and Queen Victoria for the first time in her life had to face a political crisis without the Duke's advice.

The problems were manifold. The Peelites refused to serve under their old tormentor, Disraeli. The Queen rejected Derby's suggestion that her old enemy, Palmerston, should be brought in a leader. Lord Derby in turn rejected her counter-suggestion of Mr Gladstone. In her Journal she set out Derby's interesting reply: 'Mr G. was in his opinion quite unfit for it. He possessed none of that decision, boldness, readiness, & clearness so necessary for leading a party ...'

At last the necessary compromise was reached. On 24 December the Queen heard with 'immense relief & pleasure' that Lord Aberdeen had formed a 'Liberal-Conservative Government.' The fact that Palmerston was Home Secretary and that dear Lord Aberdeen had spoilt Christmas Day itself with an interminable audience, could only diminish not destroy her pleasure. Palmerston, indeed, did

'The First of May' by Winterhalter shows the Duke of Wellington presenting a gift to his godson, Prince Arthur.

not look like being a permanent nuisance. He hobbled into the first Council on two sticks, crippled with gout, and all his friends, wrote the Queen to King Leopold, thought him breaking up.

Queen Victoria once more let fly in her Journal at the Conservatives: they were 'miserable people', except for Derby himself. The old year had ended very happily after all with a government of all the talents. The royal band ushered in the new year by playing under the Castle windows, 'Now thank we all our God.'

Despite the joyful serenade of New Year's Day, 1853 turned out to be, both for the Queen and the country, a time of unsettled feelings; of contrariness, criticism and disquiet. She expressed her own feelings on her twelfth wedding anniversary with joy tempered by '*Wehmuth*' (melancholy):

> I like not the speeding fleeting of time, – when one's bright youthful years pass away! But we have with God's mercy many yet before us, & *every* age has its advantages & its blessings!

The contrast between joy and melancholy was to be a common one in the years ahead.

A period of some strain in the Queen's family life started with the birth of Prince Leopold on 7 April 1853. The birth itself was of exceptional interest to her subjects, being the first occasion on which the Queen had taken chloroform to ease her pains. She found the effect 'soothing, quieting & delightful beyond measure'. The Queen's acceptance of chloroform won for the famous anaesthetist, Dr John Snow, his long battle against those who execrated the new pain killer on the grounds that it was contrary to the teaching of the Bible. It might well be claimed that Queen Victoria's greatest gift to her people was a refusal to accept pain in childbirth as woman's divinely appointed destiny.

Queen Victoria's rapid recovery from the birth was not, alas, crowned by an

A line-drawing caricaturing Simpson's experiments with chloroform.

equally thriving infant. Prince Leopold was always 'very delicate' and suffered from a grave and in those days mysterious condition – haemophilia, or the bleeding disease. This rare malady occurs only in males but can be handed on both through the genes of an affected male and of a healthy female. Although there is much mystery in the identification of the source by which this disease came into the Royal Family, it is probably to be traced to a spontaneous mutation in the genes which Queen Victoria inherited from her mother. Prince Leopold was the only victim in her family and therefore the only male transmitter. Three of her daughters, the Princess Royal, Princess Alice and Princess Beatrice were transmitters and their marriages spread the disease through the royal houses of Europe.

The Queen's suspense over her baby's fate led to much strain in her relationship with Albert. Small upsets could lead to hysterics as her bottled-up emotions overflowed. Albert's reaction to these scenes, though affectionate, was too clinical to be really successful. He was patient and understanding, but not sufficiently experienced in the field of female emotions to realize that all Victoria wanted was an explosion followed up by a good cry, kiss and make up.

However, all was peaceful by the autumn when the corner stone of the large, new, much turreted and battlemented Balmoral was laid. But this was to be the last peaceful holiday at Balmoral for many long months. As usual 'J. Brown' held the pony for mountain rides; as usual the Queen's Ministers sought congenial occupations. Lord Aberdeen danced a reel with Her Majesty 'beautifully dressed in a kilt' and Lord Palmerston, 'who is very old & does not see', played billiards with the Prince. Blind as he was, he could see the war-clouds in the East better than anyone.

'This sad Oriental Question', as the Queen soon came to call the Russo-Turkish imbroglio, had not greatly troubled her earlier in the year. Who is to have Constantinople when the Ottoman Empire breaks up? she asked calmly while making notes on Turkey in March. As long ago as 1840 she had decided that the Turks were too backward to last. Curiously enough, the argument constantly advanced by Palmerston and the English war party that the Russian forces in Constantinople would constitute an intolerable threat to India, did not yet move her. The Russian ambassador assured her there was no more danger of the Russian fleet going to Constantinople than of its going to Argyll House, and she particularly liked Lord Aberdeen's attitude of all-may-yet-come-right. Why not? The differences between Russia and Turkey seemed to her so small. Subsequent historians have been inclined to agree with her.

In July 1853 Russia invaded Turkey's 'Danubian Principalities'; dispirited and anxious, the Queen still half hoped that England might not become involved. On 10 October she heard that the British fleet had entered the Black Sea, without her consent having been obtained. Issues of peace and war, she felt, had been left too much in the hands of admirals. She was mistaken. In her absence from London, it was Palmerston who had persuaded old Aberdeen to make this pro-Turkish demonstration.

On 23 October a desperate Turkey declared war on Russia. Palmerston at the head of the war party urged immediate support for the Sultan, England's tottering ally, by joint action with France. The 'strong Government' on which the Queen had pinned her hopes, broke into fragments, torn between Palmerston and war and Aberdeen's obstinate faith in negotiations.

In December Lord Palmerston forced the pace and on the 16th he suddenly handed in his resignation as a protest against further Reform during a time of national emergency. As he intended, the whole country read into this manoeuvre a signal that he was prepared to lead it into war – a lead which the majority would have followed.

Palmerston's gesture was rendered superfluous by the news arriving three days after he made it that on 30 November Russia had sunk the Turkish fleet at Sinope. Even Aberdeen could not now resist the drift to war. Palmerston duly returned to office, thus ending what Lord John quizzically called his 'escapade'.

The Queen said good-bye with regret to an old year 'which seemed to have become an old friend' and whose successor might well not be so friendly.

'The year opens gloomily,' the Queen wrote on 1 January 1854. War was almost inevitable and high prices pressed upon the poor. Nearer home, 'wicked and jealous' opponents of the Government had begun to smear Prince Albert with 'atrocious calumnies'.

It was true that a fit of rare xenophobia had suddenly seized the country. Articles appeared accusing the Prince of having plotted to bring about Palmerston's resignation, of carrying on pro-Russian intrigues through his foreign relatives, and in short of keeping England out of Europe's glorious hostilities.

Queen Victoria had no doubt as to the source of these slanders. Who could it be but Palmerston? In this she was not altogether wrong, for though Palmerston did not inspire the articles he took no early steps to contradict them through the channels which he controlled.

Eventually the Queen saw no alternative but to ask Parliament, through Lord Aberdeen, publicly to contradict the lies. Aberdeen agreed and in some trepidation she opened this critical Session, prepared for hisses and groans on her way to Westminster and 'similar music' on the way back. The crowd was indeed ugly but things went better in the House than she had dared hope. The 'mad delusions' were exposed both by the Government and Opposition, and next day she was proud and happy to read aloud to Prince Albert all the nice speeches made about him.

As the country moved by desultory stages nearer and nearer to war, the Queen's attitude to the approaching conflict began to change. She saw herself now as the head of her armies in the field and found it necessary to put some stiffening into her pacifist Prime Minister, Lord Aberdeen. A war now, she insisted, would prevent a worse one later; patching up was dangerous.

The Queen had come to reflect, as so often, the opinion of the country. There was a general feeling that the long period of European cold war was over and battle must be joined – no one knew even yet exactly why. It was a kind of bellicose fatalism. Soon it took wing on a jet of euphoria. Exactly a month later, on 28 March, the Crimean War began.

18
The Unsatisfactory War
1854–56

The war which Queen Victoria had begun by calling unsatisfactory was 'incredibly popular' with her subjects, as she told King Leopold, and soon absorbed her whole being. For a start, she rose at 6.30 in the wintry dawn to watch the last battalion of Guards, 'touching & beautiful', march off. A few days later she waved farewell to the Navy at Spithead. 'The man on the topmost mast of the *Duke of Wellington* waved both his arms as we passed by!' How nobly that ardent gesture seemed to stand out against the petty quarrels of her Ministers.

As Britain got deeper into the war the Court came naturally to appreciate Palmerston's policy of using the French Emperor to defeat the Russian. In September 1854 the Prince accepted Napoleon's invitation to visit his camp at St Omer and Queen Victoria faced, with many moans, a parting from Albert which lasted five days. When the glad moment for return arrived, Prince Albert positively 'leapt aboard' the Queen's yacht to rejoin her, as an onlooker noticed, full of interesting new sidelights on their mysterious ally. Napoleon was very rheumatic, going to bed at ten so that Prince Albert's evenings were not too long; (but his cabin looked 'very blank and desolate' without 'Fräuchen'.) The French cuisine was good, servants 'respectable-looking', stables fine. The Queen felt much relieved, for up till the present she had heard only one good thing of Napoleon – that his wife, the fascinating Eugénie de Montijo, admired the purity of the English Court.

With the autumn began a long period of miserable uncertainty. For a moment at the beginning of October it sounded as if Sebastopol, the great Russian fortress in the Crimea, had fallen. Incredulous, yet bursting with excitement, the Queen and her three daughters ran up to the cairn at Balmoral and back, where a victory bonfire was to be lit. Five days later came a telegram contradicting the rumour and the Queen was going over and over in imagination the ghastly yet glorious victory of the Alma which had taken place not long before. 'Never in so short a time,' she wrote in language which would now be called Churchillian, 'has so strong a battery, so well defended, been so bravely & gallantly taken.'

Lord Burghersh, just home from the front, did his best to fit the Queen with rose-coloured spectacles: the soldiers '*really* did not seem to mind' their sufferings; the attacks on the medical profession were infamous: 'there was hardly a man who had not at least received water.' The Queen was not deceived. Lack of authentic information drove her frantic. 'If only one knew the details!' Windsor was shrouded in thick November fog but no thicker than that which hid the Crimea.

When news came she was equally on the rack. Cholera; vermin; the charge of the Light Brigade making her tremble with pride and horror; the Duke of Newcastle (Secretary for War) one moment saying that the soldiers had plenty of flannel shirts, drawers and fur caps, the next moment in tears over their privations.

Fresh from the seat of war, General Bentinck painted an even blacker picture of fever, diarrhoea, endless salt pork and no vegetables or tobacco (in any case the men could not always eat, for their unkempt moustaches froze over their mouths) or soap; 'Your Majesty's Army looks very dirty.' He told her that Sebastopol would not fall this year. Worst of all, her troops' great sufferings were 'unnecessary', since the French commissariat worked well and Napoleon's men were quite comfortable. The Generals, and indeed the upper reaches of Society from whom they were entirely recruited, were in for a rough time. In April of the following year Charles Greville was to report 'a run against the aristocracy'. Queen Victoria had no love for 'the fashionables', but a run against them might lead to dangerous social ferment.

The year 1854 had been a difficult one for both the Queen and the Prince. Beginning with the public clamour against him and the Queen's sharp criticisms of his tendency to give way under it, the first year of the war had not brought them closer together. The Queen was filled with atavistic longings to don shining armour.

This was the kind of mystique in which the Prince could not participate. He confined himself to hard work, slaving at his desk thinking up military improvements, and got fiercely criticized for his pains, especially over his idea of a German Foreign Legion. Why German? Why not Red Indian? demanded the insulted troops. Nevertheless he launched the Queen bravely and buoyantly into 1855:

Everything which disturbed our happiness in 54 shall be forgotten, and we will begin the new year in hope and confidence for the future ... Your intentions are excellent, and you will have all the help I can give you in carrying them out.

Parliament had long been on the verge of an explosion and on 24 January 1855 the blow fell. Queen Victoria invited John Russell to dine, only to receive from him his resignation. The redoubtable Radical Member for Sheffield, John Arthur Roebuck, nicknamed 'Tear 'em', intended to bring a motion of censure against the Government's conduct of the war and to demand an inquiry. Aberdeen's Cabinet would scarcely sustain this shock and Russell wanted to get out at once.

The Queen was at first 'astounded & indignant', but when the Duke of Newcastle nobly offered to be the scapegoat and give the War Office to Palmerston, she accepted this solution rather than lose all the Whigs from the Cabinet. Such an exodus of the most warlike elements would bring too much comfort to the Tsar. Lord John received a stinging note from the Queen calling him cowardly and unpatriotic, which made him exceedingly angry.

Desperate weeks followed, weeks which stretched the Queen's powers to the full but showed that she could take an active, even central part in providing the country with a government.

With the Prince disabled by a feverish chill, Queen Victoria lay awake night after night wondering what would be the result of the Roebuck debate. On 30 January, an infinitely dreary day of east wind from Russia, she heard that the Government had been beaten by 157 votes.

The next day, in a blizzard, she set off for London and sent for the Conservative leader, Lord Derby. 'It must be Palmerston,' he told her; 'the whole country wants him.' Paradoxically, he added that Palmerston's day was past; at seventy-one he was deaf, blind and no good at business. With this the Queen heartily agreed. Disraeli expressed the same opinion to a friend with gusto: Palmerston was 'an old painted pantaloon … with false teeth, which would fall out of his mouth when speaking if he did not hesitate so in his talk.' Pam's Radical following called him affectionately 'the Whiskered Wonder'.

But, in the end, Derby's advice had to be taken. Derby himself and Russell both attempted to form governments, but with no success. It was obvious to everyone that only Palmerston could succeed where they had failed. His effect could be modified by persuading 'good men', such as Clarendon, to work under him. So with Clarendon at the Foreign Office, Palmerston at last became Prime Minister.

An unexpected postscript on Palmerston's Premiership appeared in the Queen's Journal after the war was over.

Albert & I agreed that of all the Prime Ministers we have had, Lord Palmerston is the one who gives the least trouble, & is most amenable to reason & most ready to adopt suggestions. The great danger was foreign affairs, but now that these are conducted by an able, sensible & impartial man, (Lord Clarendon) & that he (Lord Palmerston) is responsible for the *whole*, everything is quite different.

The only real problem was the Queen's jealousy of Palmerston's popularity, a human frailty which was to afflict her again more deeply with Gladstone. As an intensely personal Sovereign she was bound to feel jealous of a rival.

During the course of hostilities Queen Victoria solved the psychological problem caused by her exclusion from the seat of war. At first the knitting-needle and the pen were her substitutes for the sword. Woollen mittens and scarves were posted abroad; letters of condolence no less warm went to widows of the fallen. 'All these letters,' she recorded with emotion, 'are a relief to me, as I can express all I *feel*.'

Visits to the military hospitals also stirred powerful feelings. The Queen was very shocked at the conditions in which some of the wounded soldiers were tended. After each of her hospital visits she would describe the patients in detail, narrating how she had held a ball of such and such weight and diameter, once lodged in an eye or nose. Her deepest anger was reserved for a hospital where convalescent soldiers ate their meals alongside their dying comrades; a cheerful atmosphere was essential to recovery. Many people paid tribute to the beneficial effects of the Queen's visits, including the famous Florence Nightingale, whom the Queen greatly admired and envied for her chance to do so much good.

Medals were another invaluable device for keeping her literally in touch. She

The Queen at Horse Guards Parade presenting a medal to Sir Thomas Troubridge, a Crimean veteran who had lost both his feet in action.

appeared on a dais at the Horse Guards in May 1855 wearing a lilac dress, green mantilla and white bonnet, with Lord Panmure, the War Minister, at her elbow and baskets of medals on blue and yellow ribbons between them. Crowds poured into the Green Park, bands played and a stream of noble fellows, some on crutches, some in bath-chairs, rattled past to receive the first Crimean awards. So great was her agitation that she could hardly hold the little silver pieces which Lord Panmure, fumbling desperately, passed to her. The precious core of her experience was committed to her Journal:

Many of the Privates smiled, others hardly dared look up – ... all touched my hand, the 1st time that a simple Private has touched the hand of his Sovereign ... I am proud of it, – proud of this tie which links the lowly brave to his Sovereign.

140

The charm also operated in reverse. The Sovereign's hand had touched the soldier's. When she heard that the men refused to give up their medals for engraving in case they did not get back the one she had presented, she was profoundly moved.

Tsar Nicholas died on 2 March 1855, his heart broken it was said by the carnage of Inkerman and Balaclava. Characteristically the Queen forgot that she had called him the '*one man*' responsible for the war and remembered only his personal kindness. With one Emperor out of the way it was time to bring the war nearer to an end by encouraging the other.

The Emperor Napoleon III had made various further attempts to improve his relations with Queen Victoria, chiefly through the Cambridges and Duke Ernest, but without success. By February 1855, however, the situation had changed radically: Lord Aberdeen's anti-French influence was removed, it was essential to ease the strains between the English and French armies in the Crimea, and an advance was called for by the Queen. The Emperor and Empress were invited to England.

The imperial pair arrived on a day of contrasts, at once noted by the drama-loving Queen. After a bad start in the Channel, which they crossed in such fearful fog that the British naval escort was not even seen, they received in London a truly magnificent welcome. During the first dinner party at Windsor there was a similar transition in the Queen's mood from extreme agitation at the beginning to delicious friendliness at the end.

The Empress Eugénie, tall, elegant, with a marvellous complexion, became very talkative when once at her ease, 'which she soon was with me'. The Queen was charmed to learn that Prince Albert admired Eugénie's *toilette* excessively. She had in fact brought the first crinoline to England – grey with black lace and pink bows, and a wreath of pink chrysanthemums in her auburn hair. Queen Victoria was not at first sure about the Emperor's appearance. He was extremely short, had immensely long waxed moustaches, a head far too big for his body and a gait too slow to please the energetic Queen. But there was something delightfully mysterious in his manner which immediately appealed to her. She felt an urge to get to know him. He deferred to her, flattered her, treated her as a beautiful woman. And behind his well-bred ease there was an unmistakable touch of that *outré* quality which so much attracted her. During one concert the Queen found him in such a '*causant*' mood that she dared to ask England's ally if he had really intended to invade England in 1853. '*Mon Dieu!*' gasped the first Napoleon's nephew, '*comment a–t–on pu croire à çela?*' The grand-daughter of George III replied that people *had* been able to believe it.

The visit was something of a diplomatic success. The British Cabinet had been exceedingly put out by a recent proposal of the Emperor's to take charge of the Crimean campaign in person. Indeed a major reason for inviting him to England was to extinguish this Napoleonic dream. Queen Victoria knew very well that her army would never take orders from a Bonaparte. Through the Empress Eugénie, Queen Victoria at first tactfully suggested that the Emperor's precious life must

not be risked. Afterwards at a council of war between the Emperor and the British Cabinet which the Queen attended, she boldly asked him not to go. He appeared to accept her advice with the face-saving observation that *of course* he could not leave Paris for fear of what his uncle, Prince Jérôme, and his cousin Prince Napoleon might be up to.

This council of war was another highlight in Queen Victoria's experience. She considered it 'one of the *most interesting* things I ever was present at ....' It made her feel right inside the war.

A return visit took place during the Paris Exhibition of August 1855. The Royal Family, including the Princess Royal and Prince of Wales, sailed in their new yacht, the *Victoria & Albert*. The royal party inadvertently caused some annoyance by arriving many hours late in Paris. This was the only real blot on a perfect stay in the city which had not been visited by an English Sovereign since the baby king Henry VI was crowned there in 1431.

Paris the Queen found 'the gayest town imaginable'. All was dazzle: the smoke-less brilliant air, the white reflections from the shuttered houses; the white and gold bedroom of St Cloud; the dark skinned Zouave guards; fireworks at the Versailles ball including a set piece of Windsor ('a very pretty attention'); the torchlit scene at Napoleon I's tomb where Queen Victoria made her son kneel down with her while the thunder rolled and the French Generals wept, to say a prayer over the coffin of his great-grandfather's bitterest foe ('strange & wonderful indeed!'); the orange flower picked by the Emperor for her to press; her unflagging smiles and superb curtsies and loud laughter; the transformation of Napoleon's enigmatic melancholy into glowing friendship. The wheel had come full circle as regards the Queen's feelings for this ingratiating parvenu, with whom in 1852 she could 'never for a moment feel safe'. Not only was he irresistible but dependable: 'I should not fear saying anything to him. I felt – I do not know how to express it – safe with him.'

There were a few good natured jokes at the Queen's expense. Victoria was short and stout, Eugénie tall and slender. The Parisians noticed and giggled. Orleanists also noticed that the Empress fussed over trifles, the Queen never; regal composure attended her down to the last detail as when, after bowing to the people at the opera, she resumed her seat without looking behind to see if the chair was there to receive her. Not everyone was bewitched by the *toilettes* over which she had spent so many anxious hours at Osborne, especially her plain straw travelling bonnet which she had not found time to change before her triumphal entry into Paris. General Canrobert laughed at the crude green of her parasol, her massive best bonnet, the white poodle embroidered on her handbag, and the famous dress bursting out all over with geraniums which would have done credit to Paxton's conservatory. If the General could have peeped into Her Majesty's Journal he would have found that she was equally amused by his red face, rolling eyes and copious gesticulations.

Back in Balmoral the Queen heard of a resounding victory of Anglo-French arms. Sebastopol had fallen at last. The premature bonfire still stood on the cairn from the year before. This time it was lit with a will and round the flames whirled

Opposite The clothes of the beautiful French Empress Eugénie became the admiration of London. This paper doll dressing set of her wardrobe was made in 1860.

what Prince Albert described to his brother as 'a veritable Witch's dance supported by whiskey'. The Queen's patriotic pride was later deeply wounded to hear that Sebastopol had in the end fallen to French arms, while the English attack on the Redan had failed. She could not bear the thought that peace should come before her soldiers also had won a resounding victory. After Christmas 1855, however, she accepted the fact that the French army, now riddled with sickness, would not fight on. She heard in the middle of March 1856 that a not very advantageous peace treaty was being prepared; 'I own that peace rather sticks in my throat, & so it does in that of the *whole* Nation!' She was right. The heralds who proclaimed the Peace of Paris on 30 March 1856 were hissed at Temple Bar.

The coming of peace did not assuage Queen Victoria's thirst for new, life-giving experiences with the fighting forces. Greville crustily announced: 'She has a military mania on her.' She met hundreds of returning heroes, bearded, sunburnt, knapsacked, in soiled bearskins, 'some strikingly handsome' and all giving her 'a real idea' of what life must have been out there. She yearned to run down and clasp their rough hands. Her first sight of a field day at Aldershot on 19 March 1856 was seminal. A knoll situated just outside the 'beautiful' new Pavilion built by the Prince offered a vantage ground which she eagerly seized, scrambling up to the top. 'I had never been so completely *in* anything of this kind before – surrounded by the troops, & I thought it *so* exciting.' The climax was reached in a series of great military days at Aldershot. Seated on a horse named Alma, on 16 June 1856, she wore for the first time a scarlet military tunic with gold braid, brass buttons and a gold and crimson sash, a navy blue skirt piped with white and a round felt hat with a white and scarlet plume, crimson and gold hatband and golden tassels. Surely even a nurse's uniform could not bring her nearer to her troops than this. She addressed them on 8 July in a speech of a hundred words learnt by heart (again for the first time), and on the 30th, in blazing sun, wearing her uniform and sitting on Alma she watched the march past of 'the largest force of Britishers assembled in England since the battle of Worcester!' Next day she left the camp, sorry for once to be exchanging the busy world for peaceful Osborne.

The military experience, glittering as it was, did not blind Queen Victoria to sanity and sense. When her ally, Victor Emmanuel, King of Sardinia and later of Italy, visited her near the end of 1855 the two Sovereigns compared notes on their regal duties. The burly, eccentric *roué* with eyes so wildly rolling that they looked as if they would drop out and a head carried high like an untamed horse, confessed to Queen Victoria that he did not like 'the business of king', so if he could not make war he would become a monk. In any case, he told her, another war was inevitable. The English lips were pursed and the blue eyes frosty. Kings must be sure that wars were *just*, she said severely, for they would have to answer for men's lives before God.

One must certainly aim at a just war, agreed Victor Emmanuel, but God will *always* pardon a mistake.

Queen Victoria, who could not help liking what seemed to her the bizarre relic of a bygone age, replied more gently, 'Not always.'

19
Dinner à Trois

1855–59

It was with some apprehension that the Queen saw her two eldest children move into their teens. She had learnt much as the family expanded, and she freely admitted that the two eldest had been much worse than the rest, and she herself less clever with them; everything seemed to come more naturally with the younger ones.

But the future had to be faced. In 1855 the Princess Royal was fourteen and the Queen had decided that she was – she *must* be – a woman. But proud as she was of her daughter's physical growth, she found it difficult to view her development with the calm which Prince Albert constantly advocated.

There was much at stake. One day Prince Frederick William, Vicky's prospective husband, would rule Prussia. Married to the Princess Royal, he would save Europe both from Russian reaction and French licence. This was Prince Albert's dream. The Crimean War made the marriage urgent: though France was now England's ally, Prince Albert could put no trust in Napoleon III, and Prussia's obstinate neutrality was a grave shock to his hopes of a Europe under the joint headmastership of Germany and England. On the personal side was a bogy which haunted all royal match-makers: the chosen suitor might be snatched by someone else.

Prince Frederick William arrived for a visit to Balmoral on 14 September 1855. To the Queen, he was an almost excessively interesting guest.

A becoming moustache had given Fritz a more manly appearance, though at twenty-four he was still the same amiable, unaffected creature he had been at twenty; he shot his stag on the first day, he praised the Princess Royal's artistic talents and held her in animated conversation at dinner. The Queen welcomed these good omens though as usual her feelings were ambivalent. 'The visit makes my heart break, as it *may* and probably *will* decide the fate of our dear eldest child.' Fritz, too, was uncertain. He preferred stalking Vicky to accompanying Prince Albert into the wet heather, but he wished to know her better before deciding. Four days later the pace quickened. He wrote home that Vicky had pressed his hand very hard when they were alone. That night he could not sleep.

After breakfast on 20 September Prince Frederick William was sufficiently recovered from his sleepless night to brave the Queen and Prince alone. There was a nervous pause; then he plunged. Might he have permission to talk of 'belonging to our family?' The Queen, though she had for years been dreaming of this

Prince Frederick William
of Prussia.

moment, could at first do nothing but squeeze his hand and whisper how happy
they would be. It was agreed that since the Queen did not wish her daughter to
marry '*till* she was 17', Fritz must wait till Easter to propose. But such a waiting
policy was too much for the Queen and Prince Albert. A few days later Fritz was
granted permission to give the Princess Royal a bracelet and told to tell her
something of his feelings.

There followed a nervous period of waiting until 29 September. On that day
the Queen noticed with pleased anticipation that Fritz and Vicky were lagging
behind on the way back from an expedition to the heather-covered slopes of Craig-
na-Ban. When they finally reached the carriage Fritz winked at the Queen,
'implying that he had said something to Vicky'.

At home there was a rush for the Queen's room where the whole story tumbled
out. Vicky had suspected nothing until the last two days when 'various little things'
put it into her head. Did she feel the same about Fritz as he about her? '"Oh! yes,"
with an indescribably happy look.' The Queen's burning anxiety was allayed; this
was indeed a love match like her own, not that abomination, a loveless arranged
marriage. Fritz had picked a sprig of white heather for the Princess on the way up
Craig-na-Ban in order to break the ice; on the way down he had declared his love.

Two days later it was time for Prince Frederick William to leave. Mother and
daughter had never been closer. The Princess fled to the Queen's room, they both
burst into tears and Vicky confessed that she had never been so happy in her life
as when Fritz kissed her – though how she could say all this to Mama she didn't
know. That evening she and her parents dined alone *à trois*, three adults bound
together by what they still fondly treated as a secret.

The next two years was a period of great strain for the Queen. Her longing to
square the child-marriage with her conscience meant that she pushed her daughter
right forward, pretending that she was grown up, only to find that two years of this
anomalous position was more than she could stand. She tried to forget Vicky's
rebellious tears and persistent, childish habits of laughing uproariously, gobbling
her food and waddling like a duck. She was a woman and must be treated like one.

Vicky, half child, half woman, was pushed through Confirmation, the conven-
tional gateway to adulthood. Now, it was confidently expected, she would know

her own mind. Then there was her first season to get through, always an occasion for a mother to renew her girlish agonies and triumphs. And all the time there were endless instructions from both the Queen and Prince Albert on all subjects from Roman history to what every young girl should know.

The problems of dealing with the complex anxieties and emotions of an adolescent girl in love were made no easier for the Queen by the fact that her ninth and last pregnancy came right in the middle of this period of strain. The depression and degradation of her own physical condition reminded her too closely that poor dear Vicky also would have to face the 'shadow-side' of marriage. The Queen shared the mawkish views of her contemporaries about a girl's passage from maidenhood to motherhood. Of her daughter's seventeenth birthday she wrote: 'Our poor dear Vicky's last happy birthday in our circle of Children! It is too sad. Marriage brings trials, sorrows and dangers, as well as joys!'

Prince Albert was not a great help during this critical time. His preoccupation with business left the Queen lonely and deprived. His defence, that she had plenty of companionship in eight children, she refused to accept. Her elder children were no substitute for her husband. Time spent alone with Vicky, for instance, was no compensation for the blissful dinners and evenings *à deux* that she had been used to spending with Albert. Vicky herself was a source of tension between the royal couple. The Prince was exceptionally devoted to his eldest child and dreaded the coming separation at least as much as did his wife. One day, in an unforgivably harsh note to the Queen, he accused her of wanting to get rid of Vicky. In a sense this was of course true. She did not want to share her husband with the Princess Royal. Such a feeling, though no doubt deplorable, is not uncommon among good wives, and in any case the Queen's mental processes were not nearly as simple as that.

The arrival, very late, of Princess Beatrice on 14 April 1857 went far to clear up the Queen's traumas and ushered in what she later called an epoch of progress. Immediately after the birth she made a vertical ascent from the depths of misery to the peaks of bliss.

I have felt better and stronger this time than I have ever done before … I was amply rewarded and forgot all I had gone through when I heard dearest Albert say 'it is a fine child, and a girl'!

It was worth it, if only to have Albert for a while entirely to herself again. And soon she was to have another triumph. On 25 June 1857 she created her husband Prince Consort. Prince Albert of Saxe-Coburg disappeared for ever. *The Times* sniffed at his elevation. What did it matter? On his next trip to the Continent he was given precedence immediately after King Leopold.

Husband, adolescent daughter and baby were not the end of the Queen's troubles. The engagement itself was by no means universally popular. *The Times* dismissed Fritz's family as 'a paltry German dynasty' while the Prussians were far from dazzled at this expensive commitment. By January 1856 Queen Victoria herself was having second thoughts.

I resent bitterly the conduct of the Prussian Court and Government, and do not like the idea now, of *our Child* going to Berlin, more or less the *enemy's den!*

The wedding of the Princess Royal to Prince Frederick
William took place on 25 January 1858.
Painting by John Philip.

Nor was the rest of Europe more gratified. Napoleon III, after all the junketings at Windsor and St Cloud, was offended and surprised. With a snort, Bismarck described the Coburgs as the 'stud-farm' of Europe. Further trouble came when Berlin demanded that the Princess should be married in Germany. Queen Victoria dealt summarily with this outrage in a letter to Lord Clarendon:

... the assumption of its being *too much* for a Prince Royal of Prussia to *come* over to marry *the Princess Royal of Great Britain* IN England is too absurd, to say the least ... Whatever may be the usual practice of Prussian Princes, it is not *every* day that one marries the eldest daughter of the Queen of England.

The Princess Royal's wedding day had been fixed for 25 January 1858. Eight days before the ceremony a redoubtable army of Hohenzollern relatives began to descend on Buckingham Palace. The Queen could get along well enough with the older princes but the huge, hideous young ones with their ferocious moustaches and sharp sarcastic remarks about England set her teeth on edge. Some consolation for the boorishness of her German relatives was brought by the cascade of presents, dresses and jewels that inundated the Queen and her daughter. Then came 'Poor dear Vicky's last unmarried day!' Vicky, wrote the Queen, 'clung to her truly adored father with indescribable tenderness'. Back in her own room the Queen broke down and sobbed: 'After all, it is like taking a poor Lamb to be sacrificed.'

The wedding day dawned, the second most eventful day in the Queen's life. She felt as if she were being married over again, only much more nervous. While the Queen was dressing, the Princess Royal came in and began to put on her wedding gown of white moiré silk trimmed with Honiton lace. Their hair was dressed one after the other. After the Queen had arrayed herself in the lilac and silver beloved of brides' mothers, the bride and her parents were 'daguerrotyped', the Queen trembling so much that the photograph was blurred. Then they went off. On the same spot where the young Victoria had knelt, 'our darling Flower' was kneeling now. The Queen's last fears of breaking down vanished when she saw Vicky's innocent, serious, calm face. Hand in hand the bridal pair walked out to the strains of the Wedding March written by Mr Mendelssohn, that clever friend of Her Majesty's who had once played for her the Austrian National Anthem with his right hand and *Rule Britannia* in the bass. In Buckingham Palace the young couple stepped through 'the celebrated window' on to the balcony above the cheering crowds and afterwards sat at table opposite their respective parents 'but hid by a splendid wedding cake'. When they drove off to Windsor, the two mamas settled down for a comforting, confidential gossip.

The Princess Royal's departure for Germany brought to an end the Queen's vivid but sometimes trying life *à trois*. Within three weeks she was unashamedly recording her 'great delight' in dining alone with Albert. At the same time the daily letters to her married daughter opened up a new means of self-expression which she seized upon avidly and used without any of the inhibitions she sometimes felt in face of Prince Albert's well-meaning but repressive logic. All her passions, obsessions, contrariness, practicality, immaturity, wisdom and irresistible charm

The wedding photograph of
Vicky with her parents
which Queen Victoria
spoilt by trembling.

went into this extraordinary correspondence and produced a *mêlée* of emotions,
truceless and lifelong, which only her own eldest child, who happened to be gifted
with much the same temperament, could hope to comprehend.

The Queen had devoutly hoped that her daughter would not become pregnant
for at least a year. She remembered the agonies of shame she had suffered at her
own figure, the black depression which succeeded the births of her first two children.
How much better if she and Albert had enjoyed unbounded happiness together for
twelve months. It was therefore with some alarm that the Queen heard in April
1858 that both she herself and her daughter were said to be in what she chose to
call an unhappy condition. The rumour was substantiated as far as the Princess
Royal was concerned towards the end of May. 'The horrid news' forced the Queen
to purge herself with the Princess's help of some deep-rooted prejudices. Babies,
she eventually admitted, were nicer than she used to think them, particularly
when they had got over 'that terrible frog-like action' one was expected to admire
in the bath, but she was not prepared to accept without qualification some of the
effusions of her daughter.

151

What you say of the pride of giving life to an immortal soul is very fine, dear, but I own I cannot enter into that; I think much more of our being like a cow or a dog at such moments; when our poor nature becomes so very animal & unecstatic ...

At the end of May Prince Albert hurried out to his daughter for a few days and the Queen was relieved to find herself bearing his absence better than she had ever done before. The Prince gave her a good report. In August they both visited Berlin, and the Queen, who hated to see signs of change in anyone, even an expectant mother, was delighted to discover in the Princess Royal 'quite our *old* Vicky'. Her complicated jealousy of Fritz subsided and she wrote: 'Felt as if she were quite my own again.'

Although Queen Victoria thought so poorly of nature's method of bringing a child into the world her dearest wish was to sit by her daughter's bedside when the time came and receive her first grandchild. When this proved impossible she bewailed the fate which denied to her the right of every mother, however humble – and redoubled the written advice. There must be no abandonment to malaise, no falling off in fresh air, no losing of one tooth per child. The Princess's lying-in period must last at most six weeks; after that she must forget that anything had ever happened. One parcel among innumerable others from Windsor to Berlin contained two pairs of stays with instructions how to wear them. Vicky should get a larger pair every 6 or 8 weeks, writing date of discard on each pair. 'It is of great use – hereafter.' The Queen's memoranda on the properties of elastic, bone, busk, cushions, lining and gores show her a past-master of the subject and immensely practical.

The parting of mother and daughter had brought them really close together for the first time, as both recognized. The Princess wondered anxiously whether her mutinous behaviour as a child had hidden from her mother how much she loved her; the Queen was thankful that her daughter at last understood why she had always disliked the children coming between her and dear Papa. Did not she herself admit that her greatest happiness was to be alone with Fritz? Mother and child agreed that a happy marriage was a foretaste of heaven. In buoyant mood after the Berlin visit Queen Victoria looked forward to the fun of being a young grandmama. If only she could bear all Vicky's coming sufferings for her ...

On 27 January 1859 a son, Prince William, the future Kaiser William II, was born after the kind of terrible labour which Queen Victoria had never experienced.

My precious darling you suffered much more than I ever did, & how I wish I could have lightened them for you!

It was a breech, the child's left arm being dislocated. For a time both his and his mother's life was despaired of.

The Queen was delighted to be sponsor to a 'William', having playfully warned her daughter that if the baby was a girl and received the kind of 'housemaid's' name likely to burgeon on the Prussian family tree, she would not stand over it. She was not joking when she added that forty-two godparents were excessive.

20

Last Years of Marriage

1855–60

In the same year that Queen Victoria transformed her eldest daughter with one wave of her sceptre from a child to a woman she gave unusually earnest thought to her eldest son. The thirteen-year-old Prince of Wales was not susceptible to the same magic. He seemed incapable of learning. One evening near the end of March 1855 the Queen escaped with her husband into the garden of Buckingham Palace for a walk: the future of 'our Boys' was under discussion. Prince Alfred (born 1844) presented no problem. His devotion to the Navy had persuaded his parents, contrary to their original intention, to send him to sea. Now the Prince Consort had a new idea – '*Ich habe einen Plan*' – for dealing with the Prince of Wales.

The little Prince's inert mind had been flicked into some liveliness by the Crimean War. He hero-worshipped Napoleon III, saying to him during a *tête-à-tête* drive around Paris, 'I should like to be your son.' Next year it was the outlandish King of Sardinia who dazzled him with a sword which could cut an ox in half at a blow. His first Windsor uniform made him blush with excitement; such things meant as much to him, teased his Mama, as a toy sword to little Arthur.

Prince Albert's plan of March 1855 was therefore to promise his son that if he could pass a general examination he would be allowed to train with the Guards. This innocent bribe might have borne more fruit had not the young Prince's warm affections been severely bruised a year later by the removal of Prince Alfred to Royal Lodge. Queen Victoria accepted the masculine decision that the parting of the brothers was for their own good. Sobbing bitterly, Prince Alfred departed on 3 June; the Prince of Wales, left behind and feeling 'very low', was allowed to sit with his mother throughout her dinner while she tried to comfort him. Two months later he too was pushed out of the nest. 'Pale & trembling', as the Queen observed, he said good-bye to the family when they set off for Balmoral, doomed to a long period of study and, if he worked well, a walking-tour with the unlovable Mr Gibbs.

Towards the end of 1858 a new era of freedom was painstakingly worked out. By now it was obvious that Bertie was no scholar. Gibbs was dismissed and the Prince was to have a 'Governor' instead of a tutor. In future his parents would advise rather than command. But they were unable to let him really be free. The Prince of Wales was forbidden to leave the house without reporting to his Governor, a provision which was continued later when he had short spells at the Universities of Oxford and Cambridge. Prince Albert was terrified that his son

A Royal Nursery Rhyme
for 1860:
'There was a Royal Lady
    that lived in a shoe,
She had so many children
    she didn't know what
    to do'.
In fact Victoria's ninth and
last child, Princess Beatrice,
and been born in 1857.

might have inherited some of the indecorous habits of his wife's 'wicked uncles' and was determined that the Prince of Wales should not be able to choose his own friends. To isolate his son from temptations rather than to strengthen him against them seems to have been the Prince Consort's main concern.

Some men have the gift of separating private from public anxieties; women often find it more difficult. Queen Victoria found it impossible. The birth of Princess Beatrice in April 1857 was a case in point. For months past the Queen had felt overwhelmed by her condition. Suddenly in March the Government was defeated by the pacifist John Bright on Palmerston's 'gunboat diplomacy' in China. The Queen was frantic. She implored Prince Albert to make the politicians realize that she was in no fit state to go through a crisis. The Prince obediently sent this message to Palmerston by Sir James Clark. But rule by pregnancy was disallowed. Palmerston insisted on a general election and came back with the magnificent majority of 79, the largest since the Reform Bill of 1832. The Queen cheered up. Palmerston's grip on European politics now seemed to her indispensable. When the cold weather arrived she deplored his frail appearance. What would they do if anything happened to him?

One of Palmerston's first requirements of the Queen was to cement the French

154

Victoria and Albert in 1860, a few months before Albert's death.

alliance. Her Majesty must invite Napoleon III and Eugénie to Osborne. Nothing loth, the Queen received them on 6 August 1857. All seemed to go smoothly and Napoleon even found time to gossip about his favourite hobby, the occult, describing to the Queen and Prince a spiritualist named 'Hume' with whom he was much taken up: 'he told us some certainly extraordinary things.' A week after his departure, the Prince, Queen and Duke of Cambridge set out for a cruise, calling at Cherbourg to see the French fortifications.

During the following year (in August 1858) the Queen's visit to Cherbourg was repeated in an atmosphere more martial and less friendly. Napoleon's new arsenal was inspected. Against whom were these weapons to be used? The English Press trumpeted forth that Britannia herself was the target. Napoleon, unusually silent and '*boutonné*' throughout the visit, roused himself to ask if Queen Victoria would not silence her Press. She replied that it was not in her power to do so. Next month as she rode home across the darkening hills, she saw Donati's comet flaring in the sky with a star 'distinctly through its tail'. To the country, the comet heralded war.

War had already broken out on the other side of the world. In March 1857 the mails had brought the first terrible hint of the Indian Mutiny. By July war was sweeping over India and the horrific accounts sent to the Queen haunted her as the Irish famine had haunted her ten years earlier. In August the news of bloodshed was even worse; the Queen hoped it was not true. It was true. Her blood ran cold. Palmerston's calculated sang-froid drove her into an agony of exclamation marks.

Towards the end of September the British forces began to re-establish control. At once the Queen switched her attention to the peace terms. She insisted that there should be no vindictiveness, no indiscriminate death penalty. On 14 December a 'most dreadful letter' reached her from an Indian officer describing the Cawnpore massacre, and her comment showed the restraint which she liked to think was always her reaction to great catastrophes.

The horrors of shame & every outrage which women must most dread ... surpass all belief, & it was a great mercy *all* were *killed*! It shd. never have been made known, for that no good can be done any more, & it can only distract for the life the unhappy relations.

The Queen, like the rest of the country, already realized that the Mutiny was no mere fanatical outburst against the greasing of cartridges with animal fat, as had at first been thought. It was the wholesale rejection of British rule as represented by the East India Company. On 23 November she noted a universal feeling 'that India shd belong to *me* ....' Plans were drawn up to transfer India to the Crown, under a Council, and in the new year Queen Victoria, utterly absorbed by the subject, was cosily discussing the future of the Indian Army with Palmerston, Her Majesty being most satisfied with his decision: '*all* ... to be mine ...' Two days later, on 14 January 1858, an event occurred across the Channel which put an end to her congenial Palmerstonian partnership.

Hardly had she reached Buckingham Palace to receive the first batch of guests to the Princess Royal's wedding, before the news came of an attempt by an Italian patriot, Orsini, to assassinate the French Emperor and Empress on their way to the opera. The French police discovered that the bombs had been made in England and Orsini was precisely the type of refugee whom Napoleon during his Windsor visit in 1855 had vainly begged Queen Victoria to expel. This time she was relieved to find Palmerston bowing to the whirlwind of French fury; he brought in a Bill to make conspiracy to murder a felony. At once British national pride burst into flame. The country would not be dictated to by France, Palmerston's Government was defeated in February and he resigned. The Queen found her Government's leave-taking painful and faced with foreboding the prospect of a second Derby Ministry.

Sure enough within a few months the Conservatives had torn up her understanding reached with Palmerston about the Indian Army. Instead of the delectable '*all* ... to be mine', Derby gave way to what the Queen called the 'bigotry of the older Indian officers' and put the Indian Army appointments under the Council, thus turning her into 'a mere signing machine'. One consolation was that she had been able to establish the Crown's human superiority over any bloodless Council. Derby's first draft of a Proclamation to the Indian people seemed to her cold and unfeeling. All the romance she had felt since childhood for brown skins, all the advice she had received from Indian travellers flooded her mind – the iniquity of a 'fire and sword system' of government, the 'immense field for improvement among the natives', the lies about mutilation of women and exaggeration of all kinds, the superior manners of the Indian 'lower orders' compared with ours, the ill-treatment and insulting references to natives as 'niggers' – out it all poured and was translated by royal alchemy into the moving words of a re-written Proclamation.

... Firmly relying ourselves on the truth of Christianity ... we disclaim alike the right & desire to impose our convictions on any of our subjects ... but all shall alike enjoy the equal & impartial protection of the law.

As she wrote to Lord Derby, it was 'a female sovereign' speaking from the heart to a hundred million Far Eastern peoples.

It was not long before Palmerston was back in power, at the head of the first truly Liberal Government in the country's history. But this time he was not so welcome to the Queen. For in the meanwhile war had broken out between the French and Austrians over the future of Italy. The Court, led by Prince Albert, could not contemplate the dismemberment of Austria with anything but anguish, since the Austrian court and army were full of Coburg relations. That neither England nor Prussia should become involved was the Prince Consort's burning wish and Queen Victoria shared her husband's agitation. Palmerston on the other hand was full of enthusiasm for the idea of Italian independence and was ready to bring England in against the Austrians. Fortunately an armistice was signed between France and Austria at Villafranca shortly after the fall of the Tory Government. 'Truly thankful,' reflected the Queen, 'that we are safely out of it, for we shd have inevitably committed, or tried to commit some great blunder.' But blunders were still possible, since the Queen's Ministers continued to aim at that full Italian unity which Napoleon III had thrown away at Villafranca. Indeed in Europe as a whole there was a revolutionary situation comparable only to 1848. At the end of 1860 the Queen wrote:

I felt much moved, so anxious for the future, that no war shd come, & fear for the state of Europe. My precious husband cheered me & held me in his dear arms saying, 'We must have trust, & we have trust that God will protect us.'

It was a poignant scene in view of what lay in store.

In the years leading up to 1860, Queen Victoria's devotion to her husband had become, if possible, more absorbing than ever. So had his work. Though the Queen still called him the most beautiful being on earth, he was in poor condition, running to seed, balding and wearing a wig to keep out the cold before breakfast. (Mama, as he wrote to the Princess Royal, did not approve of hot, unhealthy fires.) There were disagreements, there were storms; but more often, day after day of cloudless happiness as in some island of the blest. Even when the mundane veils were necessarily drawn down over paradise, the Queen was conscious of making steady progress under the Prince's patient tuition.

The worst storm arose out of the Queen's worries about the future of her second daughter, Princess Alice. The Queen had wanted Vicky to negotiate with the Hesse-Darmstadt family for a husband for her sister. Vicky, who wanted her sister to marry a Prussian, had fallen down on her task and the Prince had found himself in the awkward position of defending his eldest daughter against his fidgety, anxious wife. But the storm did not last for long and when the Queen's ideal young man, Prince Louis of Hesse-Darmstadt, arrived for Ascot week, Albert was tender and patient in handling his wife's nervousness. He implored her to wait and let things take their course. Six months later the Queen's suspense was ended when, on his return to England, the young suitor caught Princess Alice alone by the fire after dinner, and the Queen's second daughter found herself engaged.

The Queen seemed to be managing all right with her daughters, but what about Bertie? Perhaps Louis's sister would come up to the requisite standards of complexion, figure and intelligence. A good character and education were indispensable, rank and wealth immaterial. As for the Danish beauty, Princess Alexandra, the Prince of Wales's parents did not feel complete confidence in that particular royal house. They kept her name from their son until Uncle Ernest of Saxe-Coburg to their disgust let it out.

In the middle of the Queen's trials over the future of Princess Alice, Prince Albert had arranged for her a delightful treat at Balmoral. Thinly disguised as 'Lord & Lady Churchill & Party' (an extra dog-cart accompanied their two shabby vehicles emblazoned with the crown of England), the Queen, Prince, General Grey and Lady Churchill spent two days on an expedition to Glen Feshie, sleeping in a common inn and being convulsed with merriment when John Brown called the Queen 'Your Majesty' by mistake or Grant referred to the Prince as 'his lordship' on purpose. The Queen christened this delectable adventure 'The First Great Expedition'.

But the days of adventure were drawing to a close. In October, during a visit to Germany with the Queen to see their 'darling Grandchild', the Prince Consort had a minor carriage accident which gave a hint of the future to discerning eyes. The Queen found him lying in bed stiff and shaken with lint compresses on his nose, mouth and chin, but did not realize how near her husband had been to disaster. He seemed to her in high spirits after dinner, 'talking away'. The shrewd Stockmar, standing by his bed immediately after the crash, was shocked by his illness. On the last day in Coburg Prince Albert went for a walk with his brother Ernest and broke down, sobbing that he would never see his birthplace again. In contrast, the Queen, having contracted a violent chill, battled through three days of travelling and receptions in huge unheated German rooms without missing more than a few of her engagements.

Fortunately her last Christmas Day with Prince Albert was a glorious one, Windsor at its best. There were twenty-eight degrees of frost, windows frozen over, floods of sunshine, wild games of ice-hockey, Louis and Alice sharing a present table, Mama to luncheon, Leopold and Baby coming down to dessert and the older ones appearing after dinner; Albert telling stories, Albert cracking jokes, Albert swinging Baby in a dinner napkin, Albert, Albert, Albert.

21

'He was my Life'

1861

The man whom Stockmar considered incapable of fighting a serious illness was now forty-two. For the last three years there had been a steep decline in his health caused in the Queen's opinion by overwork. Rheumatism, catarrh and gastric attacks with fever were his constant foes, his overlove of business and melancholy fatalism their faithful allies.

On 29 January the first link was forged in the fatal chain which ended in his death. A railway crash occurred at Wimbledon. The only man killed was William Baly, a brilliant young doctor who had recently replaced the ageing Clark as physician to the Royal Family. The Prince already felt 'the greatest confidence' in Dr Baly and was 'greatly alarmed' by this incalculable loss. Unfortunately there was not to be sufficient time for the Prince to feel the same confidence in Baly's successor, William Jenner, the noted pathologist who had recently distinguished the germs of typhus and typhoid. During the Prince's last illness it was to be Clark, a veteran of seventy-three, who was really in charge.

The year continued joyless. On 16 March the Queen's mother died. Early in the month the Duchess had been operated on for an abscess: in the stark language of those days, the Queen wrote in her Journal that 'the surgeon should go to the marrow to see dear Mama's arm'. There was a brief respite; then a message came to the Queen, as she sat 'peacefully' at Buckingham Palace marking newspapers, that Mama's condition was desperate. The Prince quietly ordered the royal train and they slipped back to Windsor, reaching Frogmore at 8 pm. Prince Albert went in first. When he returned with tears in his eyes the Queen knew what to expect: 'with a trembling heart I went up, sat a long time ...' The Duchess's repeater in its tortoise-shell case struck the quarters. It was the same clock which Victoria had heard every night of her life at Kensington until as Queen she left her mother's room. With what intricate anguish she listened to its chimes again. The Prince at last persuaded her to go to bed. Twice during the night the Duchess's lady-in-waiting, Augusta Bruce, who was sleeping on the floor, saw the small, white figure of the Queen glide in and out, lamp in hand. In the morning the Duchess died, her hand in her daughter's. Prince Albert burst into loud sobs, gathered up his wife in his arms and carried her out of the room. Then he sent for Princess Alice. 'Comfort Mama.'

Queen Victoria suffered a nervous breakdown after this loss. Normal regret for lost opportunities of showing love was intensified in her a thousand times by painful memories of the past. She was too honest to pretend that her mother had

Princess Beatrice with her nurse.

been entirely blameless, but while going through the Duchess's private papers – 'almost a sacrilege' – she was overwhelmed to find how much her mother had loved her. Yet there, in her own Journal, stood the damning remark to Melbourne: 'I don't believe Ma. ever really loved me.' 'Two people' (Conroy and Lehzen) she believed were responsible for the tragedy, but tragedy it remained.

Remorse alone would not have made the Queen ill. Throughout the last years she had been in the closest touch with her mother either through daily visits or letters. Now she felt abandoned. There was no Mama to gossip about the children, to attend their birthday parties, to add an extra dimension to family life. 'I feel as if we were no longer cared for', she wrote to King Leopold. The exhausted Prince was unable, indeed unwilling to fill the gap. For the sake of his own health and his wife's happiness it would have been better if he had temporarily withdrawn from the pressure of affairs, but he had lost the power. His speeches, his journeys, his memoranda were a 'treadmill' he dared not defy.

After the Duchess of Kent's death 'everything seemed changed'. Loud noises set Queen Victoria on edge, particularly the Prince of Wales's voice bickering with the children. She shut herself up, nursing her grief. A visit to Ireland in August did nothing to cheer her. She found the climate of Killarney peculiarly oppressive. How sadly the population had dwindled since her first visit fourteen years ago. Prince Albert's birthday on 26 August was celebrated in gloom never before known on that beloved day.

> Alas! so much is different this year, nothing festive; we on a journey & separated from many of our children. I am still in such low spirits ...

She prayed as so often now that she would not survive this adored husband who was her all in all.

The annual holiday at Balmoral provided some relief for the Queen's low spirits. Two more 'Great Expeditions' into the hills seemed to restore her native capacity for pleasure, but now the Prince Consort's state began to deteriorate as steadily as his wife's improved.

In early November the second link in the chain of events leading to the Prince's destruction was forged when the Portuguese Royal Family were struck down *en masse* with typhoid. By the 12th Prince Ferdinand and King Pedro were both dead. The King was only twenty-five and like a son to Prince Albert. Like him, he had the Coburg melancholy. His death greatly increased the Prince's depression. 'We did not need this fresh loss,' wrote the Queen, 'in this sad year, this sad winter, already so different to what we have ever known.'

Swiftly another blow struck them on this same sad 12 November – the third link in the chain. A letter arrived from Stockmar reporting that the Prince of Wales's friends at the Curragh camp in Ireland had introduced him to what his father had always feared, 'the objectionable life of cavalry officers'. Bertie had had a brief affair with an actress and the news had already leaked out abroad. The Queen never forgot her husband's woebegone face as he came into her room carrying the letter. He spent the next four days in digesting the news (which was confirmed and expanded by a gossiping courtier, Lord Torrington) before sending his son on 16 November a long, reproachful yet forgiving letter which must have cost him much pain to write. It is likely that the ten days beginning with Pedro's death and Stockmar's bad news coincided with the incubation period of the typhoid germ which killed him – the last link in the chain. Owing to the disease's insidious onset it is impossible to decide exactly when it declared itself, but the Prince's doctors believed Friday 22 November to be the date.

This black Friday began and ended in a downpour. Prince Albert had been unable to throw off a cold, or, since Stockmar's news, to sleep. (Insomnia can also be an early symptom of typhoid.) Nevertheless he inspected the new Staff College at Sandhurst, returning soaked to the skin, shivering with what was considered to be a fresh chill. Windsor was filling up with guests and there was much talk of

THE ROYAL ROAD TO LEARNING.

how 'good and brave' Baby Beatrice had been when her ears were pierced for ear-rings. Albert was good and brave too. He endured a week-end of entertaining and on Monday, still sleepless and now racked with 'rheumatism' (the first typhoid pains) set off for Cambridge, where the Prince of Wales was studying, to thrash out the wretched Curragh incident. Bertie responded to affectionate appeals for frankness and his father arrived home next day with an easier mind but a body aching more wretchedly than ever. In order to prevent embarrassment he had informed his son that Mama did not and must not know of the affair. Had he not died, the matter, so far as the Queen was concerned, would have been closed.

Next day the Queen confessed to King Leopold that Albert was irritable and trying. A mixture of fear and faith – fear of even so much as contemplating a serious illness in her beloved and faith in fresh air – led her to spur him on just as she had spurred on her mother. Her role, as she once told the Princess Royal, was always

A Punch drawing of the Prince of Wales's arrival at Oxford. He was the first Prince of Wales to attend a university since Henry v.

to raise flagging spirits. On Friday the 29th Prince Albert could neither shoot nor attend luncheon, but to please her he walked round in the afternoon while she inspected 200 Eton Volunteers and then watched them eating an 'ample' luncheon in the Orangery – 'a pretty sight'. Poor Albert was not a pretty sight: even the Queen had to admit that he looked terrible.

It was in this condition that the Prince suddenly found himself faced with the task of preventing a major international crisis, a side effect of the American Civil War, now in its eighth month. The Confederates had dispatched two envoys to plead the Southern cause in England. On the way their English ship, the *Trent*, had been chased and boarded by the Federal forces and the envoys kidnapped. The Palmerstonian hackles were aroused by the insult to England and the country was behind him. Unless there was immediate release of the envoys, our ambassador would be recalled from Washington and there would be war. Prince Albert was aghast and resolved to redraft the terse, staccato message to the Federal Government, if he died in the attempt. So weak that he could hardly hold the pen, he skilfully concealed the bleak outlines of the draft in courteous verbiage, so that what had seemed a strident ultimatum was now an invitation to negotiate. Then he left his desk for ever. Fortunately the Cabinet accepted the Prince's amended draft and the Federalists saw that a way had been left open for them to retreat with honour. The *Trent* case, thanks to Albert the Good, passed into peaceful history.

On the following day, Monday 2 December, Dr Jenner spoke out: though there was still no fever it was likely to develop. Waves of anguish swept over Queen Victoria. The Prince, meanwhile, was given the harrowing details of Pedro's death by two gentlemen just returned from Portugal. It was as well, he muttered to his equerries, who with his valet were all he had for sick-nurses, that *he* had no fever, for he would never recover from it. The Queen begged him not to say such foolish things. Restless and petulant, he decided to sleep in a small bed at the foot of their large one. The Prince tossed all night in his small bed; Victoria offered him drinks and listened to the clock striking the hours. Towards morning he went into his own room. She followed him. He knew he was getting a low fever, he moaned, he knew he would die. Tuesday night, 3 December, was no better. The Prince walked from room to room, the Queen again following him; at six she sent for Jenner 'in an agony'. For an hour and a half opiates brought him 'blessed relief'. She swung at once from agony to hope, especially when she noticed that on waking he dressed completely as if for a normal day. The improvement was short-lived, though the physicians continued to assure the Queen every day that 'there was no cause for alarm' and every day letters left Windsor carrying to relatives this soothing message.

It is tempting to blame the Prince's doctors for what transpired and posterity has not hesitated to do so. From the beginning, old Dr Clark had decided on a 'psychological' treatment which consisted of keeping from the Prince, the Queen and therefore the world, the nature and gravity of the case. He knew from of old that Prince Albert worried about himself. Since King Pedro's death his fears had sharpened into an obsession that typhoid in particular would prove fatal. The

word 'fever', therefore, must neither be whispered in his hearing nor written in the Queen's face. If Prince Albert saw her looking panicky he would guess all and give up. According to Clark, the calm repetition to the Queen of 'no cause for alarm' was imperative. He remembered, as well he might, her 'fidgets', her 'nerves', her hysterics and recent breakdown. But he disregarded her own saying that 'great events make me calm'. Even without his well-meant deception it is probable that she would have controlled herself in front of the Prince, for his sake. As it was, having endured over three weeks of unavoidable anxiety, she suffered a violent shock at the end.

Clark's determination not to frighten the Prince at whatever cost almost certainly prevented him from being properly nursed. No one was better equipped to treat typhoid than William Jenner, but he had done his great work in hospitals and been with the Royal Family only during the last nine months. He was in no position to challenge the family doctor. One cannot help feeling that if young Dr Baly had been in charge there would have been less of the patient walking about, talking, showing pictures to little Arthur and hearing Baby's French verses between bouts of delirium.

By 6 December the Queen had endured five of the most terrible nights in her life. The Prince could not sleep without ether drops; he coughed and moaned, continually changing his bed. With tears streaming down her cheeks she hovered just outside the bedroom, watching the candles flicker and Dr Jenner's figure huddled near the door. By day the Prince still refused to go to bed; his expression strange and unsmiling, he hardly noticed her but kept asking his doctors, 'How long will it go on?'

On the 7th Dr Jenner at last told the Queen that the Prince had gastric or bowel fever – 'the thing they had been watching for all along.' Both were contemporary names for the dreaded typhoid. Jenner assured the Queen that they knew exactly how to treat it: it would take a month, dating from 22 November. His confidence was somewhat optimistic. When the Prince was taken ill one man in every three died of an infectious fever, and the drains at Windsor were as foul as any in the land.

Next day when Queen Victoria came into the sickroom the Prince did not know her but called out to Löhlein, his valet, '*Wer ist das?*' The Queen, her heart breaking, kissed his forehead and said it was '*Weibchen*', his little wife. Whereupon he recognized her for a moment – '*Das ist recht*' – only to drift away again, angrily imagining that she had opened a letter addressed to him containing bad news about Prince Leopold. He called continually for General Bruce, the Prince of Wales's Governor. After wandering about the passages, occasionally rattling at a door-handle, he at last decided to settle in the Blue Room – the King's Room where both George IV and William IV had died.

Bulletins were issued on Wednesday 11 December for the first time. To the Queen this was an overwhelming sign of doom; she dropped her Journal and did not resume it until 24 December. (To the public the bulletins appeared so mild as to be scarcely interesting.) The Prince's alterations of clarity and incoherence kept her on the rack. He laid his head on her shoulder murmuring, 'It is very comfortable like that, *dear Child*.' But in a moment he was gazing wildly round the room. His restlessness continued and, to placate him, the physicians had him moved from bed to sofa and wheeled from room to room.

His condition continued to fluctuate for the next two days. For an hour on Friday Jenner had despaired but then he rallied. Later he relapsed again and when the Queen came to say goodnight the doctors would not let her approach.

She was allowed to sit at the foot of the bed with Princess Alice on the floor, while brandy was administered every half-hour and the doctors said he continued to improve. Dr Watson, a specialist called in at the instigation of Lord Palmerston, whom the poor Queen found 'very kind', explained that it was a crisis, a trial of strength. He had seen infinitely worse cases recover: 'I never despair with fever.'

To describe the Prince Consort's death proved a task for many years beyond Queen Victoria's powers. She tried once on 24 December 1861 and again on 27 March 1862; it was not until February 1872 that she at last wrote the date 'Saturday, December 14th' and found the courage to describe from notes scrawled at the time 'this dreadful day'. The struggle between Queen Victoria's emotions and her ruthless, self-imposed duty to her Journal was one of the strangest elements in her sufferings.

After a night of hourly, hopeful messages, she was visited at 6 am by another of the doctors with good news: 'I've no hesitation in saying ... that I think there is ground to hope the crisis is over.' At seven she came to the Blue Room door, saw the 'sad look of night-watching', the candles burnt down to their sockets, the group of doctors with anxious faces. Then she went in.

Never can I forget how beautiful my Darling looked lying there with his face lit up by the rising sun, his eyes unusually bright gazing as it were on unseen objects & not taking notice of me.

At last after weeks of fever, the Prince's face had recaptured the ethereal lines of youth.

In the course of the bright, calm morning the invalid was wheeled through into the other room. The Queen needed a breath of air. Yes, she might go out for half an hour if she stayed close by. With Princess Alice she went on to the Terrace but the trumpets of a military band playing at a distance were too much for her and she came in crying bitterly. Dr Watson could only say that he was not worse. 'We are very much frightened but don't and won't give up hope.'

In the later afternoon the children were called, even the Prince of Wales whom the Queen thought might agitate his father. All, except the baby, came in and kissed his hand. He took no notice. She sent for General Bruce and gave him her hand. He kissed it, kneeling. 'She then took his hand and placed it on the Prince's, holding it there for some time. His eyes were closed, and there was no recognition.' Later he revived and asked for Phipps, his private secretary. Then the Keeper of the Privy Purse and Master of the Household took leave; both broke down but the Queen with heroic self-command remained quietly sitting at his side. Dr

Watson motioned her to offer him a sip of brandy. She shook her head. Her hand was the only thing she could not control.

At 8 pm Francis Seymour wrote to his father that the Prince had just got out of bed himself. 'The Doctors took this opportunity of testing his lungs, and although there was much congestion there is little organic mischief, and if they can but get the blood purified and the lungs restored to a more healthy action he may yet recover! The Doctors however dread a crisis like yesterday and are little hopeful ...'

They changed his bed. Having got out by himself, he could not get back again unaided. The Queen went to lie down next door. Suddenly she heard heavy breathing. She ran in.

'*Es ist das kleine Fräuchen*' she whispered tremulously, leaning over him; he moved his head. She asked for '*ein Kuss*' and he moved his lips. For a moment she rushed out of the Blue Room, throwing herself in anguish to the ground. The brave, faithful Alice called her back, for the end was near.

'Oh, this is death,' cried the Queen, taking his left hand, already cold, and kneeling down. 'I know it. I have seen *this* before.'

Princess Alice knelt on the other side, the Prince of Wales and Princess Helena at the foot, the doctors and members of the Household close by.

Two or three long but perfectly gentle breaths were drawn, the hand clasping mine, & (oh! it turns me sick to write it) *all all* was over ... I stood up, kissing his dear heavenly forehead & called out in a bitter agonising cry: 'Oh! my dear Darling!' & then dropped on my knees in mute, distracted despair, unable to utter a word or shed a tear!

The time was a quarter to eleven. The Queen was carried into the Red Room where she lay half-stunned on the sofa. 'We heard her loud sobs as she went off to her solitary room,' wrote Dean Wellesley to his brother. After a short while she was able to see her children, promising to live for them. The Prince of Wales ran into her arms.

'Indeed, Mama, I will be all I can to you.' She kissed him again and again.

'I am sure, my dear boy, you will.' Her Household filed past.

'You will not desert me? You will all help me?' They pledged unswerving devotion to her and received in return her pledge of unswerving devotion to duty. Lord Alfred Paget sobbed out that he had been in waiting at her marriage and was in waiting *now*. Then Sir James Clark came for her and led her back into the Blue Room.

Oh! that I can even now write it – & that I did not go out of my mind! – I went in alone with that kind, fatherly old Friend – who so loved us both ...

At first she dared not look. Then she took courage and kissed his forehead.

The worst moments were to come. 'I went to my room & there sat gazing wildly & as hard as a stone on my Maids ...' They got her to bed. Princess Alice had her own bed moved into the room but the Queen could neither weep nor sleep. The Princess sent for Jenner who gave the Queen a mild opiate. For a little while she closed her eyes, then awoke and at last the agonizing, comforting tears poured down. She cried and cried and slept.

PART TWO

22

Still December

1861–64

When the Prince Consort died a despairing cry broke from the Queen that a whole reign was finished and a new one begun. In a sense she was right. Hitherto the routine business of the Crown had been shared by a man; a conscientious, analytical man whose religion was work and who held that every human being, including his wife, was capable of unlimited improvement if they only tried hard enough. Now the Queen was on her own. How would she manage without her beloved husband at her side?

Prince Albert himself had been slowly teaching the Queen one lesson which might help her to live through her despair, to 'take things as God sent them'. Apart from occasional paroxysms of weeping, her Household were astonished at her submissiveness. On the Sunday following the Prince's death she wished to take the Duchess of Sutherland into the Blue Room. Her doctors warned her not to kiss the body. Meekly she obeyed, embracing his clothes instead. One more visit later that day; then she decided not to go again lest this 'sad though lovely image' should be printed too deeply on her mind. The room was meticulously photographed so that it might be cleaned but not changed. She slept with his night-shirt in her arms and a cast of his hand within reach. Over the empty pillow she hung his portrait crowned with a wreath of evergreens. The borders of her handkerchiefs and writing-paper, already black for her mother, had to be increased to almost half an inch. Her Household could not conceive how she would carry on alone; they expected a breakdown and told their friends so. 'The poor Queen, the poor Queen', they murmured as they passed one another in the silent Corridor.

King Leopold lost no time in getting her away from Windsor to Osborne. Before leaving the Queen had walked down to Frogmore. There, near her mother's tomb, she chose a spot for the Mausoleum, 'for us'. As she pined alone at Osborne, getting back old letters, appointing guardians for her younger children, making her will, working at unintelligible State papers, she felt certain that by the time the Mausoleum was complete she too would be inside it. Such despondency may well have been increased by her uprooting from Windsor, and many people, including Princess Alice, felt that the Queen's abrupt removal from the scene of her suffering greatly delayed her recovery from her grief.

Overpowering lassitude prevented the Queen from taking proper exercise, talking to more than one person at a time, getting up for breakfast or dining with the family. It did not prevent her from covering the landscape with Albert memorials. Forgotten was the advice once given by Melbourne never to waste her

The Queen and Princess Alice in deep mourning around a bust of Prince Albert.

171

money on memorials. There was one stone to mark where Prince Albert had shot his last stag at Balmoral and another for his last shoot at Windsor; there was the colossal statue in the Horticultural Garden whose neck, she thought, was too thin and shoulders 'not quite right'. Most absorbing of all was the great national memorial in Kensington, though here, as elsewhere, she desperately needed the help of the Prince's critical faculties. The Albert Memorial, with her Angel holding the catalogue of the Great Exhibition against his dear knee, was not entirely worthy of its object. The chest was too hollow, the back too round and the left leg drawn up too high; but at any rate – 'It can be seen from a great distance.'

Queen Victoria's feelings about death are generally dismissed as plain morbid. But her attitude should be judged against the background of her times. Frank interest in death-bed scenes was quite normal. So was the cult of the death-chamber and the Mausoleum. Queen Victoria at least tried to make them cheerful. The Blue Room had its ceiling 'beautifully though simply' redecorated and was embellished with new china, pictures and the Prince's bust between the two beds which had shared his last hours. *Our* Mausoleum at Frogmore was unique precisely because it banished gloom.

The explanation of the Queen's particular reputation for morbidity must be found in her failure to reconcile the claims of public life and private grief. Had she fulfilled her State functions adequately, few would have criticized her for having the Prince Consort's clothes laid out each evening, with hot water and a clean towel. Many bereaved Victorians were going almost as far. Even King Edward VII left undisturbed the last tube of tooth-paste used by his dead son, Prince Albert Victor. He is not a by-word for morbidity.

Not unnaturally the country hoped that Her Majesty would soon be able to resume her official life. They did not realize how depleted were her resources even before the blow fell. She herself had almost forgotten her anxiety about the Prince's health during his last years. When Stockmar died in July 1863 her old letters were returned to her and she was surprised to find them so full of alarm, especially over 'his poor dear stomach'.

Courtiers who had to bear the brunt of a house of mourning tended to accuse her doctors of prescribing seclusion purely because Her Majesty ordered them to do so. They suspected that the spirit was weak but the flesh was strong. The public could not imagine any mourning lasting more than three years. Yet there seems reason to believe that the shock to Queen Victoria's system caused the kind of temporary physiological changes which modern drugs can alleviate. There are many indications of this. After Prince Albert's death she lost weight, yet her legs would hardly carry her. She felt the cold, though in the past her passion for low temperatures had been legendary and many were the shivering courtiers who longed to modify her partiality for draughts. She suffered from neuralgic head-aches and became engulfed in a lethargic depression from which all the time she longed to escape.

It is often suggested that the trouble was her time of life. There is no evidence for this theory. When the Prince Consort died she was only forty-two and felt younger; despite her violent attitude towards childbearing she was hoping for

The Blue Room at Windsor where Prince Albert died.

Planting a memorial tree for Prince Albert in Windsor Great Park, November 1862.

The Prince of Wales in 1863, a photograph from Queen Victoria's album.

Centre The Royal wedding guests at the marriage of the Prince of Wales to Princess Alexandra. Queen Victoria still stricken with grief at Albert's death would not attend the wedding breakfast but 'lunched alone'.

another child. The Princess Royal, indeed, emphasized that much of poor Mama's misery was due to bitter disappointment. The onset of the change could only have increased not caused a neurosis which already had her in its grip.

The first clash between grief and duty occurred when the Queen professed herself unable to receive her Ministers personally; they must communicate through General Grey or Princess Alice. (General Sir Charles Grey, the late Prince's secretary, was now acting in this position for the Queen. It was characteristic of a certain obtuseness, not to say jealousy, in Ministers that the harassed widow had to wait until 1867 before her need for help with government business was recognized and Grey formally appointed private secretary.) Lord Russell promptly rapped her over the knuckles. She submitted with a good grace, commenting on Lord Palmerston's kindness at a subsequent audience and tactfully ignoring his green gloves and blue studs.

Underneath she was steeling herself against the next thrust. They intended to push her, she believed, always a little further than she could go. This became the growing-point of her neurosis. As the pressures increased so she would brace herself against them, refusing in the end to perform public duties of which she was perfectly capable for fear of being pressed into others beyond her strength. Her early seclusion, at any rate, shows an instinct for self-preservation. She knew and 'they' did not how near she was to a breakdown. Three times during her first visit as a widow to Balmoral she feared that the pressure of incomprehensible

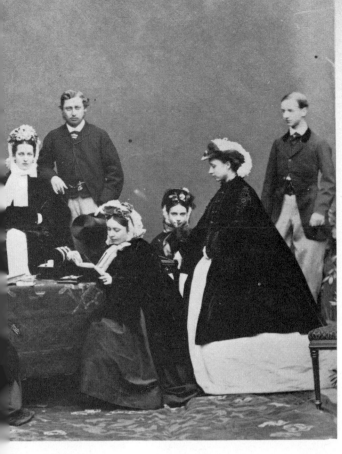

Princess Alexandra of
Denmark.

business on top of her frantic grief was driving her insane. Considering the
Prince's many warnings of what would happen if she lost control, her alarm was
understandable.

The next clash quickly followed when the Queen was required to attend a Privy
Council. She declined. A solution was found by the new Clerk who bore the
encouraging name of Arthur Helps. Queen Victoria was persuaded to station
herself in one room while Helps and three Privy Councillors occupied another,
with the door open between them; as each item was read out, Helps solemnly
replied on her behalf, 'Approved'.

If Queen Victoria had reflected she would have seen that many of dearest
Albert's laws were already being broken. Instead of seeking outside interests, she
was withdrawing; instead of cultivating the present, she was dedicating herself
to the past. He used to chide her for 'looking before and after', building castles in
the air or sighing for past delights. Now she was not even building castles. 'It is
terrible,' she wrote to the Princess Royal, 'never to look forward to the future but
only backwards.'

In other respects, however, she clung tenaciously to Prince Albert's law. He
had mapped out his eldest son's future before he died. In the spring of 1862 the
Prince of Wales would make a tour of Palestine followed by marriage, it was hoped,
to Princess Alexandra of Denmark, who had finally been chosen as his prospective
bride shortly before the Prince Consort's death.

The Prince's departure was fortunate, for his mother could not look at him without a shudder. At first she shuddered at the 'disgusting details' of his affair at the Curragh. But when the Princess Royal leapt to her brother's defence – dear Mama must try to see his good qualities also – the Queen shifted her ground: her shudder was due to the result of the affair. Bertie had broken Papa's heart.

No attitude could have been more unfair, or hurtful to the Queen herself. For despite the slashing attacks she launched at intervals against most of her offspring, at heart she wanted to think the best of 'our children'. At the root of her trouble with the Prince of Wales lay her old obsession about his being a 'caricature' of herself. How could a caricature occupy the throne? Yet she was daily praying for death to take her, when precisely this situation would arise. The Queen's monomania had landed her in a dilemma as pathetic as it was futile.

When the Prince of Wales returned from abroad no more was heard of the Queen's shudders and she settled down to the job of getting him married. Though he seemed 'much improved', she still felt it right to inform Alix's family that Bertie was 'a regular *mauvais sujet*' lest 'the poor girl' be trapped into a life of misery.

Any doubts the Queen might have felt about Alix herself vanished when she met her on the way to Coburg in September. Her only fear was that the Princess was still growing and would be taller than her future husband, who was spreading outwards and looked like a farmer.

On 5 March 1863 the marriage took place in St George's Chapel, Windsor. The ceremony was in striking contrast to the funereal conditions in which poor Princess Alice, in a black trousseau, had been married a year earlier. Guests were staggered by the magnificence of the proceedings and appalled by the lack of rehearsal. Lord Palmerston and Lady Westminster had to travel back third class on the special train, the latter loaded with half-a-million pounds' worth of diamonds, while Disraeli had to sit on his wife's lap. For little Prince William of Prussia it was a first opportunity to defy the English. He threw his aunt's muff out of the carriage window and when his youthful uncles reproved him he sank his teeth into their bare knees. His sombre grandmama he addressed familiarly as 'duck'.

The Queen's personal arrangements were flawless. Having reached the Chapel by a specially constructed covered way which led direct into the darkness of Catherine of Aragon's Closet, high above the altar, she stepped forward when the ceremony began, shaking with nerves but able to smile at Princess Beatrice and appreciate the Princess Royal's deep curtsey. It was only when the sound of silver trumpets pierced her as never before that she suddenly felt faint. The wedding breakfast was not graced with her presence; '*I* lunched alone.' After the guests had departed she drove to the Mausoleum '& prayed by that beloved resting-place, feeling soothed & calmed.'

The marriages of her children soon forced the Queen to concern herself with political problems which, although they caused her much anxiety, had the beneficial effect of renewing her confidence in herself. The Prussian slogan to unite Germany – 'blood and iron' – was about to clang through Europe, incidentally ringing the knell of peace and goodwill in the Queen's family. At first the Queen's sympathies were for Prussia whose ambitions she failed to understand. Prussia was the home of Vicky and Fritz, now engaged in a political struggle with Bismarck, his father's chief minister.

In 1863 the Queen misinterpreted a subtle move by Bismarck and thought that Prussia was being squeezed out by Austria. She forced herself to visit Germany and interviewed both the King of Prussia and Emperor of Austria in the hope of bringing them together. That her interviews accomplished nothing she was candid enough to realize, her most significant recollection being of Bismarck's 'horrid expression' when she happened to run into him afterwards; he deeply resented her interference.

In the same year the Queen was faced with a more difficult problem. She found her two eldest children ranged on opposing sides in the complex debate between the Danes, the Prussians and other parties over the future of the Duchies of Schleswig and Holstein. Bismarck's solution to the problem was a simple one which showed little concern for the anxieties of a widowed lady with a Danish daughter-in-law and a Prussian son-in-law. The Prussian armies invaded and occupied both Duchies in early 1864, inflicting so catastrophic a defeat on the Danes that Palmerston and Russell feared an attack on Denmark itself. 'God forgive you for it,' wrote Queen Victoria bluntly to her eldest daughter. At home the Queen, committed to Prince Albert's former watchword of British neutrality, suffered agonies as it seemed that Britain would get involved on the Danish side. Scuffles with Palmerston and Russell followed as she pressed her opinion on them; they were only ended by an armistice signed in April 1864.

Despite the failure of her attempts at intervention, the troubles abroad convinced the Queen of her right to eavesdrop, so to speak, on Cabinet discussions and to use her knowledge for pushing her own views. But she was still not prepared to perform her public functions at home. Things had got to such a state that posters appeared in March 1864 outside Buckingham Palace.

These commanding premises to be let or sold, in consequence of the late occupant's declining business.

This and similar attacks stung the Queen, but did not force her out into the public eye, for Sovereign and people were estranged by a genuine misunderstanding. To the Queen, desk-work was enough. If she stuck to her boxes and kept England at peace, what more could she do? Surely they did not want her to ape the showmanship of George IV? Her popularity in the past had depended on 'hard work and domestic purity'. It still did.

The Queen forgot that a monarch must not only work but be seen to work. Or as King Leopold put it: 'the English are very personal; to continue to love people they must see them ....' Cunningly he fanned her jealousies. Bertie and Alexandra were '*constantly before the public* in EVERY IMAGINABLE SHAPE. *and* CHARACTER, and *fill entirely the public mind*'. Princess Alice added her gentler pressure. At last for the first time since Prince Albert's death the Queen drove on 21 June 1864 in an open carriage. It was just in time, for all the talk abroad was about her forthcoming abdication. How *really* pleased her good people seemed – 'though my poor sad face & garb *must* tell its tale.'

23
Brown Eminence
The 1860s

Queen Victoria at last faced a new year in 1865 with the will to live. Remembering her children, her country and Europe she wrote, 'For all this I must try & live on for a while yet!' Fate, as if to mark this step forward, promptly removed two more of her old props, at the same time presenting her with two powerful new ones.

Lord Palmerston died on 18 October 1865. '... I *never* liked him,' she wrote to her moribund uncle, King Leopold, though his death had snapped another link with 'that bright happy past'. A week later she was definitely lamenting Palmerston's loss in a letter to the Princess Royal, citing against him only his 'addiction to earthly vanity' (presumably now cured) and praising his strong will, hard head, knowledge of history, courage and other 'great qualities'.

Within two months, on 10 December, King Leopold himself died. 'Now you are head of all the family,' wrote Princess Alice to her mother. Queen Victoria's matriarchal sense was forthwith affronted by a refusal on the part of the Belgian authorities to grant King Leopold's wish for burial at Windsor. 'All you tell me of the Funeral,' the Queen fumed to the Princess Royal, 'is vy painful & caused by that atrocious Catholic Clergy! Nasty "Beggers" as Brown wld say ...'

Queen Victoria had begun to quote John Brown. He was indeed a new and formidable influence in her life. But before embarking on Brown's strange story it is necessary to introduce a second person who played a leading part from 1865 onwards.

Henry Ponsonby, one of the Prince Consort's equerries, was thirty-seven when the Queen took him over in 1861. For thirty years he was to pepper Queen Victoria with Liberal ideas and spice her Court with humour. What the *Greville Memoirs* do for the first half of Queen Victoria's reign the Ponsonby Letters do for the second. They are of exceptional value for the five years (1865–70) when the Brown scandal flared.

John Conroy was picked out by the Duke of Kent to serve the Duchess. John Brown was picked out by the Prince Consort to serve the Queen. Conroy became known as 'King John'. By the year 1867 it was widely believed that another 'King John' ruled. Three or four years later the scandal was dead. It has never been buried.

At the time of the Prince Consort's death, Brown had been Queen Victoria's 'particular gillie' as she said, for nearly three years, 'combining the offices of groom, footman, page, and *maid*, I might almost say, as he is so handy about

Sir Henry Ponsonby who was equerry to the Queen for thirty years.

cloaks and shawls ...' In one sense he was less exalted than the chief gillie, Grant, but he waited at table on expeditions when not too 'bashful', i.e. tipsy, and made the Queen's safety out riding and driving his especial care. Otherwise he was only one among several favourites. Not until the autumn of 1863 does Brown's name begin to stand out from her Journal. A series of carriage accidents brought this about. Once the leading horse fell and Brown saved the day by sitting on its head. A few days later Brown rescued her when her coachman drove her into a ditch at night, giving her a black eye and permanently crooked thumb.

John Brown was a rough, handsome, intelligent Scot of thirty-nine with a strong arm, big stick, long legs, curly hair and beard, blue eyes and firm chin. Brown's brusque manner gave her confidence. His admonishments to keep still while he tucked in her rug or pinned her cape and his habit of addressing her as 'wumman' seemed the plainest guarantee of devotion.

At the end of October 1864 the Queen, Dr Jenner and Sir Charles Phipps, Keeper of the Privy Purse, hatched an idea which was to change her life. They decided to bring John Brown to Osborne for the winter. Dr Jenner, she wrote, wished her to keep up her riding and a strange groom would never do. Soon the Queen felt that there were other ways in which Brown could make himself useful, 'besides leading my pony as he is so very dependable ...' A memorandum of 4 February 1865 describes Brown's new status. He is henceforth to be called 'The Queen's Highland Servant', taking orders from none but the Queen herself and attending her both indoors and outdoors. He is to continue as before cleaning her boots, skirts and cloaks unless this proves too much. Brown's duties remained similar for the next seven years though he had rapid promotions in status and

John Brown with Queen
Victoria at Osborne.
Painting by Landseer.

salary. By 1872 the Queen was addressing him as 'John Brown Esq.' and his salary had more than trebled to £400.

Brown's magic began to work, speeding Queen Victoria's recovery. Sometimes, indeed, she worried that the service provided by 'honest Brown' was too much of a comfort. Ought she to reproach herself because her grief for the Prince was becoming less violent?

The country worried too. A whisper soon arose that Queen Victoria had married. In elegant drawing-rooms jokes were made about 'Mrs John Brown' and a scurrilous pamphlet with this title went the rounds. On 30 June 1866 *Punch* prepared the ground for an attack by publishing *An Imaginary Despatch* from Balmoral in which the Queen lambasted her Ministers for excluding her from public affairs.

A French caricature of the
relationship between the
Queen and her Highland
servant.

This piece of heavy sarcasm was followed on 7 July by an imaginary *Court Circular*:

Balmoral, Tuesday.

   Mr John Brown walked on the Slopes. He subsequently partook of a haggis. In the evening, Mr John Brown was pleased to listen to a bag-pipe.
Mr John Brown retired early.

   Other journals, both at home and abroad, took up the tale. The trouble was that Queen Victoria's seclusion provided the perfect climate to sustain it. Who could say what was happening in the Scottish hills or on the Island in the Solent? Though her public appearances were steadily increasing, the improvement was never quick enough to overtake fresh criticism.

   Queen Victoria, naïve and obstinate as ever, kept providing fresh evidence of her infatuation. Brown, for example, complained in 1868 that royal smokers kept him up too late. The Queen, therefore, wrote to her long-suffering equerry, Lord Charles Fitzroy:

Lord Charles would perhaps simply mention to Prince (Christian) *without* giving it as a *direct order* that the Queen felt it *necessary* for the sake of the *servants* ... that the smoking room should be closed ... by 12 o'clock – not later.

In any household, royal or otherwise, the servant whose convenience appears to come before that of the family will not be popular.

Gradually the hubbub subsided, though there continued to be rows caused by jealousy of Brown or by the latter's outspoken manner to the Queen's relatives and staff. In 1870 it seems that he had taken secret steps to make his escape from his somewhat ambiguous position by marrying one of the Queen's dressers, but nothing came of it. The Queen's torrential woe may have persuaded him to drop it or perhaps he decided that he was too grand for a dresser. One fact emerges from this attempt of Brown's to free himself. If it was true that he thought of marrying in 1870 he could not have become the Queen's husband in 1866, as the gossips declared. And if he did not marry her before 1870, there is no reason to think that he did so afterwards. By 1871 the Brown crisis was over.

That the Queen was neither John Brown's mistress nor his morganatic wife should be clear from a study of her character. Her passionate nature, as we have seen, did not require physical ardours so much as intense, undivided affection producing a sense of safety and comfort. She needed a man to lean on, not to marry. And if she had ever been tempted to marry again, a sense of propriety would have ruled out Brown. He was a servant. It would *never* do. An entry in her Journal dated 24 May 1871, Brown's heyday, proves that she did not marry again:

My poor old birthday, my 51st! Alone, alone, as it will ever be! But surely, my dearest one blesses me.

Four years before her death she made her last will:

I die in peace with all fully aware of my many faults relying with confidence on the love, mercy and goodness of my Heavenly Father and His Blessed Son & earnestly trusting to be reunited to my beloved Husband, my dearest Mother, my loved Children and 3 dear sons-in-law. – And all who have been very near & dear to me on earth. Also I hope to meet those who have so faithfully & so devotedly served me especially good John Brown and good Annie Macdonald who I trusted would help to lay my remains in my coffin & to see me placed next to my dearly loved Husband in the mausoleum at Frogmore.

Perhaps it is surprising that two servants got into this exalted company at all. That was the Queen's way. The point is that John Brown was coupled with the wardrobe maid, no place for a second husband.

One other role besides lover and keeper was cast for Brown – that of the Queen's medium through whom she made contact with Prince Albert. The age was deeply interested in spiritualism and some of Queen Victoria's friends and even family became involved in psychical research. But the evidence put forward that the Queen ever attempted to make contact with Albert or used Brown as a medium is so circumstantial and conflicting as to be useless.

On the other hand the Queen certainly had a thirst for knowledge of that 'unseen world' beyond death, which was much intensified by the loss of her mother and husband in 1861. For one reputed to be unbookish, she turned in 1862 with pathetic eagerness to the help of books. In May she sent the Princess Royal her copy of the book she had found most useful: *New Philosophy* – 'all about the future'. Published anonymously in 1847, its author defended mankind's right, contrary to orthodox teaching, to speculate about the hereafter and predicted that spiritual progress would not come to an end with death: 'each will have to make up where he was wanting.'

Other books were to follow and the Queen's spiritual advisers soon saw which way the wind was blowing. They ministered to the Queen's imperious need for a clear picture of the hereafter or comforted her when she had doubts of its very existence.

These '*flashes* of doubtfulness' often racked her, one outstanding cause being the Almighty's apparent disregard of her reiterated prayer that if Albert were taken she should go too. Years afterwards she related to the Princess Royal a psychic experience she had undergone which had much strengthened her:

I too wanted once to put an end to my life *here*, but a *Voice* told me for *His* sake – no, 'Still Endure'.

This experience, unique in the Queen's life, made an indelible impression. 'Still Endure' became her motto.

By dint of reading, prayer and congenial conversation Queen Victoria rebuilt her beliefs into a shape so definite that gossips on the fringe of her Court assumed they must be based on personal experience: spiritualism was Society's vivid new interest – why not the Queen's?

What was the position of Brown in the Queen's system of beliefs? As we have seen there is little evidence that he was a medium, but it is probable that the Queen credited him with two well-known gifts of the Highlander – second sight and that poetry which lifts one up 'above the heavy Clay wh clogs our Souls!' Poetry and premonitions are far from being mediumship but they are enough to build on. A combination of John Brown's *ambience* and the Blue Room, where she was known to pray, should be sufficient to explain away the rumours of this aspect of Her Majesty's relationship with the Queen's Highland Servant.

Yet the rumours existed. What has been said already about the Queen's morbidity applies also to the Queen's John Brown. No one would have deprecated her cult of the Blue Room if she had been at the same time a bustling public figure. Similarly, she might have been excused John Brown if her drives round London had been more frequent. The people needed to see more of Brown sitting on the box not less. All the Queen's troubles went back to the same source: her seclusion.

24
Granite and Rock
1865–68

Palmerston's death in 1865 left Lord Russell, the younger of Queen Victoria's 'two dreadful old men', at the head of affairs. The prospect of a political reshuffle as usual seemed unbearable. She would have to interview a new Prime Minister, for the first time since her marriage, alone, weighing every syllable, recording every word. She had never found Russell sympathetic. Gladstone, she reckoned, would make a prudent but an unpopular Leader of the House – a source of future instability. Worst of all, she would have to leave Balmoral for Windsor several days early. 'Alas, alas,' she wailed to the Princess Royal, 'I dread it more than words can express'. Once more, reality was less black than imagination painted it. The Russell audience went off splendidly and she felt that Prince Albert's blessing rested upon her labours.

If anyone had had the nerve to cross-question her at this date about her politics, she would probably have answered that she was a Liberal or a Liberal-Conservative. She had lived almost one third of her life steeped in Whiggery and until nearly the end of the second third she was still breathing Liberal airs. Most of the prominent members of her Household were Liberals, or even Radicals. Later some Tories were introduced, such as her new physician, Sir William Jenner, or Sir Theodore Martin, who was to prove useful amongst other things in his ability to explain Gladstone's explanations of political affairs to the Queen. But the Queen obstinately refused to consider herself a Tory. Throughout her subsequent battles with Gladstone she retained a maddening habit of asserting that no one was more truly Liberal than she.

The Queen announced her intention to open Parliament for the first time since her widowhood on 6 February 1866. So cynical had people become that many thought she would seize the excuse of King Leopold's death to cancel it. But the eternal problem of persuading Parliament to provide financial support for her children was pressing in 1866 and the Queen was determined to submit herself to what she now described as a sacrifice, a '*Show*', through which the broken-hearted widow was to be 'dragged in *deep mourning*, ALONE *in State*.'

Despite a high wind she drove with both carriage windows open so that she could be seen, but she refused the State coach, banished the trumpets and bypassed 'that terrible Gallery, with staring people', in the House of Lords. Discarding the crown she adapted the black cap of Mary Queen of Scots. Her long veil and dress were black, her crimson robes were draped over the throne like a cast-off skin, while the Lord Chancellor read her speech. Utterly expressionless,

WHERE IS BRITANNIA ?

A nineteenth-century coalmine. An 1842 commission revealed that in some mines children were employed from the age of five and earned, at most a few shillings a week.

she stared in front of her as if she did not hear a word. The Monarch seemed to have abdicated in favour of the Mandarin, but a Mandarin who did not even nod.

This same year she made a number of other official appearances, including one or two 'alarming' breakfasts (garden parties) at Buckingham Palace, where she had to recognize hundreds of people. After so many years' seclusion it was 'very puzzling & bewildering'. There were also visits to hospitals and prisons. She still felt the urge to tend the poor and the sick, and indeed if she could have been left to potter about on her good works, she would have felt adequate.

As it was, politics forced her into public life. The urge for a second instalment of electoral reform was creating a ferment in the country and in Parliament. Russell himself was committed to introducing a Reform Bill but there were acute divisions in his Government on the subject. What would happen if he was beaten? Lord Derby would refuse to take over, Clarendon explained, not wanting 'to be made a fool of a 3rd. time by his Govt. not being able to stand'.

Her old nightmare was upon her – the prospect of no government at all; but now she went into action alone. And a fear unknown to Prince Albert lent wings to her pen. A war between Prussia and Austria for the mastery of Germany was impending. Not the moment for a political crisis in England. The Queen's attempts to prevent a crisis failed. Lord Derby would not support Reform, nor would Russell drop it. Meanwhile Europe darkened. 'War seems inevitable,' she wrote on 12 June. Two days later she left for Balmoral, thankful to get away from it all, 'if only for a short time'.

The Seven Weeks' War between Prussia and Austria had indeed broken out and proved to be one of the century's great watersheds, ending as it did in the rout of Austria at Sadowa. Queen Victoria had striven with tears, prayers and pen to avert a conflict in which her children would be fighting on different sides. At the eleventh hour her niece, Marie Leiningen, put into German for her an astonishing plea for peace to the King of Prussia: 'Beloved Brother, – At this

The Frenchman Gustav
Doré came to London in the
mid-nineteenth century and
vividly recorded the dark
squalor and misery he found.

A drawing of one of the
new industrial areas, the
'Black Country' round
Wolverhampton in 1866.

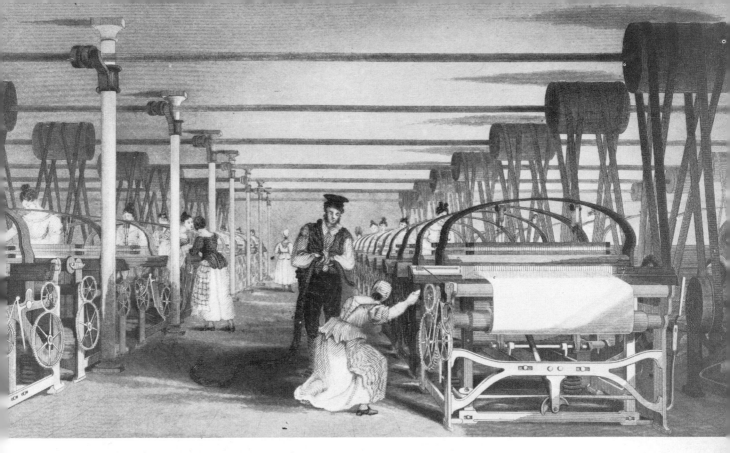

The introduction of power-driven machinery meant women could now perform tasks formerly undertaken by men. This drawing shows them handling power-driven looms.

fearful moment I cannot be silent … You are deceived …' by '*one man* [Bismarck] …' But the responsibility for war rests on '*you alone* …' Princess Louise put the matter more epigrammatically. When the Princess Royal wrote to ask what she should give Lenchen for a wedding present, Princess Louise promptly suggested, 'Bismarck's head on a charger'.

All in vain. The Queen's 'beloved brother' showed her letter to Bismarck and under the monster's eye composed what Queen Victoria called a 'deluded' answer. Lord Clarendon, the Foreign Secretary, had to explain away her intervention as a personal impulse.

War was declared. For a time Princess Alice completely lost touch with her soldier husband. She had just given birth to a third daughter. 'Poor dear Alice,' wrote the Queen in her Journal, '*what* a position for her!'

The respite at Balmoral in June was as short as Queen Victoria expected but too long to please the politicians. Russell's Government was defeated within five days. As it was by only 11 votes she declined to accept his resignation, dispatched a certificate of sickness from Dr Jenner and blocked her ears to the growls from the South. But she could not escape. The Princess Royal's little son Siggie died while the Queen was up there and she longed to be with her daughter. Her place was neither in Berlin, comforting Vicky, nor at Balmoral cosseting herself, but at Windsor.

She arrived back on 26 June, saw Russell, contemplated 'the peaceful face' in the Mausoleum and, on return, found a laconic telegram from the Prime Minister:

'Proposition no. 2' (we had agreed upon 2 numbers) which meant resignation! So here we are! but think it is perhaps after all, better so.

Here we are indeed. Prussia was engaged upon annexing the first instalment of German states which had sided against her in the war with Austria, among them Hanover. Hesse-Darmstadt, Princess Alice's home, had also mobilized against Prussia. The Queen could do little to help except send bandages for Princess Alice's hospitals and give her children asylum. On 27 June, while the little Hesses scampered up and down the Corridor, the Queen held a Council declaring England's neutrality. Just as she finished a violent thunderstorm burst.

Contrary to Clarendon's expectations Lord Derby was now struggling to form his last Ministry. By 3 July as the Queen lay gasping on her sofa in the appalling heat, sending and receiving messages, she knew that he would succeed. With the Prime Minister in the Lords, Disraeli would be Chancellor and Leader of the House: '… all these changes are very trying.' Her hatred of upheavals hid from her the brightness of the future.

The Tories no more than the Liberals could drop Reform. Gigantic outdoor meetings made it clear what the country wanted. Derby's justification of his party's *volte-face* was that it would 'dish the Whigs'. But it was Disraeli who had the monumental task of steering the second Reform Bill through, against violent opposition from both sides of the House, in the course of which three Ministers resigned.

The significance of the Reform, by which one million new voters were added to the rolls, was interpreted by Disraeli to the Queen. It was to have a profound influence on her own development. She pictured a nation reshaping itself in forms ever more favourable to a benevolent Monarchy, but hostile to Society. The Queen passed on her thoughts to the Princess Royal.

> The Lower Classes are becoming so well-informed – are so intelligent & earn their bread & riches so deservedly that they cannot & ought not to be kept back – to be abused by the wretched ignorant Highborn beings, who live only to kill time.

What the upper classes needed was a frightening shock before the 'dreadful crash'.

She saw herself as Queen of 'the lower classes', the loyal poor who cheered her most and sympathized most with her grief. And their prophet was to be Benjamin Disraeli, the man who had created the concept of the 'two nations', rich and poor. In February 1868 the gout finally disabled Lord Derby and Disraeli became Prime Minister. 'A proud thing', Queen Victoria wrote to the Princess Royal, 'for a Man "risen from the people" – to have attained!' His father, after all, was not only a Jew, but a 'mere man of letters'.

The Queen's division between lower and upper classes ignored the middle class – the class *par excellence* of the Victorian era. The truth is that though Queen Victoria was *bourgeoise* enough for the middle class to claim her as their own, she herself was no more interested in the minutiae of classes than of religious creeds. She distinguished broadly, like the rest of the aristocracy, between those who worked for a living and those who did not. The 'upper classes' did not. According to this categorization even Disraeli was a man of the people. 'Yes, I have climbed to the top of the greasy pole', said Disraeli with a gay, plebeian flourish.

It is a remarkable fact that Disraeli's and Brown's periods of influence on Queen Victoria almost coincided, Brown over-running Disraeli by two years at each end. Those who would attribute her revival exclusively to one or the other must find room for Brown's 'wumman' and Disraeli's 'faery' inside the same skin at the same time.

Queen Victoria's most romantic relationship had begun in the best tradition, with repugnance. 'Mr Disraeli (!) *high office*', she exploded in 1844 when the young Tory dandy asked for and was refused a job under Peel. By 1849 he was Opposition leader in the House of Commons but for every speech of his which she considered 'most brilliant', another was 'disgraceful'. As Chancellor of the Exchequer in 1852 he was at last able to woo her with his pen. Never had she received such Parliamentary reports. He described speeches as 'elaborate', 'malignant', or 'languid' instead of merely good, bad or indifferent. When he wanted to call a speaker's style elegant, he said it had 'concinnity'. A little dazed, she was nevertheless grateful.

Dizzy was so 'odd'. Odd he remained in her eyes, with his black ringlets and skin like a Dead Sea scroll, until he became Prime Minister at the age of sixty-four. Whenever Mrs Disraeli came with him, she only added to the oddness. 'Mrs Disraeli was very odd.' Nevertheless Queen Victoria had manifested a weakness for the *outré* ever since her girlhood, and given the right circumstances, Dizzy's oddities could turn out to be irresistible. Even his peculiar appearance was unlikely to disturb the niece of King Leopold, who had recently gone to the grave in a rich black wig and with wrinkled skin brilliantly rouged. Queen Victoria accepted the many grotesque faces which surrounded her with stoicism, reserving her comments for the handsome ones.

Prince Albert had no taste for the *outré*. He had written off Disraeli as an imposter and his conversion to Free Trade as dishonest. But if the living Albert had kept Queen Victoria and Disraeli apart, the dear departed brought them together. No one's condolences pleased her more than Dizzy's. His speech on the Albert Memorial made her weep. While Gladstone delayed its construction by haggling over the cost, Disraeli carried the vote through Parliament. The Irish refused to subscribe to a public memorial and later tried to blow up the Prince's statue in Phoenix Park. She heard that they also had held up the Albert Memorial in Kensington by not carrying out their contract for granite. Gladstone would excuse the Irish. Disraeli reiterated his assurance, given as long ago as January 1861, that she could always rely on the Conservative Party 'as on a rock'. Should she choose Gladstone and the Irish granite or Disraeli and the Conservative rock? When Disraeli struck water from the rock in the form of Tory democracy – the union of Queen and People – Queen Victoria drank eagerly.

Disraeli kissed hands as Prime Minister on 27 February 1868. He gracefully summed up his future relations with the Sovereign as 'on her part perfect confidence; on his, perfect devotion'. Complimenting her on her great experience which surpassed 'all living princes and most living people', he entreated her not to withhold from him the benefit of her guidance. All great matters he would submit to her; the burden of all trivial affairs should be borne by him alone. In point of fact Disraeli found it more convenient to reverse these chivalrous principles, permitting Her Majesty to settle minor matters and reserving the great decisions for himself.

Disraeli quickly showed himself able to manage the Queen. No head-on collisions but a patient assumption that she would see reason. The reason was skilfully mixed with flattery. On one occasion Disraeli thanked her fervently for redrafting one of his speeches 'in a liberal sense'. In the spring the Queen showed her gratitude for this new happy relationship by sending Disraeli primroses from Osborne. He thanked her in language no less flowery and in return sent her his novels and letters crammed with gossip. For the first time in her life she felt really on the inside, confiding to Lady Augusta Stanley (Bruce) that 'she never before knew *everything*'.

In November a general election brought the idyll to an end. When his government had been defeated earlier in the year he had offered the Queen a choice between his resignation at once or dissolution later. She chose dissolution later, gambling on the chance of Disraeli getting back. Great was Liberal rage, for his constitutional duty was to offer not a choice but advice. Dizzy, however, intended to demonstrate two points: the Sovereign's power to choose – and to choose him.

Despite Disraeli's warnings the Queen hoped for a Tory victory. Though she heard 'a great ringing of bells' on 17 November as polling proceeded, there was less noise from the newly enfranchized voters than she had feared – surely a hopeful sign. Nevertheless the Tories were soundly beaten. As a tribute to her retiring Prime Minister and at his earnest request, she created his wife the Viscountess Beaconsfield and reluctantly yielded herself to Gladstone's political embrace. Her new Prime Minister was already known to the masses by a name singularly unpleasing to their Queen: 'The People's William'. But with the propriety habitual to her, she received him graciously. 'He is completely under the charm,' wrote Granville delightedly to Grey.

William Ewart Gladstone was ten and a half years older than the Queen. At fifty-nine he was a striking figure: tall, upright, with flashing eyes, commanding features and a voice even more remarkable than her own. Beginning as a Tory, he had become a Peelite over Free Trade and finally moved to the Liberals in 1859.

On paper Gladstone was all set to be a royal favourite. He was clearly in line with Prince Albert, Peel and Aberdeen. The Prince had admired his moral character, choosing his son Willie to accompany the wayward Bertie abroad. Queen Victoria appreciated Gladstone's virtue. After a dinner at Balmoral a sincere tribute appeared in her Journal:

He is very agreeable, so quiet & intellectual, with such a knowledge of all subjects, & is such a *good* man ...

But his goodness took many forms, some of them unacceptable to the Queen. His habit of resigning office for unintelligible reasons of conscience she considered hypocrisy. Soon she was to find some of his more extreme activities 'strange' – a word she often used to denote mental derangement. Later she was to become more explicit in this opinion.

Any good intentions which the Queen may have felt towards Gladstone were immediately shattered by his determination to disestablish the Protestant Church in Ireland. He saw this as the best way of bringing peace to that distressful island with its vast majority of Roman Catholics. Although the Queen wanted peace in Ireland no less than Gladstone himself, and like him was alarmed by the terrorist activities of the Fenians (Irish-Americans determined to destroy British rule in Ireland for ever), she was unable to accept the Prime Minister's policy.

Disestablishment struck directly at her prerogative as head of the Irish Church. And where would it end? Many people prophesied that the Church of Scotland would be next to fall. Furthermore she had no faith that the policy would lead to peace, observing 'that the tenure of land was of far more importance [than Disestablishment] to the Irish.' As a result of her personal opinion of Gladstone's policy she refused to open Parliament and thus seem to approve the Bill, coolly informing the enraged Gladstone that he could say she had a worse headache than usual. When the Princess Royal among others deprecated this backsliding, the Queen tartly summed up her attitude: '... I will not appear to have turned quite round.' She forgot that it was the Ministry which had changed, not the Sovereign. In the same breath, however, she remembered her constitutional duty, promising to support her Government 'to the utmost extent'. She was largely, if not to the utmost extent, true to her word.

While Queen Victoria was worrying about the upbringing of her children, the education received by her subjects varied greatly.

Mr Williams's Academy in Lewisham.

Rugby, one of the earliest English public schools whose reputation in the nineteenth century flourished under the headmastership of Dr Arnold.

When Gladstone's Bill reached the Lords, she urged moderation upon the Opposition peers while secretly agreeing with Dean Stanley that they '*must* amend the Irish bill, as much as they can'. Their Lordships proceeded to show that they could amend it so drastically as to provoke a constitutional crisis. Whereupon the Queen took fright and all sides ran for compromise. On 22 July 1869 she recorded with unspeakable relief: 'Everything is settled!!!' The Irish Church was duly disestablished. When it came to the pinch, she desperately wanted the machinery to work, even if she deprecated the product.

How did Queen Victoria stand at the end of 1869 *vis-à-vis* the two new forces which were to dominate the second half of her reign – Tory Democracy and Liberalism emergent from Whiggery – each with a leader of genius?

Gladstone was falling behind. Though his last speech on Disestablishment was 'very fine and very *handsome*', her compliments to him were academic rather than heartfelt. Those personal idiosyncrasies of the great man which so exacerbated later struggles already fretted her: she could not find him agreeable, '& he talks so very much'. Disraeli might not be so 'noble' and earnest nor have such strong convictions, but if anything he was 'even more unselfish' and his ideas were larger.

The duty of expounding Tory Reform to the Queen having fallen to Disraeli, he had inevitably stolen an ideological march on his rival. His 'large ideas' grew larger in her imagination as she mulled them over. In reforming the Constitution he would force Society to reform itself; the working classes would educate their masters. There would be no more misbehaviour on the steps of the Throne, once Society was reformed. Of all Queen Victoria's present anxieties, the greatest was her unreformed family.

25
Head of all the Family
1865–69

Queen Victoria's forty-seventh birthday (24 May 1866) was marked by the restoration of a pious act which had fallen into abeyance. She counted her blessings. They made an interesting short list. Affectionate children and friends; the ability to make others happy and to be of use. Up till now she had performed her matriarchal duties more as a martyr than a mother. When the Prince was alive she had not been able to choose a bonnet alone; five years later she could not trust her family, her Court, her country, Europe itself, to choose a children's nurse, a new fashion or a foreign policy without her advice. The remark dropped by Princess Alice at the time of King Leopold's death had gone home. 'Now you are head of all the family.'

The Prince of Wales and his family kept the Queen's matriarchal feelings in a state of perpetual flux. One day she would expatiate on their charming natures; next, she found the whole family wretched, ill-behaved and selfish. Nonetheless her relations with her eldest son showed a gradual improvement, despite the gloomy prognosis of Sir James Clark at the end of 1865.

> No one who knows the character of the Queen and of the Heir apparent can look forward to the future without seeing troubles in that quarter ...

Even her over-anxious heart could not fail to recognize his devotion to herself. 'Really dear Bertie is so full of good & amiable qualities,' she wrote to the Princess Royal in 1867, 'that it makes one forget & overlook much that one would wish different.' Nevertheless one did wish much different, indeed, almost his whole way of life. The 'Marlborough House set' who frequented his London home were the fast set. Knitting in public (as Princess Alix had been seen to do) was one of their least offences. Gambling, racing, smoking, associating with Americans and Jews – he had learned all these deplorable habits from Society.

Queen Victoria had by now shifted the sin of parricide from her son's shoulders to Society as a whole. As she warmed to him she grew colder towards his circle. But though she wished for more of his company she considered him still too indiscreet to share her State duties, apart from the ceremonial ones. She longed to receive generous, undiluted confidence from her heir while retaining the right to ration with extreme caution the amount of confidence she gave in return. Despite her son's desire to understand more of the business of government she continued to thwart him. For close on thirty years she obstinately kept Prince Albert's golden key to the Foreign Office boxes out of hands which seemed to her both grasping and incapable. In the meantime the Prince of Wales, twenty-eight in 1869, still had no occupation worth the name.

The temptations of Society were no threat to the Princess Royal. Her trouble was being too stiff and brusque. At the Paris Exhibition of 1867, for example, she caused great offence by taking only three old gowns, studying nothing but surgical instruments and sanitation and leaving early. She also made trouble through her continued desire for one of her sisters to marry a Prussian prince and help her in Germany. But Queen Victoria was no longer so keen on Prussians nor on losing another daughter abroad.

Two more daughters were married during these years. At twenty-two the artistic Princess Louise fell in love with the Duke of Argyll's heir, Lord Lorne, a Liberal Member of Parliament and 'a subject'. The Queen swallowed her doubts and defended the engagement against the criticisms of her family. The Royal Family could not afford to marry penniless foreigners, since 'our Children have (alas!) such swarms of children'; nor could the Queen afford to entertain large foreign suites, all babbling German at table. Dearest Papa had been able to keep them in order. She could not.

Prince Arthur with Princess Helena and Princess Louise at the opening of the Royal Infirmary in 1865. Painting by Sir A. Helps.

Princess Louise in her wedding gown. Her marriage was to end in separation.

The country was pleased, apart from the diehards whose violence made the Queen wonder whether Lorne ought not to resign his seat, thus saving her from accusations of Liberal partisanship. The Duke of Argyll put his foot down. The Queen soon liked everything about the subject except his voice, though she remained doubtful whether her daughter's Bohemian tendencies would be cured by a husband who wrote poetry.

Then there was the question of a husband for Princess Helena. The Queen was determined that the invaluable Lenchen should remain in England. This meant a son-in-law who would live at Frogmore, where she intended to settle her daughter for life. With considerable trepidation, the Queen finally accepted Prince Christian of Schleswig-Holstein. On one point only was she quite easy: Lenchen would be personally very happy with her upstanding, sensible, not very exciting, bald German who smoked twenty-four cigars a day. The political aspects of the marriage were more alarming since it revived the antagonisms over Schleswig-Holstein which had split the family two years before. The Queen did her best to mend the breach. The business, however, of reconciling the divergent interests of her large family would have been beyond many matriarchs with a calmer temperament than hers.

The most difficult children during these years were Princess Alice and Prince Alfred. Remembering that it was Princess Alice above all others who saved the Queen in her hour of desolation, it is sad to have to record a long breach. Much of the trouble arose from her continued criticism of the Queen's seclusion. But there

Princess Beatrice, a
drawing by Noel Paton.

were other, more petty, difficulties. Alice was critical of Princess Helena's marriage and afterwards jealous of her comparative opulence at Frogmore. She failed to write on her sister's birthday – an omission little short of a crime – and as a reprisal the Queen refused to invite the Hesses to England during the following year for fear of ruining Lenchen's first months of happy marriage. This breach was mended through the mediation of the Princess Royal, but Darmstadt and Windsor were to continue to argue. Nevertheless the strains would have been negligible but for the Princess's having criticized her mother's seclusion.

Prince Alfred's 'ruin' was another matter. Like his elder brother he was a victim of Society. In 1862 he had got into a scrape with a lady in Malta, but the Queen had recovered from this. Soon afterwards she was showering him with compliments: 'Dear Affie is a very dear, clever, charming companion – & I think he gets liker & liker to blessed Papa!' The problem was to get him married. Various attempts failed, and at Windsor in the autumn of 1866 he displayed the most difficult side of his difficult character. He was rude to the servants and so reserved with his mother that she suspected him of hiding a guilty secret. In contrast the Prince of Wales was kindness itself and immensely popular with 'the people [servants] here'. Then the atmosphere improved again, Prince Alfred confessing his secret to Princess Helena – he was hopelessly in love with a commoner – and his mother forgiving him. Had not dearest Albert often said that it was no sin to fall in love, only to go in the way of temptation? London must be avoided; 'that Society has done him incredible harm.'

And so the wheel spins round according to changes in the Queen's volatile nature and the chance of some peccadillo having come to her ears. One moment (August 1868) Affie is 'a gt grief' – 'he don't see or feel what is wrong!' – whereas Bertie is 'so anxious to do well – tho' he is sometimes imprudent – but that is all ...': the next (September 1868), Affie pays 'a very happy visit to Balmoral', reformed – need it be said? – by a strong letter from his Mama.

The Queen's three youngest children brought her more pleasure than pain. Princess Beatrice at eight was still 'Baby' and had no faults save that of behaving occasionally like a child.

2nd June 1865 – Baby's liveliness & fidgetyness was beyond everything, & she ended by throwing all the milk over herself.

With Prince Leopold, now struggling through his precarious adolescence, it was a running battle to prevent him from doing too much. The Queen gave him the Garter a year earlier than his brothers because

he was far more advanced in mind & I wish to give him this encouragement & pleasure, as he has so many privations and disappointments.

At various times she tried to see a replica of her husband in one or other of her sons. In 'little Leo' she discovered his father's brains. When in 1868 he was 'given back from the brink of the grave', she vowed to make him henceforth the chief object in her life.

200

The Prince Consort's character, if not his brains, was reflected in her favourite son, Prince Arthur. She found no blemish in him and determined to keep him that way. The Prince's Governor was instructed to keep the thermometers in her son's room at 60°; to prevent him from going behind the scenes at the theatres and to the Derby with Prince Alfred, from wearing 'frightful *stick-ups*' or a centre parting or putting his hands in his pockets. He must keep a daily journal, like the Queen his dear mother.

Grandchildren were multiplying. Despite her aversion to natural processes she insisted on being called to the birth of each grandchild, sitting for hours by the pillow, rubbing the arms or gripping the hands of the mother-to-be. Presents and loans poured from Windsor: everything from a bassinet to a little sarcophagus, from a quilt knitted by 'Gangan', as Queen Victoria was called by her grandchildren, to the family christening robe of Honiton lace which scarcely held together. Nothing was wasted. Vicky would like a new hot-dish for baby Charlotte? Then she must kindly return the old one for visiting grandchildren.

In certain moods she deplored the naughtiness of little Victoria and Ella Hesse or Eddy and Georgie of Wales. More often she would nurse a baby granddaughter with croup – 'it seemed to do her good' – and spend hours with one or other of the Wales boys alone in her room. 'One at a time is much the best.' Small girls were allowed in together to help Gangan change her dress. 'Dear little things, I like to see them so at home with me.' With human ambivalence she faced the sudden blank after Christmas: 'It is always sad, when a large family party disperses, but on the other hand, I need a little quiet.'

As the grandchildren grew older she sighed for the memoranda which Albert would assuredly have provided but did her best to supply the want. Let Vicky refrain from pushing little Henry's education:

nothing is gained by it – & it weakens their brains. We found this, & taught the younger ones all later.

Let Vicky also beware of arrogance in Willy. There had been an incident at Osborne when he had objected to a back seat in the pony carriage, refusing to speak a word to his attendant. His Grandmama tactfully professed herself 'much amused' at this 'little tinge of pride' in a five-year-old; but ever afterwards she issued periodic warnings.

A hundred minor matters pressed upon the busy matriarch. Often she did not go to bed till one o'clock and the feeling that she could not get up for breakfast was buried with her early widowhood. There were liveries to be chosen for Princess Helena's footmen – a 'slight diversion' from Lord Russell and Reform; fashions to be criticized, especially the hideous tight gowns which prevented ladies from curtseying and sometimes caused them to trip and fall flat. Reading material at Balmoral needed checking. At one time there were 26 guide books, 32 *Ladies of the Lake* and 12 *Rob Roys*. The Librarian had to send up some new books.

In 1868 the Queen herself had brought out a new book, her *Leaves from the Journal of Our Life in the Highlands*. The book, illustrated with her own sketches and bound in moss green covers adorned with golden antlers, sold 20,000 copies at once and quickly went through several editions. 'We authors, Ma'am', was the gallant phrase with which Dizzy addressed his Sovereign.

Queen Victoria attributed the book's success to its simple narrative, its expression of marital love and the 'friendly footing' on which she lived with her Highlanders. It would reform 'Highborn beings' by showing them the example of a good, simple life at the summit. There is more than a hint that she believed the *Leaves* would in future look after her popularity, rendering a drastic alteration in her way of life superfluous. For this very reason many of her family deplored the Queen's publications.

Always the Queen's thoughts returned to the contrast between the proud and the humble, the high and the low, Society and servants. She maintained an ingenious distinction between what she called 'John Bullism' and what might be called 'John Brownism'. John Bullism was an arrogant form of bullying prevalent among smart 'slangy' cavalry officers. In the domestic field, John Bullism created class hatred, in the international field, war. 'John Brownism' stood for all that was fine and noble in human nature: unselfishness, dignified humility, honesty and devotion.

The year 1869 marked the end of an epoch. In the course of it Queen Victoria reached her fiftieth birthday. 'Have completed $\frac{1}{2}$ a century now!' She regretted the passing of the 'sixties, hallowed as they were by Prince Albert having lived in them. All her self-confidence and sense of moral purpose would be needed to face the 'seventies, for a new enemy had appeared on the scene. John Bull was to be joined by John Ball, the arrogant cavalry officer by the rank republican.

A photograph of Queen Victoria with her eldest grandchild, the future Kaiser William II of Germany.

26

The Royalty Question

1870–74

The Queen again declined to open Parliament in February 1870. She would catch cold wearing a low-cut dress in her carriage. (Two years later Gladstone suggested clothing herself in ermine up to the neck. She laughed scornfully: the House of Lords was too hot.) In the same month she was punished by the spectacle of a much more painful opening – that of the Mordaunt case.

A member of the dreaded 'fast set', Sir Charles Mordaunt, brought a divorce suit against his wife, as a result of which the Prince of Wales was subpoenaed. Twelve letters from the Prince to Lady Mordaunt (who now occupied a lunatic asylum) were read out in court. So patently innocuous were they as seriously to disappoint the garbage-pickers; nevertheless a whirlwind of condemnation arose. The Lord Chancellor said 'it was as bad as a revolution as affecting [the Prince of] Wales'. London was black with the smoke of burnt confidential letters.

The Queen unburdened herself to the Princess Royal. She had never doubted Bertie's innocence, she wrote, and his appearance in court did great good, but the whole thing was 'painful & lowering'; the heir should never have got mixed up with 'such people'; she hoped that the trial would teach him a lesson; in future she would constantly remind him of it.

One evil result of the Mordaunt case was that it interrupted the Queen's slow process of reconciliation with her own physical nature. Dwelling on Bertie's delinquency she found herself warning Vicky against having too many children:

Believe me, Children are a terrible anxiety & the sorrow they cause is far gter than the pleasure they give.

From here she went on to attack marriage:

I am equally shy of marriages & large families ... better a 1000 times never marry, than marry for marrying's sake, wh I believe the gter number of people do.

Finally sex and childbirth came under the lash:

The animal side of our nature is to me – too dreadful ...

Queen Victoria was unfortunate in running into an acute international crisis – the Franco-Prussian War – soon after the Mordaunt case. The campaign, she knew, would again be fought in miniature by a divided Royal Family and she feared that Germany, not yet united, would be beaten by the Napoleonic hosts. Her efforts for peace were as unsuccessful as in 1866, for England, having opted out of

European affairs, was no longer an influence. For all that, the proclamation of England's neutrality was promptly followed by reproaches from Queen Victoria's Prussian relatives. As before, she played her delicate role with discretion and sympathy. She would send the Princess Royal linen for the wounded but not under her own name: whatever happened she must not 'swerve from the steep and thorny path' of neutrality or 'separate herself or allow herself to be separated from her own people'.

The total defeat of the French was to moderate the Queen's former Prussian sympathies. Delight at Fritz's great victory over Marshal MacMahon gave way to agitation when she learned that beautiful, wicked Paris was besieged and bombarded. Vainly hoping that the Prussians would not retain any French territory she again interceded with King William. The only result was a snarl from Bismarck about 'petticoat' interference. Her position had become an unenviable one by the time an armistice was signed on 28 January 1871. In Germany she was accused of turning the Princess Royal against her adopted country, in England of having a pro-Prussian bias. She had to warn her daughter that whereas people were formerly 'very German', now they were 'very French'.

Prussian aggression on top of the Mordaunt case and the Queen's seclusion formed a dangerous combination. The news of a republican meeting in October 1870 at which the Court had been derided as 'a pack of Germans', was laughed off by Ponsonby: 'We had better sacrifice Sahl and Bauer', the Queen's German librarian and governess. Next year he was not inclined to be what his mistress had once called 'so funny'.

As a result of the Franco-Prussian War one new Emperor appeared in Europe (the German Emperor William I) and another vanished (Napoleon III); Germany became united and France a Republic. These events had their repercussions in England. Republicanism was in the air and clubs to further it were founded up and down the country. Queen Victoria was deeply concerned by this disloyalty but as usual ignored her own contribution. 'Democratic feeling,' she wrote, 'is caused by the fact that the sins of the upper classes are forgiven while the lower classes are punished.' That made it easy to 'mislead' radical-minded artisans about the Monarch. Why pay nearly forty times as much as a President would cost, said 'wicked people', for a Queen they never saw?

A Queen they never saw. This was once again the main burden of the attack on the Sovereign, taken up by working-class newspapers and given its most outspoken airing by Sir Charles Dilke, a Radical Member of Parliament, in a speech at Newcastle on 6 November 1871. After denouncing Queen Victoria's dereliction of duty, he incited his audience to set up a Republic – 'let it come'.

The reaction of the Queen's advisers to these increasingly dangerous attacks was to try and draw her out of her seclusion. As early as 1868 General Grey had advised Gladstone to order the Queen in a '*peremptory*' tone to do her duty. It was not in Gladstone's nature to be peremptory towards Royalty. Prodding, however, was well within his compass. He had made it his mission to pacify Ireland. In 1869 he accepted a second mission, to energize the Queen. Along with

A satire on Queen Victoria's prolonged absences from the capital.

the Army, Church and other institutions he filed Queen Victoria, under the heading of the 'Royalty Question'.

However, after some small successes, the 'Royalty Question' lapsed in 1870. Ponsonby, who had taken over Grey's position after the latter's death in March, was well aware of the pitfalls and was resolved not to lose all influence by going too far. Gladstone himself was too immersed in political business to have much time to activate the Queen.

But in the following year he was prodding again. On 8 August 1871 the Queen received a letter from Gladstone asking her in her 'wisdom' to postpone her departure from Osborne to Balmoral until the House of Commons had been prorogued, a fortnight later than usual. The Queen was evasive but put her case strongly in a letter to the Princess Royal. The more she gave the more was asked; she had '*not prorogued* Parlt *in person* since the year: 52. That would *next* be asked!!' (It was.)

When the Queen finally did leave for Balmoral in mid-August it was as a sick woman. The illness turned out to be serious. An abscess on her arm which would not respond to treatment was accompanied by gout and rheumatism. On 22 August the Queen wrote in her Journal that she had never '*felt so ill since typhoid in 35*'. On 4 September the great Professor Lister, who had been called in by Jenner, lanced the abscess, but it was not until the end of the month that she really began to recover. She had lost two stone in weight and when she emerged again all were startled by the change in her manner and appearance. Even now her convalescence was to drag on for several weeks.

The initial reaction to the Queen's illness was that she was shamming. Gladstone summed up the Queen's behaviour as his most 'sickening' experience in forty years of public life, though later, when he realized how ill she was, he wrote that he was 'extremely concerned' to hear of Her Majesty's 'suffering state'. Other people were not so quickly convinced. It was not till 18 September that *The Times* printed an apology for its attacks on the Queen. It had taken six weeks of illness, said Ponsonby, and 'a vast amount of bodily suffering to convince people she was not shamming.'

Scarcely had the Queen recovered from her own illness when she received a telegram from Sandringham saying that the Prince of Wales had a feverish attack. Next day the Queen heard it was 'mild' typhoid; news followed of a high temperature and delirium. Obsessed with '10 years ago', she drove to the Mausoleum and then, on 29 November, hastened to her son's bedside.

Superstitious dread swept the house as the fatal 14 December, tenth anniversary of the Prince Consort's death, approached. The Queen watched her son from behind a screen, not daring to leave the house for more than half an hour each day. On 12 December she went to bed 'with the horrid feeling I may be called up'. The Prince of Wales, however, in contrast to his father was attended by professional nurses and his ravings revealed a robust temperament. His pillows went flying about the room as he laughed and sang, one of them felling his wife. At moments he thought he had succeeded to the throne, proposing reforms in the Household which made his attendants' hair stand on end.

On the 13th, the crisis was at hand. Queen Victoria was allowed to sit without a screen by his bed. 'In those heart-rending moments I hardly knew how to pray aright, only asking God if possible to spare me my Beloved Child.' Her prayers were answered. Next day the Prince took a turn for the better. On the following day, when only the nurse was with him, she was allowed to go in. He smiled, kissed her hand 'in his old way' and said, '"Oh! dear Mama I am so glad to see you. Have you been here all this time?" … I was so thankful & comforted.'

A letter of thanks to her people for their sympathy was the way Queen Victoria naturally chose to express her overflowing feelings. The Government, however, insisted on a public Thanksgiving Service at St Paul's. She conveyed her dislike of 'public religious displays', which were apt to degenerate into '*merely a show*', at the same time demanding an open carriage 'to enable the *people* (for *whom this is*)' to see properly.

Next month the persistent Dilke urged the Commons to delve thoroughly into Her Majesty's expenditure. He was howled down. Typhoid fever, which had just failed to dispatch her son, destroyed Dilke's campaign and dealt republicanism a crippling blow. Gladstone, too, was soon to recognize the failure of his attempts to prod the Queen. The prolonged correspondence had made the Queen ' "shut up" (so to speak)' towards him, and by 1873 he had other things to think about as his first and greatest Ministry tottered towards its fall. In March Disraeli defeated him by three votes on an Irish Universities Bill but refused to form a Government himself. He intended to keep the humiliated Liberals in the stocks, throwing abuse at them for a few more months.

To Queen Victoria, by far the most overwhelming event of 1873 was the engagement of Prince Alfred, Duke of Edinburgh, to the Tsar of Russia's only daughter, Marie. This final solution to the problem of Affie was not reached without difficulty. He had finally set his heart on the young Russian Princess in 1869. But his suit failed to prosper either with the Russians or his mother and in 1872 the affair lapsed. To Queen Victoria's dismay, in January 1873 she heard that negotiations had been reopened. The reason, according to unsubstantiated rumours picked up by the British ambassador, was because Marie had compromised herself with Prince Golitsyn, if not others, and her family were ready to see her settled. The Queen, no less ready to 'avert' the match by applying her customary family and diplomatic pressures, could not believe that Marie really loved her son. A marriage into the Russian church would mean priests constantly running in and out of the Edinburgh's home, Clarence House. Above all, Russia was 'unfriendly' to England and the Romanovs were personally 'false' and 'arrogant'. Was it likely that a princess with '*half Oriental* Russian notions' of self-indulgence would make the kind of unaffected, hard-working partner she always desired for her children? In the end, however, the Queen accepted the engagement and Marie dispelled most of this accumulated anger by her warm spontaneity. As long as she quickly learnt English ways – 'good not fast' – she would be 'a treasure'.

A private treasure, be it understood, not a political one. For the Edinburgh marriage, despite much international speculation, was never one of those 'great foreign alliances' which Queen Victoria had already abandoned by 1870.

One subject upon which the Queen and Gladstone saw eye to eye was that of Women's Rights. In 1870 she enlisted his aid in keeping women out of the medical profession, impressing on him 'what an *awful* idea this is – of allowing *young girls* & young men to enter the dissecting room together.' Gladstone agreed that it was 'repulsive'. More vehemently still she urged Sir Theodore Martin, her late husband's biographer, to assist his Sovereign in checking 'this *mad*, *wicked folly* of "Women's rights" with *all* the attendant horrors on which her poor, feeble sex seems bent, viz: in forgetting every sense of womanly feeling & propriety.' Remembering the activities of one suffragist, Lady Amberley, mother of Bertrand Russell, she added: 'Lady Amberley ought to get a good whipping.'

Gladstone's Ministry continued to run downhill throughout 1873 until it fell early in 1874. Queen Victoria took an uncharitable view of his fall:

I cannot help thinking, as many do, that the proposal to remove the Income Tax was a bait, to catch the electors, in which he has signally failed.

She sweetened his last audience, however, with a reference to his loyalty to the Crown, and he left once more 'quite under the charm'.

On 10 February 1874, the anniversary of her wedding day, she recorded Disraeli's arrival at the head of a 'healthy' Conservative majority – the first since Peel. Disraeli, tottering and wheezing in the east winds, nevertheless came to her like a second bridegroom.

27
The Faery Queen
1874–78

Disraeli during his five years in opposition had kept in touch with Queen Victoria at a distance. He had written assiduously during her illness of 1871 and defended her in speeches in 1872 and 1873. All these things made their mark and when she saw a copy of his election manifesto she turned her back on Ponsonby for venturing to criticize it.

What attracted her about this mediocre document was the promise it held out of a more active foreign policy. Disraeli's election victory of 1874 was a post-dated reward for the votes he had bestowed on thousands of heads of households in 1867 who were not unwilling to see Britain once more throwing her weight about, much as they themselves lorded it over their own families. Queen Victoria shared their feelings. The mood was not yet jingoism and certainly not aggression. The two words which expressed her ideal best were 'high tone', a blend of the high horse and high principles.

Disraeli treated his friend Lady Bradford to an idyllic version of his first visit as Premier to Osborne in August 1874. 'The Faery', as it amused him to call the plump, graceful little being who now dominated his burlesque imagination, greeted him so warmly that he half expected to be kissed. 'She was wreathed with smiles and, as she tattled, glided about the room like a bird.' He was offered a privilege not accorded to a Prime Minister since Lord M.: he was asked to sit down. Disraeli deemed it judicious to decline on this first occasion.

Those who watched the tropical growth of this bizarre friendship were apt to see in it nothing beyond masculine guile and feminine infatuation – one of the stock man-woman relationships of Victorian mythology. Disraeli's confession at the end of his life to Matthew Arnold – 'You have heard me called a flatterer, and it is true. Everyone likes flattery and when you come to royalty, you should lay it on with a trowel' – might suggest that they were right. Disraeli, however, like many highly-strung people in positions of great power, genuinely needed the support of women, and Queen Victoria occupied as real a place in his affections as any of his other female friends. Indeed they all had something in common. As the Russian ambassador once remarked, Dizzy's ladies were '*toutes grand'mères*'. The majority were also widows. Both Disraeli and the Queen venerated that deity of Victorian England – the bereaved spouse. Both indeed understood the other's needs well and knew how to savour the delicious fictions of their relationship. When Disraeli said: 'I am fortunate in serving a female Sovereign', he was quite genuine. But there are different kinds of service. He probably echoed the Queen's

own sentiments in his famous pronouncement: 'Gladstone treats the Queen like a public department; I treat her like a woman.'

Disraeli was often to exploit his influence over the Faery to forward his own policies. But at the beginning of the new Ministry it was the Queen who created two opportunities for establishing Disraeli's compliance.

Early in 1874 the Queen took her revenge on all those who in her opinion were undermining the Anglican Church. From behind the scenes she drove through a Public Worship Bill, introduced by Archbishop Tait, to purge it of Romish practices. After the Bill's passage she hoped there would be no more 'bowings and scrapings' and above all '*confession*'. The Bill aroused opposition from all quarters and Disraeli considered this unwise bit of legislation to be the hardest nut he ever had to crack. To her it brought a satisfying sense of personal power and ministerial obedience.

The year before the passing of the Public Worship Bill the Queen had tackled Ponsonby on the subject of a Royal Titles Bill, a subject that had been in her mind ever since the transfer of India to the Crown in 1858, after the Mutiny.

I am an Empress & in common conversation am sometimes called Empress of India. Why have I never officially assumed this title? I feel I ought to do so & wish to have preliminary enquiries made.

But when Ponsonby made the enquiries they fell on stony Liberal ground.

Problems of precedent lay behind the Queen's question. The King of Prussia had recently become an Emperor and tactlessly showed that he considered his son grander than hers. Her feeling of indignation was strengthened by many clashes with the Russian Imperial Family after Prince Alfred had married the Tsar's daughter.

Politics as well as precedence were involved in the Titles Bill. The Duke of Cambridge warned Queen Victoria that Britain would soon be fighting Russia for mastery of the East. What better way of crying 'Hands off India' than by declaring her Imperial title? Her oriental brothers, the Shah and Sultan, were particularly encouraging.

Unfortunately, neither of these gentlemen sat in Parliament and the Bill had an extremely rough passage. The Queen was appalled, having been led to believe that everyone was in favour of it. Disraeli had not dared to tell her that nobody wanted a Faery Empress. In the end he was forced to explain to the House that the Queen would only be Imperial in connection with India. This was just wishful thinking. The Queen was soon signing herself, 'V.R. & I.' – *Victoria Regina et Imperatrix* – here, there and everywhere, instead of reserving it, in the words of an angry critic, W.S. Blunt, 'for communications east of Suez'.

On May Day 1876 Victoria was declared Queen-Empress. She celebrated with a family dinner in honour of the Prince of Wales who had just returned from a very successful tour of India. He had gone before she had time effectively to deploy her instinctive objections to his going anywhere. But his success impressed her: his tiger and elephant shoots, his sabbatarian rectitude and his speeches. He returned in triumph, his ship stuffed with presents for dear Mama, of which the best was a copy of her own *Leaves* translated into Hindustani with covers of inlaid marble.

In 1875 the Queen happened to be studying Theodore Martin's new volume of the Prince Consort's *Life*, dealing with the Crimean War, just as the Eastern question flared up again. In consequence she found herself much better up in the history of the Middle East than her advisers.

Inevitably the new 'crises' as she called them, seemed a continuation of the old. Had the world not learnt its lesson? Disraeli was cast for the role of Palmerston, Russia was still the enemy, Turkey the ally. Then two new features appeared in the situation which she had not bargained for. The Bulgarian peasants rose against their Turkish masters and Gladstone rose from a bed of sickness to denounce the atrocities perpetrated against them by the Turks. There was no role for which Queen Victoria could cast Gladstone's demonic apparition except Satan.

News of the peasants' revolt in 1875 turned the attention of Europe to reforming its Sick Man – Turkey. Disraeli, however, made it his first business to snatch a plum from the dying tree. With the help of the Rothschilds he bought 177,000 Suez Canal shares out of a total of 400,000 from a bankrupt Turkish vassal, the Khedive of Egypt. It cost the country £4 million and, as the Queen truly remarked, 'may have far-reaching consequences'. Disraeli's announcement of his triumph shows what he meant by treating the Queen as a woman. 'It is just settled,' he

The Royal family in 1875. Queen Victoria was quickly becoming the matriarch of an enormous and ever-growing family. By 1875 she had seventeen grand-children. Her first great-grandchild was born in 1894.

wrote on 25 November, 'you have it, Madam.' Gladstone would never have thought of depositing anything as a personal gift at the Faery Queen's feet. Next day in a letter to Theodore Martin Queen Victoria re-emphasized the differences she had already noticed between Disraeli and Gladstone. Disraeli had '*very lofty views*' of England's destiny. His mind was so much 'greater' and 'quicker' than that of Mr Gladstone.

Yet not quick enough, as it proved, to distinguish between authentic news of a monstrous crime and 'coffee-house babble' – Disraeli's phrase for the Bulgarian atrocities. Mr Gladstone, on the contrary, was to demonstrate a physical and mental quickness almost inconceivable in an old gentleman approaching seventy who had retired that year from his party's leadership.

Queen Victoria hoped that her Government would organize a European solution to the Eastern question. Disraeli preferred to act alone. He dispatched the fleet to Besika Bay and by this unilateral action prevented the possibility of an inter-national conference. The Queen was not impressed. She dreaded having to fight alone for the delinquent Turks, especially when she began to learn more details of their behaviour. It was with profound horror that she heard about the 'Bashi-Bazouks' – savage bands of Turkish irregulars who had murdered 12,000 Bulgarian Christians. The very name Bashi-Bazouk, like 'Gauleiter' in a later age, suggested unspeakable cruelties. The Queen described them in her Journal as 'horribly cruel mutilators, with narrow faces, pointed beards, no uniform & knives stuck about in their belts'. It was therefore disturbing to her that Disraeli con-tinued to refer to the 'Bulgarian atrocities' in inverted commas, as if they were a Liberal invention.

Meanwhile on 11 August 1876 Disraeli, satisfied that Gladstone would never again lead the Commons, considered it safe to take a peerage. The first boxes which arrived for the Queen signed 'Beaconsfield' contained confirmation of the Bulgarian atrocities.

The Government's sceptical sang-froid disintegrated, a Liberal flood of moral indignation broke loose and every conscience in the country, from Gladstone's High Church precision instrument to Shaftesbury's Evangelical pickaxe and the indefatigable road-drill of the *Daily News*, got to work on the Government's façade. On 6 September Gladstone issued his famous pamphlet, *The Bulgarian Horrors and the Question of the East*. The finest invective of the century, it sold a thousand times faster than any royal *Leaves* and swept the masses into monster rallies at Blackheath, St James's Hall, Piccadilly, and elsewhere.

Let the Turks now carry off their abuses in the only possible manner, namely by carrying off themselves. Their Zaptiehs and their Mindirs, their Bimbashis and their Yuzbachis, their Kaimakams and their Pashas, one and all, bag and baggage, shall, I hope, clear out from the province they have desolated and profaned ...

The Queen's dilemma had been excruciating. 'She don't like the Turks,' wrote Ponsonby towards the end of August, ' – hates them more because of their atrocities', and wants the Government to 'speak out at once'. But she could not bear to blame Beaconsfield. His levity last June, she argued, 'was not his fault but that of his Cabinet who disagreed with him.' Ponsonby drily suggested that Beaconsfield should now correct what Disraeli had said.

It took her a month of anxiety and rheumatism to find the way out. By the end of September her rheumatism had gone and so had Turkish responsibility for the Bashi-Bazouks – on to the shoulders of the Russians. She wrote to Beaconsfield:

Hearing as we *do* all the undercurrents and knowing as we do that Russia *instigated* this insurrection, which *caused* the cruelty of the Turks ... the world *ought* to know that on *their* shoulders and *not* on *ours* rest the *blood* of the murdered Bulgarians!

The final step was easy. Who had instigated the Russians? None other than that 'disgraceful ... mischief-maker', that 'fire-brand', that 'half madman', Gladstone. *His* meetings and pamphlets, his furies and frenzies, his St James's Halls and Blackheaths had inflamed the Russians. Let *him* clear out, to Hawarden Castle, bag and baggage.

Her pen worked incessantly to prevent a Russian attack upon Turkey and when Russia declared war in April 1877 she felt as if the Tsar's challenge had been thrown down, not to the Sultan, but to herself. Beaconsfield ruthlessly exploited this tendency in his Sovereign to see political events as a personal struggle. While at the end of 1876 Ponsonby reckoned that she was not 'unreasonably anti-Russian', by the time Beaconsfield had done with her she was rabid.

To show her support for Beaconsfield she volunteered to open Parliament in February 1877 and stoically bore 'the long trying pause' till the Members of the Commons 'came along with a great rush'. For the same reason she ostentatiously lunched with the Prime Minister in his home at Hughenden, a public demonstration of friendship not shown since she had visited Melbourne at Brocket Hall in 1841. Beaconsfield's comparison between 'our' policy and Gladstone's was diligently quoted in her Journal. Ours was 'the Imperial policy of England', Gladstone's 'the policy of crusade' – mere 'sentimental eccentricity'.

Even Beaconsfield's policy soon did not seem dynamic enough to the impassioned Queen. The Russian atrocities had put 'the so called Bulgarian atrocities' into the shade. When the Russians were unexpectedly held up before Plevna the Cabinet saw it as a breathing space but the Queen as a breathless opportunity for checkmating their next advance. Occupy Gallipoli – send the fleet to Constantinople – join the Turks in the field – join the Austrians – only let the Government decide what to do and dó it.

Yet even in this tornado of emotion she did not altogether lose her head. When the Princess Royal excitedly suggested that Britain should annex Egypt, Queen Victoria replied crushingly:

Why shd we make such a wanton aggression . . . ? It is not our custom to annexe countries (as it is in some others) unless we are obliged & forced to do so – as in the case of the Transvaal Republic.

Forced, that is, by the cruelty of the Boers to the natives.

To her disgust she realized that Beaconsfield was having trouble with two 'deplorable' colleagues. The Foreign Secretary, Lord Derby, and the Colonial Secretary, Lord Carnarvon, were for 'peace at all price', while Beaconsfield longed to take the highest possible tone with Russia – or so he made her believe. Not for an instant did she suspect that he was playing on her bellicosity to push his Cabinet

The Congress of Berlin in 1878 achieved a settlement in Europe which was not dismantled until the First World War. Disraeli can be seen standing to the left of the picture.

forward while trading on their reluctance in order to hold her back. It is sometimes a help to steer between Scylla and Charybdis. With feverish excitement she bent herself to the task of disembarrassing Beaconsfield both of his hesitations and his colleagues.

The torture was not to last much longer. At the beginning of March 1878 Russia forced upon Turkey the secret Treaty of San Stefano, which was suspected of threatening British interests. The Queen, together with a vociferous section of the country, demanded warlike action: Derby and Carnarvon must go. The reserves were called out and Derby and Carnarvon went of their own accord. Theirs were not the only resignations flashed around in the crisis. The Queen herself threatened to abdicate five times between April 1877 and February 1878, rather than see the country 'kiss the feet of the great barbarians ...'

The Russian ambassador described the partnership of Queen Victoria and Beaconsfield as 'this conspiracy of a half-mad woman' with a 'political clown'. Schouvaloff was mistaken. The 'clown' was in control, the woman though agitated was quite sane, and there was no conspiracy. In fact Queen Victoria, for all her frantic activity, did not materially change the course of events. At times she was Beaconsfield's fulcrum; never his partner.

Lord Salisbury, who succeeded Derby, proved in Queen Victoria's words 'up to the occasion' – an occasion which after all did not necessitate war or 'the Dizzy brink'. A conference was agreed upon in Berlin under the chairmanship of Bismarck.

The Congress of Berlin met in June. It was hard to say which of the old men in charge seemed in worse shape – Gortchakoff withered by age, Disraeli racked by disease and Bismarck flatulent with overeating. Between them, however, they achieved a solution for Europe which was not finally dismantled until 1918. Disraeli represented the result as a surrender by the Emperor of Russia to the Empress of India. Queen Victoria was shrewd enough to feel reservations. It was all 'vy triumphant', she wrote to the Princess Royal, but she regretted 'that Russia had got anything'. On the other hand, the Liberals would have done far worse. Her dislike of the Liberals, and Gladstone in particular, had taken on a new, unpleasing dimension. His family's commercial background was subtly invoked to explain his politics. 'Sordid gain' was the sole inspiration of his fiery crusade. The 'so called, but not real, Liberals', she wrote, 'wld make England a mere Cotton spinning Country.'

Every detail of the Congress enthralled the Queen, from the 'ceremonious and costumish' opening to Bismarck's last dramatic *tête-à-tête* with Beaconsfield, the former drinking oceans of champagne and stout, the latter fraternally choking himself with cigars. Most of all she enjoyed the account of Bismarck's family dinner given in Beaconsfield's honour. The Iron Chancellor poured a stream of indelicate stories into his guest's ear, while Beaconsfield fixed his mind steadfastly on '*her*'. Put not your trust in princes, was Bismarck's advice: his own health had been broken by the German Emperor's 'horrible conduct'. Beaconsfield retorted that he 'served one who was the soul of candour and justice, and whom all her Ministers loved.'

28
'I Had No Alternative'
1878–80

'My auspicious sister of sublime nature to whose wishes events correspond' – thus exquisitely did the Shah of Persia address a business letter to Queen Victoria in 1874. From then onwards events did indeed begin to behave more as they ought.

The Queen's health at sixty was much better than it had been at fifty. 'My nerves' no longer dominate the pages of her Journal. She was in fact working with more zest than ever before in her life, and duty had overcome her earlier tendency to self-pity. The entries in her Journal at times like the New Year, when she tended to be introspective, illustrate these emotional changes. For a period after her husband's death she felt that the first day of January no longer seemed to be a 'new chapter'. Towards the end of the 'sixties she was still immersed in self but with an impulse to 'fight on'. By the end of the 'seventies the wheel had come full circle. On 31 December 1879 she sat quietly writing, her thoughts not at first upon herself but on those families bereaved in the Ashanti war; when she did turn to her own record it was with sorrow for her failings rather than for her misfortunes. 'I wish I felt I had got the better of many weaknesses and faults!' Here speaks the old Victoria, once more strong enough to risk contemplation of her sins.

It was inevitable that the new woman now emerging should be a different creature from the one who had gone into seclusion in 1861. In the interval much of the Prince Consort's laborious legacy had been forgotten. Apart from penitential pilgrimages to the Horticultural Garden, she now carried on his cultural crusades with frank boredom. A visit in 1873 to an international exhibition was typical: while waiting unwillingly for a demonstration of how to cook an omelette she had to listen to 'a rather tiresome lecture'.

Some of Prince Albert's taboos were lifted, if only on special occasions. Smoking was one of them. In the 'fifties it was considered out of the question for the Queen, a woman, so much as to touch with her lips an oriental pipe of friendship on board an Egyptian ship at Southampton. Protocol demanded that the twelve-year-old Prince of Wales should take a ceremonial puff on his Mama's behalf. Twenty years later Queen Victoria, Princess Beatrice and Horatia Stopford were blithely smoking cigarettes on a picnic at Balmoral to keep the midges away.

Political impartiality, as taught by Melbourne and preached by the Prince, was the most serious casualty of the Queen's renaissance. She convinced herself, however, that circumstances, not she, had changed: the Liberals had become socialistic while the Conservatives were now the sole repositories of 'true Liberalism'. In her defence it must be emphasized that few of her Ministers tried to re-educate their Sovereign in political neutrality. Party warfare had grown fiercer with the coming of democracy and Ministers themselves felt less inclined than Melbourne had been to give opponents their due. Gladstone, who had once been a Conservative and always admired them, probably stood alone in trying to be fair to his enemies. Disraeli's early flirtation with Radicalism simply enabled him to defame its exponents more effectively.

An unnatural striving after intellectuality, painstakingly nurtured in her by Prince Albert, had also passed peacefully away. Novels and biographies such as Disraeli's *Coningsby* and *Endymion* or Mrs Gaskell's *Life of Charlotte Brontë* were read, but there was no more constitutional law. The kind of title which now features prominently in her reading list is *Aunt Margaret's Troubles* or *The Unkind Word*. Who can blame her? It was restful to be herself again.

Left to herself the Queen's judgements on art became a matter of hit or miss. Landseer's early works, particularly his sketches, she rightly valued above his later productions; George Richmond's new style of portraiture – 'green flesh & blue lips & Chinese sorts of leaves as a background!!' – repelled her. She refused to be painted by Watts or Millais, quite apart from the fact that she understood the latter had seduced his future wife while painting her. Indian art she found beautiful except when it descended to 'rather tasteless' imitations of Europe. Her 'misses' were most apparent in the frenzied bijouterie of her private apartments. Queen Victoria never pretended to elegance in her sitting-room; her aim was to make it 'cheerful' and 'cosy' or, when it got a new carpet, 'very gay'. But if a total absence of empty spaces on walls, floors, tables, chests and desks can create the charm of an over-stuffed cottage garden, it possessed charm as well. The crowd of miniatures, medals, photographs, lithographs, engravings, water colours, bronzes, marbles, plaster-casts, embroideries, woolwork, beadwork, pressed flowers and a hundred other knick-knacks kept it vibrating with the chirpy folk-music of humanity.

Not only Albert's ideas but also the places which he had blessed by his presence were no longer sacrosanct. By 1869 she was glad to abandon the old railway coach, hallowed by the Prince's occupation, for a new smart one with all the compartments interconnecting: no more steep clambering down on to the line for ladies-in-waiting, necks and legs exposed to every kind of risk and indelicacy, to reach the Queen. During the previous year she had built for herself the first house since her marriage in which the Prince had never lived – the Glasallt Sheil – a small (fifteen-roomed) villa planted on smooth turf at the far end of Loch Muick. The Queen actually preferred its sitting-room to the one designed for her at Balmoral by Prince Albert.

Some of her best holidays were now in southern countries abroad where she and the Prince had never been together, her initial qualms at 'doing anything now without Albert' having been stifled in the pious thought that he would 'rejoice in seeing me take an interest in all I see'. She had not forgotten his homilies on her need to get out of herself.

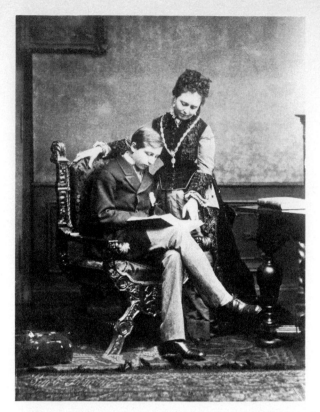

Vicky with her son the future Kaiser. Queen Victoria often warned her about his arrogance.

Queen Victoria now recognized in herself a certain toughness of character and capacity to handle human situations which her beloved one had lacked. There was her conviction that he could never have faced up to the realities of the new Prussia. As the years passed, she added to the list of 'inevitable' changes which she had accepted philosophically but which the Prince would have opposed, thereby only injuring himself: disestablishment of the Irish Church, Army reform and the 'style of life of Bertie & Affie'. In some ways Papa, she told Vicky in 1872, could have helped her; in others his difficulties with his sons would have been even greater than hers.

Queen Victoria was growing fonder of the Prince of Wales. Whereas she had written in 1870, 'no one looks up to him, though all like him', her approval three years later was unqualified: 'he is loved by all above & below ...' The Prince of Wales's geniality towards those 'below' endeared him to his mother even more than his patent devotion to herself. For the Queen's tenderness towards servants was one of the things in her life which never changed. An obstinately drunken ghillie was dismissed in the 'seventies but the event was so rare that the Household discussed it with bated breath.

In the middle of 1875 the over-protected Prince Leopold was the subject of a new, good resolution. Having recovered from a long illness, he hoped at last to live as other young men. Queen Victoria began by muttering angrily about 'undutifulness' and 'base ingratitude' to God, herself and his doctors. Then, on 1 July, a new note was struck:

218

Alice and Louis of Hesse with their family. Alice was the first of Queen Victoria's children to die, on 14 December 1878, the seventeenth anniversary of Albert's death.

... if I show gt indifference to his movements excepting when my authority must be obeyed, I don't think his love of opposition (a family defect) will be roused & he will learn what he owes to me.

This reasonable parental line was normally effective, though there were of course occasional storms. The worst was in 1878 when Prince Leopold perpetrated a crime which in his mother's eyes placed 'the whole authority of the Sovereign & Throne' in jeopardy: he expressed an 'intense aversion' to Balmoral and refused to go there. But even this storm abated after two days when she decided to 'leave him alone & take no notice of him for some time' – unless he got into mischief.

Between the Queen and her eldest daughter the understanding deepened each year. The Princess Royal's difficulties with Prince William were instrumental in bringing mother and daughter together and in making the Queen see her own children in a rosier light. His behaviour caused increasing anxiety. 'Why does Willy always sign himself "William Prince of Prussia"?' – the Queen asked her daughter – 'his father never does.' In fact she knew very well it was Willy's pride, fostered by Bismarck and his grandparents. Prussian arrogance had taught him to listen with approval to their insulting remarks about his English mother. How fortunate she herself had been compared to Vicky.

The Queen's good fortune was about to receive a tragic check. On 10 November 1878 she received a telegram from her daughter Alice with the news that one of her children had diphtheria. Soon the whole family – children and parents – had caught the terrifying disease. First the baby died, and then on 14 December, the anniversary of Prince Albert's death, the Queen received a telegram announcing Alice's death that morning. The heartbroken Queen was not one to overlook the dramatic element in this tragedy. That the child who had supported her should be 'called back' to the father she had tended on this of all days seemed to her 'almost incredible & most mysterious!'

But death no longer had the power to crush her. The Queen herself voluntarily shouldered the task of breaking the dreadful news to each member of the family. Next day, feeling pathetically deprived, – 'I was so proud of my 9!' – but comforted by the therapeutic business of commissioning a statue of mother and child for the Mausoleum, she paid a significant tribute in her Journal to Princess Alice's 'talent, initiative & energy' combined with a character 'so friendly to those in the house, always simple, never proud or haughty'. This was the kind of woman Queen Victoria truly admired: one with spirit who was also kind to the servants. 'High tone' without 'John Bullism'.

Queen Victoria's sixtieth birthday occurred on 24 May 1879, twelve days after she became a great-grandmother – 'Quite an event'. Her own anniversary produced a somewhat tremulous response:

My poor old 6oth birthday. I feel that I am getting old, & that these last months, & the loss of my beloved child have aged, & shaken the elasticity out of me.

She prayed once more for improvement 'in every way'.

Improvement in one way, at any rate, had come. It was only a pity that the Queen's increased patience with her children seemed to go with a more peremptory spirit towards those of her Ministers with whom she disagreed. Gladstone was to find that the elasticity had by no means been shaken out of her.

The Queen soon found that when Gladstone had risen from his sick-bed to defend the Bulgarian peasants it was but the beginning of a long crusade against Disraeli's aggressiveness overseas. The Queen felt herself included in these criticisms. Was not Beaconsfield's militancy inspired by her? The results of Beaconsfield's African and Far Eastern policy – the Zulu, Ashanti and Afghan wars – seemed to her the necessary concomitants of holding enviable possessions.

If *we are* to *maintain* our position as a *first-rate* Power ... we must, with our Indian Empire and large Colonies, be *Prepared* for *attacks* and *wars, somewhere* or *other*, CONTINUALLY.

Mr Gladstone would not accept this position. In a series of great speeches in his Midlothian constituency he attacked the First Afghan War and the whole policy of imperial aggrandisement. 'Remember the rights of the savage, as we call him', he thundered at Dalkeith on 26 November 1879:

Remember that the happiness of his humble home, remember that the sanctity of life in the hill villages of Afghanistan, among the winter snows, is as inviolable in the eye of the Almighty God as can be your own.

Every word of Gladstone's Midlothian oratory, every act in the stage management of his heroic campaigns seemed to search out the Queen's tenderest spots and jab them. 'Mr Gladstone is going about Scotland, like an American stumping orator, making most violent speeches,' she wrote in her Journal on 2 December 1879. British annexations of territory which even Bismarck had lauded as 'progress', Gladstone stigmatized as 'false phantoms of glory'. Gladstone demanded a Chancellor of the Exchequer who would save the candle ends and a Prime Minister with a gospel of honest work, thus prostituting the creed of dearest Albert in order to belabour dear Lord Beaconsfield. The 'Empress of India' came in for specific abuse: Gladstone denounced the title as 'theatrical bombast and folly'.

Disraeli was unmoved, dismissing Gladstone's oratory as just 'a waste of powder and shot'. At the end of February 1880 the Prime Minister took a snap decision to go to the polls in April. Queen Victoria had opened Parliament in person on 5 February, resplendent in a new State coach topped by a crown, lavishly gilt and furnished with so much glass that the people could see her from every angle. Lord Beaconsfield, ignoring the ill-omened fact that he was too weak to carry the Sword of State in the procession, banked on the fervour created by a State opening enhanced by two remarkable by-election successes, to bring him victory. An immediate dissolution was announced on 8 March. The country gasped; the Queen spiritedly looked forward to the Tories coming back 'stronger than ever'.

Who could have foretold that Gladstone would at once set forth on a second Midlothian procession which made her gilded coach rumbling down the Mall look like Cinderella's pumpkin? Again the monster crowds surged round the 'People's William'; again the bonfires blazed and the fireworks banged; again Lord Rosebery, Scotland's greatest magnifico, acted as Gladstone's host. Was the Sword of State too heavy for Beaconsfield? The Grand Old Man swung an axe in Lord Rosebery's park and having levelled the Tory Party to the ground, scanned the splendid election news and wrote in his diary: 'It seemed as if the arm of the Lord had bared itself for work ...'

If Gladstone confused himself with the Almighty, Queen Victoria had reason to suspect that he also confused himself with the Sovereign. What did he mean by appealing beyond the aristocracy, beyond the landed interest, beyond the Established Church, beyond all wealth and rank to '*the nation* itself'? The right to speak directly to the people over the heads of faction had always been her own prerogative. Nothing could explain such colossal, such imperial arrogance but the presumption that Gladstone had gone mad.

Insane, insulting, arrogant, un-British – she might call Gladstone all these things but he did not yet seem dangerous. The fact was that he had resigned the Liberal leadership to Lord Granville, with Lord Hartington in charge of the party in the Commons. It never entered the Queen's head that Gladstone might become dangerous in the sense of becoming Prime Minister again. But as the Liberal successes piled up during the following April it became obvious, in the blunt words of Prince Arthur, that the Liberals were 'mad about' Gladstone and none but he could head a new Government. Gladstone shared this view: if God called him back it was not to play second fiddle to two colleagues like Granville and Hartington whose very nicknames proved their remoteness from Mount Sinai – 'Puss' and 'Harty Tarty'.

The Queen was in Baden-Baden when she heard the stunning news of Lord Beaconsfield's electoral defeat. So great was her shock and mortification that her courtiers congratulated themselves on having her tucked well away where the first bitterness might break its edge on them. Again and again they heard that she was losing in Beaconsfield the only Minister since Melbourne who had become her 'friend'. As for Gladstone – 'she will sooner *abdicate* than send for or have any *communication* with *that half-mad fire-brand* who wd soon ruin everything & be a Dictator.'

On 15 April the Queen left Baden-Baden. Three days later Beaconsfield gave what seemed to her the right advice: 'irrespective of any personal feelings I might have', to send for Hartington. Hartington was sent for – and gave the wrong answer. Neither he nor Granville, he feared, would succeed without Gladstone, while Gladstone would decline a subordinate position. Further interviews with both Hartington and Granville confirmed the impossible situation. Only Gladstone could succeed but the Queen could not give Gladstone her confidence.

Nevertheless the country had to have a government and in the end the Queen, despite her threats of abdication, knew that she must support the constitution. She seated herself squarely at her desk and dismissed the double audience in her Journal as 'a trying ordeal'. Then she prepared herself to face Mr Gladstone at 6.30 that evening. She had no alternative. Even the Prince of Wales told her so. But while the Liberal leaders relaxed she braced herself. Like the war-horse in the *Book of Job*, she saith among the trumpets, Ha, Ha, and smelleth the battle afar off.

A caricature on Queen Victoria's reluctance to accept Gladstone as premier.

29
Among the Trumpets
1880–83

Gladstone's audience was brief, quiet and tense as the moment between the lightning flash and the thunder. He noted afterwards that the Queen had been 'natural under effort'. A contemporary sketch of him kissing her hand suggests that the effort was greater than the naturalness. A look of detached disgust is depicted upon the royal features, as if the hand which suffered such indignity could no longer be her own.

She did not ask Gladstone why he had won. Beaconsfield had already declared that like Napoleon he had been 'beaten by the elements' – six bad harvests running. The Queen wondered how people could be so perverse as to expect a change of government to change the weather. Sir Stafford Northcote listed hard times, love of change, lazy candidates, Gladstone 'getting hold of the common people' and the Ballot which tempted them to promise one way and vote another – 'a very bad thing'. The Queen summed up the Conservative defeat as 'over-confidence'. In future they promised to spend money and organize like the Liberals (a reference to their famous 'Caucus'). She hoped this would be a lesson, 'so that such a thing should not occur again.'

She did not mention Lord Chelmsford's catastrophic rout by Cetewayo, the Zulu king, in the burning gullies of Isandhlwana (1879); nevertheless this fearful blow to British arms played a part in turning the masses temporarily against Beaconsfield's exhibitionist imperialism.

Since Queen Victoria admitted no connection between Beaconsfield's policy and the Conservative defeat, she did not hesitate to spend most of the few minutes allotted to Gladstone in telling him that the foreign policy he had just pulverized at the polls must on no account be changed. Never had an incoming Prime Minister received a stranger mandate. Gladstone, however, pleased the Queen by the meekness with which he accepted her ukase. She relied on Lord Hartington to keep him meek. Beaconsfield had told her that Hartington was 'in his heart a Conservative'.

Disunity, she knew, was the Liberal Party's fatal weakness. One wing relied on rich, blue-blooded Whigs like Princess Louise's father-in-law, the Duke of Argyll; the other wing included Radicals, Socialists, Republicans, Irish, atheists and immoral exponents of other 'horrid things' – a dark reference by the Queen to the fact that Charles Bradlaugh, Radical MP for Northampton, stood for 'anticonception' (as it was then called), besides being anti-God.

In the Queen's opinion nothing held the two wings together but sheer office-seeking. She hoped their leader would soon collapse. During Gladstone's first audience he told her 'he should not be able to go on for long' and she remarked how 'ill & haggard he looked'. Queen Victoria was to continue to indulge in wishful thinking about the state of her Prime Minister's health, though Gladstone himself confided to Lord Granville that he felt better at the end of the stormy 1881 session than after any other he could remember.

The enemy which was to defeat the G.O.M. was not old age but a new age of violent protest against the old ways. Besides Bradlaugh, there was Parnell with his Irish Home Rulers and Lord Randolph Churchill with his Fourth Party of Conservative hatchet men whom Dizzy appropriately called his Bashi-Bazouks. Joseph Chamberlain, the Radical, helped to stir the pot.

Comforting rumours reached the Queen that Gladstone's first Cabinet appointments had infuriated the Radicals. With Lord Granville as Foreign Secretary and Lord Hartington at the India Office, they accused him of forming 'a Tory Government'; why did he not include 'some of them'? The Queen heard with delight that Gladstone would not listen and meant to fight it out.

Gladstone failed to fight it out and 'some of them', to put it mildly, got into his Cabinet. Old John Bright she could tolerate but Joseph Chamberlain, the steely screw-maker who had risen to the top in Birmingham, cast a Jacobinical glare over the Board of Trade.

Life under the Liberal Government was not at first as bad as the Queen sometimes liked to make out. She still considered 'the People's William' a most disagreeable person. He, for his part, predicted more than once that the Monarchy must fall with such a Monarch. But, when it came to the point, by no means all the Liberal reforms provoked her. And when politics became particularly tiresome she could still correspond with Beaconsfield, either directly or through his faithful secretary, Monty Corry, now Lord Rowton. This correspondence could have led to considerable scandal. The aged statesman realized, however, that what his beloved Sovereign chiefly required was soothing affection. On one occasion only did his gift for phrase-making lead him into unconstitutional paths.

Apparently Lord Hartington, foolishly hoping to avoid trouble, had omitted to show the Queen in advance her Speech for opening the session of 1881. It contained the controversial decision to evacuate Kandahar in Afghanistan. A scene of unexampled bitterness took place in the Council Chamber at Osborne, which left the Queen 'shaken' and her Ministers on the point of resignation. She refused to approve the Kandahar paragraph; they refused to submit the Speech to her without it. The fifteen-stone Home Secretary, Sir William Harcourt, was already in a bad temper, having been fetched from Cowes with three colleagues squeezed into a small, one-horse bathing-carriage. Eventually Her Majesty agreed to reserve the expression of her disapproval for a memorandum to Gladstone. 'I spoke to no one,' she recorded in her Journal, 'and the Ministers nearly tumbled over each other going out.' Harcourt, however, had left behind a dart which stuck quivering in the Queen's *amour propre*: 'the Speech of the Sovereign,' he announced, 'is only the Speech of the Ministers.' The Mandarin must nod but not argue.

This made no sense to Queen Victoria. Why had they ever made her read the Speech herself if Harcourt was right? Prince Leopold must ask Lord Beaconsfield for his opinion. The old oracle produced a remarkable verdict. The principle of Sir William Harcourt, he declared, was not known to the British Constitution. 'It is only a piece of Parliamentary gossip.'

Thus the pillar of the Constitution – ministerial responsibility – and the crime of the century – the Bulgarian atrocities – were both dismissed by Beaconsfield as 'Parliamentary gossip' and 'coffee-house babble' respectively. But before the great magician could palm any more political facts, death played the vanishing trick on him.

Lord Beaconsfield died on 19 April 1881, choked by the grime of London borne on unrelenting east winds. Lord Rowton performed the last act of a perfect secretary by giving to the world his master's 'last words': 'I had rather live but I am not afraid to die'. Raising himself as if to address the Commons, he fell forward and was dead. Other 'last words' have been attributed to the weary old man who sometimes found his energetic Faery a little too much for him. Would he like a royal visit? 'No, it is better not. She'd only ask me to take a message to Albert'.

After he was dead a huge memorial tablet arrived over his pew at Hughenden Church, 'placed by his grateful Sovereign and Friend, Victoria R.I.' – to the scandalized amazement of the country. 'His Favourite Flower' was written on the card attached to a primrose wreath for Beaconsfield's grave.

How much did Queen Victoria owe to Disraeli? Her good spirits, certainly, without which no one can do a good job. A renewed conviction also that she had a vocation: that her letters, her telegrams, her tirades were the things which persuaded statesmen from pursuing 'downward' policies. Did Disraeli carry the good work too far, giving the Queen-Empress an inflated sense of her own importance? Lord Derby thought so, and so of course did Gladstone. On the whole, however, they exaggerated the harm she could do as much as Disraeli exaggerated her right to do it. The royal prerogative was a failing force and the Queen too sensible to insist on it in practice, despite her paper protestations.

Nothing but a grand, even exaggerated conception of her vocation could have roused her from lethargy. One side of her never liked politics. To make her exert herself in this uncongenial sphere, brilliant colours and bold designs were necessary. It was easier to be a Queen-Empress with the world to save than a constitutional Monarch who was required only to sign and drive. Without Disraeli the Queen might have gone down to the grave an unpopular recluse, carrying with her a discredited British Monarchy. Disraeli's audacious magic, though not of a kind to transform a neurotic widow into an unimpeachable, sober figurehead, lifted the Monarchy out of the trough which was its greatest danger. Dizzy's Faery was a stage on the way to Queen Victoria's apotheosis.

Beaconsfield died and the withdrawal from Kandahar took place. It was to be followed by further retreats, rumoured and real. Theodore Martin alarmed the

Queen with the report (false) that Cyprus was to be abandoned. A statement that Gladstone would fulfil his election promise to give independence to the Transvaal was the painful truth – painful because the Transvaal Boers had just wiped out a British force at the battle of Majuba Hill.

Queen Victoria disapproved of withdrawals: she held that they always led to hasty, improvised returns at enormous cost. To make peace immediately after a defeat like Majuba, before honour had been 'retrieved', was especially short-sighted: 'I fear future difficulties are being laid up there.' Above all, she loathed the idea of handing over African natives to the Boers – 'a most merciless and cruel neighbour, and in fact oppressor', just like the southern slave-owners in *Uncle Tom's Cabin*. In the light of after events who is to say that Gladstone had all the right on his side?

Disagreeable as the Queen found this retreat from Empire, it was nothing to the indignation that was raised by the sight of English administrators dithering in Ireland and Irish politicians rampaging at Westminster.

The Queen was shockingly ill-informed on the state of Ireland. Her advisers concealed from her the starvation, arrears and evictions, and brought to her notice only the crime engendered by the disgraceful conditions. 'In few counties is there real distress', she read in a report of November 1880, 'but in few no crime.' The Land League, she heard, founded by the Irish leader, Parnell, to fight rack-renting, was the cause of all the mischief, while the only remedy was force. The Queen agreed with the men on the spot, the Irish were impossible and it was no use trying to satisfy them.

Gladstone, on the contrary, brought in a Compensation for Disturbance Bill to mitigate the hardships of evicted farmers and did not renew the Peace Preservation Act. These two measures, known as the 'Land Bill' and 'Coercion' respectively, represented the fundamental division between government by the carrot and the stick. They also represented a fundamental division within Gladstone's Cabinet. The Prime Minister and the Radicals were pledged to a Land Bill first; after that carrot they fondly believed the stick would be unnecessary. The big property owners in his party, many of them with Irish land, demanded coercion first, a view shared by Queen Victoria. When Gladstone pressed ahead with the second reading of the Land Bill, Lord Lansdowne resigned from the Government, a move which shocked the Cabinet but delighted the Queen.

Gladstone faced opposition not only from the Tories and his own Cabinet but from the very people he thought he was trying to help. Not satisfied with the provisions of the proposed Land Bill, the sixty Irish Nationalists in the British Parliament, led by Charles Stewart Parnell, used every form of 'brutish' obstruction, as Gladstone called it, to oppress their oppressors. In Ireland itself Parnell convulsed English rule by his invention of the 'boycott'. Lord Erne's agent, Captain Boycott, had been spontaneously outlawed by his whole community for evicting tenants; he could not even get a shirt washed or a letter delivered. His punishment was now methodically applied by order of Parnell's Land League to all subsequent evictors.

Eventually the breakdown of law and order in Ireland forced the Government to pass a Coercion Bill in February 1881, after some of the wildest scenes ever remembered in Parliament. Queen Victoria was much relieved. 'Firm' measures were the only solution. She also advocated restriction of the sale of dynamite, which was so easy to make; just a cupful of nitrate acid and sand mixed with glycerine and you could blow up anything.

Far from instituting such measures Gladstone reintroduced a Land Bill. The Duke of Argyll promptly resigned. To Gladstone this was a fearful loss on top of Lansdowne's defection, casting grave doubts on his treasured belief that the best of the aristocracy were with him. Whigs and Radicals must go together like faith and works; Gladstone was temperamentally unwilling to save or be saved through Radicals alone.

The Land Bill was not a part of Gladstone's programme which the Queen criticized, for a measure of reform was by now inevitable. In accordance with past

Charles Stewart Parnell, leader of the sixty Irish Nationalists at Westminster.

practice, the Queen exerted pressure on the Lords not to oppose it, and Salisbury had to apologize for so misinterpreting Her Majesty's wishes as to meditate a constitutional crisis. On 22 August 1881 the greatest Land Act of the nineteenth century reached the Statute Book, too late. As an experiment in Land Courts it increased the excitement in Ireland while, as a compromise mangled by the Peers, it disgusted the Land League.

Matters now went from bad to worse. Parnell's attacks on the Government led eventually to his arrest and imprisonment. Soon the Irish rebels, freed from his discipline, were plunging Ireland into chaos. Hoping to restore some semblance of order Parnell negotiated his own release, unfortunately over the head of the Irish Secretary, Forster, who promptly resigned. A final scene in the tragedy remained to be played. Forster's replacement, Lord Frederick Cavendish, adored husband of Gladstone's niece, Lucy Lyttelton, and his Under-Secretary, Frederick Burke, were knifed to death in Dublin's Phoenix Park.

Gladstone, broken in appearance by the tragic failure of his policies, could not but be pitied. The Queen noted, however, that he 'is still always excusing the Irish'. Her feelings were soon as violent as ever against him and his Government. Already bruised by Ireland, Gladstone faced an adversary whose self-confidence was constantly increasing.

As Irish affairs moved to this climax, the Queen's efforts to get her last son married came to a successful conclusion. The ailing Prince Leopold's ambition had met with the same frustrations as all his other attempts to lead a normal life. The Queen could not believe that anyone suitable would have him. This was perhaps a sublimation of a selfish desire to keep him at her side. In any case the Queen relented and found him a bride, Princess Helen of Waldeck. Prince Leopold was created Duke of Albany and the young Duchess turned out to be 'quite a personage'; she insisted on conducting all arguments with her mother-in-law face to face. The wedding on 27 April 1882 gave further evidence of the popularity of the Queen, who was now within sight of public deification. She herself honoured the occasion by wearing over a black dress her white wedding lace and veil for the first time since 1840.

The wedding was a happy interlude in a troubled year. A week later came the Phoenix Park murders. Next month the Queen heard that Arabi Pasha, the Egyptian Foreign Minister, had revolted against the Khedive's authority. Britain's efforts to suppress Arabi were hampered by the hesitation of her partner in Egypt, republican France, to put down a popular leader. '*Egypt* is VITAL to us', the Queen dashed off to Ponsonby, – for the passage to India. By 1 July there were still no improvements:

Already 6 months of the year passed! How terribly time flies! and in what awful times we live! Ireland no better ... Egypt in a dreadful state, – the Sultan unmanageable and the other Powers behaving very ill!! God help & guide me! – a very fine day.

Then Gladstone unexpectedly decided that military operations against Arabi would be a holy war and ordered the fleet to bombard Alexandria. Anger and exaltation met in an explosion of passions which rocked the whole country. 'Gladstone?' shrieked W.S. Blunt in his diary, 'Great God, is there no vengeance for this pitiful man of blood, who has not even the courage to be at the same time a man of iron?' John Bright sent in his resignation – 'The old leaven of the Nonconformist will break out,' said Gladstone acidly to Ponsonby – but the Queen quivered with pride at her Navy's firmness. Next day the Duke of Connaught (Prince Arthur) left at the head of the Guards to take part, on 3 September 1882, in Arabi's defeat at the battle of Tel-el-Kebir. A bonfire roared on Craig Gowan, as after Sebastopol, and for a time all was joy: black was black and white white, just as the Queen liked things to be. Her son distinguished himself; the Khedive proved to be a non-smoker with only one wife, while Arabi and the Sultan were scoundrels, bribing a tobacconist to poison the Khedive.

A letter of congratulation on the victory of Tel-el-Kebir from Gladstone to the Queen gave less than satisfaction. He failed to say one word about the Duke of Connaught's part. She made up for Gladstone's omission by personally receiving the victorious troops on 17 November with her son taking pride of place. 'He looked so like his beloved Father I felt quite overcome.' Next to the Duke she praised the 'brilliant contingent' of Indians. The admirers of Sir Garnet Wolseley, who had commanded in Egypt, were much annoyed.

The rest of the year was a whirl of social duties and celebrations: a State dinner, State opening of the new Law Courts, where she recognized the great Florence Nightingale sitting near the dais in order to see *her*; endless decorating of war heroes and visits to hospitals. Netley Hospital seemed comfortable except for a shortage of arm-chairs.

I gave the Egyptian medal to a number of them (wounded), it was very touching to bend over the beds of these brave, noble, uncomplaining men, & pin medals on their shirts. Took good care to prick no one.

Haslar Hospital was less satisfactory: there were no nurses and an air of severity.

Everything was so like the dear past, so interesting, from the Indians' magnificent turbans over which she struggled to push their decorations, down to the peculiar appearance of Colonel Home who had commanded the Blues in Egypt though 'slightly off his head'. When 14 December came round and found her busier than ever, she could scarcely believe that she had once longed to die. On Boxing Day the Christmas tree was lit for the last time and stripped of its presents as of old, her little granddaughters drawing lots for the fairy doll at the top.

How much has happened during this year. I have to thank God for very much, & only wish I was more worthy of His great mercies & goodness to me.

Among the mercies had been a Government reshuffle in December. The raising of Dilke and Derby to the Cabinet was more than counterbalanced by Lord Hartington's appointment as Minister of War. At least, the Queen had thought so. But when she congratulated Hartington on his important new responsibilities he replied that there would not be much for him to do: 'I think everything has been done; & the Army should rest now.' Less than ever could she rest.

30
The Bitter Cry
1883–84

During the first months of 1883 the Queen began to hope that her Prime Minister was in for a period of rest even longer than the British Army's. Temporarily broken by insomnia, Gladstone went abroad in January and Harcourt told her that if he returned at Easter it would be only to resign. The Queen gathered that Harcourt for one would not be sorry. He was busy rounding up the Phoenix Park murderers whose identity had been betrayed by an informer; whatever 'delusions' Gladstone might cherish, Harcourt assured Queen Victoria that Ireland would have to be governed under a Crimes Act for the next twenty years.

Hartington and Goschen, a right-wing Whig who had gained the Queen's confidence, also expressed nervousness at the prospect of Gladstone's return: though a genius, the Government was doing 'wonderfully well' without him. When the Prime Minister finally reappeared Harcourt reported that he looked as if he couldn't do much work. The Queen agreed. Had not Gladstone at a drawing-room failed to hear what she said to him? 'The Diplomatic Corps are numerous today,' she had said. The Siamese suite happened to be passing and Gladstone replied, 'Yes, they are very ugly.'

The ever-present hope of his retirement brought a crumb of comfort to the Queen during a sudden wave of misfortune which now smote her.

A fall downstairs at Windsor on 17 March 1883 started up a succession of painful rheumatic attacks. After a week spent on a sofa she was carried by John Brown and a footman into her little pony-chair 'which I used to use long ago'. With Jenner's help she tried to walk but failed. Next day was Easter Sunday. A sad entry in her Journal greeted this festival. 'Had not a good night. Vexed that Brown could not attend me, not being at all well, with a swollen face, which it is feared is erysipelas.' He had caught a chill combing the grounds for Fenians. Bad days and nights followed, Brown getting worse and the Queen no better. He was nursed in the Clarence Tower by Sir William Jenner and Dr Reid, the Queen's most valued new physician whose father, to add to the gloom, suddenly died on the 27th. 'He is greatly upset but said he would rather not leave me just now.' On the 29th Prince Leopold told her that John Brown had died.

The Queen was crushed. Just at the crisis of her own pain she had lost not only an excellent servant but a real friend. It was like 'one of those shocks in 61', she wrote to the sympathetic Ponsonby; she had not been able to walk before Brown's death, now she could not even stand. Lord Rowton, whose master had always treated 'Mr Brown' with studied respect, called on the Queen personally to condole; so did Tennyson, much to Ponsonby's alarm who feared an official elegy. The Prime Minister paid a tribute to 'Mr J. Brown' and the Queen filled half a column of the *Court Circular* with his praises. All the tributes were collected in a special scrap-book.

As the weeks passed the Queen's spirits began to recover but the double burden of her own pain and Brown's loss would suddenly plunge her in the middle of lively conversation into gloom. On 28 June she wrote, 'I walked just a little but my attempts were very unsuccessful. How I miss my good Brown's strong arm to help me along'. It was not till 13 July that she could get in and out of her carriage at Balmoral without a 'platform'. She remembered that the Duke of Orleans had been killed by falling out of his carriage exactly forty-one years ago; to that tragedy she attributed all France's troubles. *She* must not fall. A masseuse, Madame Charlotte Nautet (known to the Court as 'the Rubber'), came from Aix-les-Bains and 'kneaded & worked backwards & forwards' every limb, muscle and joint, leaving the Queen rolled up in flannel for fifteen minutes: 'it made me very late & feel tired.' At the end of the year she was still very lame and very sad.

Queen Victoria had been working on a further instalment of her *Leaves* throughout 1883 and it was published on 12 February 1884 under the tile of *More Leaves from a Journal of Our Life in the Highlands*. Everyone was kind about the Queen's book except, as before, her own family. But the Queen swiftly demolished their criticisms: having reigned forty-five years she knew what her people liked and what was good for them; her *Leaves* had done good in 1868 and *More Leaves* would do more good now; publication of the truth caused 'false biographies & lives (endless ones have been published of me)' to 'fall into the background & vanish altogether.'

Ponsonby had received an advance copy of *More Leaves* as a New Year present. On 23 February another parcel arrived for him. It contained a manuscript with a covering note from the Queen announcing that she was engaged upon the enclosed 'little memoir' of John Brown. Her object was to show by her gratitude and friendship that Brown was a 'gt deal more' than a devoted servant. Its circulation would at first be private.

Ponsonby was in a quandary. He thought the 'little memoir' calamitous, but it was not till the 28th that he dared to reply. He made two main points: the memoir was 'invested with a degree of interest which must be felt by all who knew Brown', but Sir Henry doubted whether 'this record of Your Majesty's innermost and most sacred feelings' should be published to the world; passages would be misunderstood and unfavourably criticized by strangers, causing the Queen pain.

Sir Henry's view was shared by everyone who knew of the manuscript. But few had the courage to tackle the Queen on such a delicate subject. It was left to the intrepid Dean of Windsor, Randall Davidson, to incur the royal displeasure. The opinion of his colleague, Dr Lees of Edinburgh, had convinced him that publication of the memoir would be 'most undesirable'. He therefore seized the opportunity on 6 March, while thanking the Queen for a presentation copy of *More Leaves*, to hint that yet more leaves would be a mistake. Queen Victoria expressed haughty surprise at this view and announced her intention to proceed with publication. The Dean then wrote again with more vigour; the Queen ordered him, through Lady Ely, to withdraw and apologize for the pain he had caused and the Dean, having apologized in writing for the pain only, offered to resign.

There was a long, terrible silence. Offended Majesty retired for a fortnight into a deep thunder-cloud and Davidson ceased to exist – another preached on Sunday from his pulpit. Suddenly, a few days later, he was sent for. A smiling goddess received him 'more friendly than ever'. The memoir was never mentioned again. As the Dean realized, Queen Victoria never bore a grudge, actually preferring those people who, from the highest motives 'occasionally incurred her wrath'.

Dr Lees heard later in the spring that John Brown's memoir had been 'postponed'; according to Sir Henry's biographer, Arthur Ponsonby, it was destroyed. Or was it? There is a legend that the Queen's memoir and Brown's diaries are both still lying closely guarded in some royal cupboard. The private life of royalty has always fascinated the curious and this legend is just another example of that strange mythology of Brown the Highlander which has embellished the equally remarkable truth from his lifetime down to the present day. There is no historical evidence that the papers were not destroyed.

There do remain some fragments of the kind which the Queen might have included in the memoir if she had ever finished it. These alone are enough to make it crystal clear why Davidson, without for a moment believing in an immoral relationship between the Queen and Brown, nevertheless risked his whole career to prevent publication. A few greetings cards have survived, some garish, some charming in lacy frames, all addressed by Queen Victoria to John Brown.

On 1 January 1877, for example, Brown received the following verses printed beneath the picture of a dashing little parlour-maid:

> *I send my serving maiden*
> *With New Year letter laden,*
> *Its words will prove*
> *My faith and love*
> *To you my heart's best treasure,*
> *Then smile on her and smile on me*
> *And let your answer loving be,*
> *And give me pleasure.*

In the Queen's handwriting was written:

> To my best friend J.B.
> From his best friend. V.R.I.

The tone of this and similar effusions is echoed in a letter of Queen Victoria's announcing John Brown's death to her grandson Prince George of Wales.

> ... I have lost my *dearest best* friend who no-one in *this World* can *ever* replace ... *never forget* your poor sorrowing old Grandmama's *best* & *truest friend* ...

No doubt the Queen's advisers were right at the time to stop publication, but today it can only be regretted that the *Life of John Brown* is lost to history. As the Queen herself always insisted, true biography drives out false.

Deprived of the comfort of writing Brown's memoir, Queen Victoria contented herself with having dedicated her own *More Leaves* to him, after inserting a paragraph about him at the end. Even this mild expression of her feelings had worried a Court determined to have no revivals of the old scandals.

Brown's later years at Court had in fact passed without undue commotion, something of a miracle considering his addiction to the bottle. As a Scot living in the raw Highlands he thought nothing of it and it was due to his cheerful frankness that the world now knows how Queen Victoria liked her tea. One day a maid-of-honour was told by Brown that she could have two hours off as the Queen was going out.

'To tea, I suppose?'

'Well, no, she don't much like tea – we tak oot biscuits & sperruts.'

When sober, Brown's duties were remarkably wide, from receiving doctor's reports on the health of royal employees and undertakers' reports on their funerals, to dealing with the mud at Cowes Harbour and collecting donations from the Household for a monument to Lord Beaconsfield. His 'strong arm' was always in evidence. Times without number he saved the Queen from horses with staggers, runaway horses, horses driven by drunken coachmen into the ditch. His speed in seizing the pistols of madmen put her equerries to shame.

Ponsonby, who knew the best and worst of Brown, summed up his influence fairly on 26 May 1883, after escorting the Queen in a low state to Crathie churchyard:

Wreaths from Princesses, Empresses & Ladies in Waiting are lying on Brown's grave. He was the only person who could fight and make the Queen do what she did not wish. He did not always succeed nor was his advice always the best. But I believe he was honest and with all his want of education – his roughness – his prejudices and other faults he was undoubtedly a most excellent servant to her.

'I cannot cease lamenting', wrote Queen Victoria in her Journal on 27 March 1884, the first anniversary of John Brown's death. That same day a telegram arrived from Cannes where Prince Leopold was holidaying while his wife waited for her second baby, to say that he had hurt his knee. Next day came the news that he had died from a haemorrhage of the brain. The Queen's stiff, aching limbs were still being massaged by the Rubber and incessant, alarming telegrams from Egypt made her head swim. Now to all this was added a new and terrible heartache. Though Prince Leopold's faults had never escaped her, in her agony after his death she called him 'the dearest of my dear sons'.

The Queen's immediate reaction to death was, as ever, clear-sighted and true:

For dear Leopold himself we could not repine … there was such a restless longing for what he could not have; this seemed to increase rather than lessen.

But insight, however clear, could not lift the shadow and it may have been the sorrow of these years which helped to turn Queen Victoria's thoughts to the distress of the poor – now again at a dreadful peak. She made a determined effort to find out what was really going on in the slums of London and among the unemployed. *The Bitter Cry of Outcast London*, an enquiry into the slums by a group of Noncomformist missionaries, had stirred her deeply. She put questions to Gladstone about the homes of the poor. If improvements had indeed been made (as she was constantly being told) we surely need not despair of making more? The Prime Minister replied by dilating yet again on past improvements without showing much enthusiasm for future experiment. The same thing was to happen later when Queen Victoria suggested public works to mitigate unemployment. Gladstone again stalled. His old-fashioned Liberalism in home affairs had not caught up with the needs of the 'eighties.

Housing was not the only subject on which the Queen chose to disagree with her Prime Minister. There was indeed little that he could do right. He preferred High Churchmen; she preferred Low Churchmen with large-minded ideas. He felt that Cabinet secrets were secrets. She persisted in her assertion that past Prime Ministers had revealed to her the details of Cabinet conflict. Gladstone considered the Queen's claims 'intolerable', 'ill-judged', 'inadmissable', and her Court 'oriental' and 'Byzantine', due entirely to Disraeli's encouragement. For the Queen the only ray of hope was the thought that the Grand Old Man, seventy-four in December 1883, surely could not go on much longer.

Gladstone arrived at Osborne at the beginning of February 1884, full of good resolutions for the future. After the longest audience he could remember (one hour and a quarter) he brought up the subject of retirement with the Queen's private secretary, declaring vehemently that only the Bulgarian atrocities had 'dragged' him out of his privacy and 'forced' him back into the front rank ten years ago.

'I regretted it but I couldn't help it. I could not keep silent and I did not.'

After next year he would for ever hold his peace. His business would cease, he declared, in the summer of 1885 when Parliament would be dissolved. Nothing would induce him to go through another general election.

Neither the Queen nor Ponsonby took this with the scepticism which long experience of the Grand Old Man should have taught.

31
Gordon and the Tup-Tupping

1884–85

Arabi's defeat in 1882 brought no peace to Egypt. The revolt moved southwards into the Sudan and found a new leader in a fakir calling himself the Mahdi, the Expected One. As soon as Queen Victoria realized what was afoot, letters and telegrams began again to descend on the Government, urging them to crush this false prophet without delay. But Gladstone wanted no more African adventures and Hartington was for giving the army a rest. Throughout the following year the country was divided between those like the Queen who wished to keep British troops in Egypt and the mass of Liberals clamouring for evacuation.

Things were brought to a head by terrible news from the Sudan. Ten thousand Egyptian soldiers under Hicks Pasha had been slaughtered and the Expected One was at the frontiers of Egypt. Gladstone's Cabinet announced on 3 December that they must abandon the Sudan, rescuing only the garrisons scattered over the country with Khartoum as their centre.

The Queen shuddered at this humiliation. She concentrated her energies on goading the Government into doing something. By the middle of January she appeared to have been successful. While Gladstone was laid up with a chill, a Cabinet presided over by Hartington took the momentous decision to send out General Gordon.

Gordon's instructions seemed explicit enough: to report on the situation in the Sudan with a view to evacuation. Nothing whatever was said about re-occupying the territory; nevertheless vague references to performing 'such other duties' as Sir Evelyn Baring, the Controller of Egypt, might require, made the orders less explicit than they sounded. Besides, Gordon did not listen very intently to human sounds. 'We are pianos', he wrote to his sister; 'events play on us'. He was a mystic and a fatalist.

Charles George Gordon was just fifty-one; the wrong man for the Sudan but one after the Queen's heart. He had earned the nickname of 'Chinese' Gordon from victories, not evacuations, in the Far East. Like Napoleon III he had blue, magnetic eyes and 'destiny' seemed to him, as to Napoleon and Disraeli, more important than human will. He carried a cane into battle like a later man of destiny in Africa, Cecil Rhodes, and called it his 'wand of victory'.

Gordon took a hero's departure from London on 18 January 1884, the crowd of Jingoes taking it for granted that he would not stick pedantically to his orders. Khartoum welcomed him on 18 February as their Expected One and kissed his feet. Four days earlier the Queen had received his sister at Windsor – 'very anxious

General Gordon who was killed at Khartoum in 1885. Queen Victoria was furious with Gladstone for not acting more quickly in sending an expedition to relieve him.

about him, but great confidence in his will to be preserved'. On that same day she discovered from Foreign Office telegrams that Gordon thought reinforcements would 'help him'. Help him to do what? Smash the Mahdi? The Government desired him to do one thing only – evacuate the Sudan. They were convinced he could do this without any more help. This and further messages were ignored and on 18 March the Mahdi closed in. Khartoum was besieged.

Everyone knew that 'poor Gen. Gordon', as the Queen now called him, was in greater danger than the garrisons he had been sent to save; everyone, except the Government. They still believed that sheer cussedness prevented him returning to Cairo. Next month Gladstone was hissed in London and on 19 May he suddenly told the Queen that an expedition might after all have to be sent from England to Gordon's relief.

In the midst of worrying about 'poor Gen. Gordon' the Queen made her last eruption into politics which was both on a grand scale and entirely beneficial.

A great increase in the franchise, extending the vote from the boroughs to the counties, had been promised by the Liberals in 1880. Now, four years later, Gladstone passed his Reform Bill through the Commons. Lord Salisbury refused to accept it unless a 'Seats Bill' was also introduced, redistributing the Parliamentary constituencies so as to save his Tory party from being swamped by new voters. Gladstone stuck by Reform first, Redistribution afterwards. The Lords therefore threw out the Reform Bill on 9 July 1884.

The country immediately faced a constitutional crisis as the Radicals saw their chance to attack the whole institution of the Lords for their obstructive behaviour. The Queen, not frightened by reform of the franchise but much alarmed by reform of the Lords, worked desperately for peace. At last the 'impulsive' Salisbury and the 'imprudent' Gladstone were brought together and the obvious compromise was reached. A Reform Bill passed through the Lords while an agreed Redistribution Bill simultaneously came before the Commons.

Gladstone's reaction to Queen Victoria's intervention is significant. He began by impatiently declining to argue with 'her Infallibility' and ended with an almost gushing letter of thanks. The Queen telegraphed a characteristic reply: 'To be able to be of use is all I care to live for now.' But the Reform Bill was the last great problem which Queen Victoria and Gladstone worked out in harmony. A few weeks later the issue of the Sudan, now fast approaching a decision, opened a new and terrible chasm between them.

Gladstone had delayed sending a force to relieve Khartoum until the last possible moment. He held that since Gordon had no right to be in danger, danger did not exist; moreover, the Mahdi's followers (unlike Arabi's) were 'rightly struggling to be free' and so an expedition would be wrong. At last in September 1884 when Gordon had been besieged for nearly six months Gladstone was forced by public opinion to send Wolseley to Egypt, but it was October before the relief force started up the Nile. On the 24th Gordon wrote in his Khartoum Diary:

If they do not come before 30th November the game is up, and Rule Britannia.

Food was almost gone. Day and night he swept the desert from the palace roof with his old telescope, picked up for £5, but it showed him no rescuers. Then on 12 November he heard the sound of drumming.

This is our *first* encounter with the Mahdi's personal troops. One tumbles at 3 a.m. into a troubled sleep; a drum beats – tup! tup! tup! comes into a dream ... The next query is, where is this tup tupping going on. A hope arises it will die away. No it goes on, and increases in intensity.

Gordon's last entry was made on the 'fatal' 14 December:

now Mark THIS, if the expedition ... does not come in ten days, The Town May Fall, and I have done my best for the honour of our country. Good bye. C. G. Gordon ...

The first of the ten thousand rescuers arrived before Khartoum on 28 January 1885. They were just too late. Two days earlier the Mahdi's soldiers had burst into the palace and speared Gordon to death.

A year earlier the Queen had written to Gladstone: 'the Queen trembles for Gen. Gordon's safety. If anything befalls *him*, the result will be awful.' She was true to her word. She telegraphed identical messages to Gladstone, Granville and Hartington *en clair*:

These news from Khartoum are frightful, and to think that all this might have been prevented and many precious lives saved by earlier action is too frightful.

Gladstone was handed this open rebuke by the station-master at Carnforth on his way back to London. Holding himself blameless, his indignation was colossal and he wondered whether he ought to resign.

Unforgivable as the Queen's action was, it was prompted by the intensity of her suffering, which in turn was due to her romantic view of the Sovereign's responsibility. Owing to 'the old Sinner', she wrote to the Princess Royal, 'we were just too late as we always are – & it is I who have as the Head of the Nation to bear the humiliation'.

As so often, the Queen's pangs reflected those of her people. Gordon had been the idol of the young army officers and they nicknamed the Grand Old Man the Grand Old Spider. On the music-halls he became the M.O.G. – murderer of Gordon. Gladstone did nothing to make amends. He appeared thoughtlessly at the theatre while the whole country was in mourning and the nearest he could get to a tribute in Parliament was the cold phrase, 'the lamented Gordon'.

For a few weeks it seemed that public clamour would force the Government into reconquering the Sudan. But the sudden threat of a third Afghan War frightened the Government into cancelling Wolseley's second expedition to the Sudan, and concentrating on forcing the Russians to come to terms. Agreement in Afghanistan and the unexpected death of the Mahdi in the Sudan enabled the Liberals to return to their wonted policy of peace.

Gladstone's conduct of foreign affairs, though it avoided war, did not stengthen his hold over the Cabinet. Soon they were once more acutely divided over a new Coercion Bill for Ireland. It was the stick and carrot all over again. The Radicals, led by Dilke and Chamberlain, insisted on modified forms of Home Rule before any new Coercion Bill, a policy unacceptable to the landowning Peers.

But before the Liberal split could go further a Budget proposal to increase the taxes on beer and spirits was defeated by a combination of Tories and Irish Nationalists in a snap division on 9 June. The beaten Ministers thankfully escaped from the tumult which broke out in the House and later presented their resignations.

Queen Victoria's last exchange with Gladstone was sharp. She shook hands with Hartington and Granville but not with Gladstone. Humbly he asked if he might kiss her hand. She gave him her fingers but there was no forgiveness.

The last days of Gladstone's Ministry coincided with a crisis in the Queen's domestic life. At the centre of the crisis lay the susceptibility of the younger members of her family to fall in love with the clever and handsome Battenberg brothers. The four Battenbergs were minor princelings on the father's side. His morganatic marriage to a mere Countess deprived his sons of their Hessian rank but they were granted the title of Battenberg without an H.R.H. The Germany of the *Almanack de Gotha* disapproved of such people marrying into the Royal Family. The Queen however thought that 'great matches do not make happiness'.

The Queen's granddaughter, Victoria of Hesse, the eldest daughter of poor Alice, married her cousin Prince Louis of Battenberg in April 1884. The wedding at Darmstadt was disturbed not only by the expected bickering of the bride's German relatives but also by the general alarm aroused by the behaviour of the bride's father. Queen Victoria was shocked to discover that the widowed Grand Duke Louis had been 'entrapped' by a 'depraved' and 'scheming' woman of Russian origin, named Alexandrina Kalomine.

Meanwhile, a second ill-starred love affair was occupying the Queen's mind. Another granddaughter, Princess Victoria of Prussia ('Moretta' or 'young Vicky') had fallen in love with another Battenberg, Prince Alexander of Bulgaria ('Samdro'). Unfortunately for young Vicky, her Sandro had quarrelled with the Tsar. Bismarck, determined not to upset Russia, violently opposed the marriage, dragging with him the Princess's grandparents, father and brother, Prince William, the future Kaiser. On the lovers' side in this 'Romeo and Juliet' affair were only the Princess's mother, the Princess Royal, and her English grandmother, Queen Victoria. But these two were a formidable alliance. During the house-party for the Darmstadt wedding, Fritz was packed off to shoot capercailzie so that the billing and cooing of Sandro and young Vicky should not be disturbed.

With all this going on Queen Victoria may have missed the signs of yet another Battenberg romance. It was therefore with something like panic that she heard from her only remaining unmarried daughter, Princess Beatrice, of her wish to marry Prince Henry of Battenberg ('Liko'). For months the Queen refused even to discuss the idea, telling herself that it was nothing but an aberration which would never have happened if Princess Beatrice had not lost her dear brother Leopold. In time, however, she realized the strain of this situation on her daughter's health. Prince Henry came to England, and having promised to make his future home with the Queen so as not to deprive her of Princess Beatrice's services, received her consent. The engagement was announced on 30 December 1884. Four days later Ponsonby reported: 'She [the Queen] is beaming and proud of him'.

On 7 January she wrote to the Princess Royal:

The marriage is immensely popular here & the joy unbounded that she, sweet Child, remains with poor, old shattered me!!

(If by 'here' she meant the Court, this was true. In the country another German marriage was severely criticized.) She expressed surprise at her own complete

The wedding of Princess Beatrice and Prince Henry of Battenberg. Queen Victoria gave her consent on condition that the couple should live with her in England.

Opposite The Duchess of Kent in old age by Winterhalter.

serenity, after the 'horror' and 'most violent dislike' of 'my precious Baby marrying at all'; it was all due to Liko himself having won her heart by his modesty and consideration.

Once again the Queen's German relatives behaved badly. Queen Victoria had conferred upon Prince Henry an H.R.H. for use in England. Several of her German kinsmen refused to employ this title when answering her invitations to his wedding. Her blood boiled. How dared they say that Liko was not '*geblüt*', not pure bred?

240

Particularly offensive were Prince William of Prussia, his wife and his brother, Prince Henry. Willy needed a good 'skelping', as the Scotch said, she wrote furiously to his mother, the Princess Royal.

Queen Victoria's championship of the Battenberg family did not interfere with her vigilance in other directions. There was always 'tup-tupping' on the periphery of the huge family: scandals in Coburg, Teck debts, the Brunswick fortune, Hanover exiles. Queen Victoria corresponded tirelessly about them all. Opportunities to display her increased tact with her children were not wanting. As early as 1881 the magazine *Truth* had drawn attention to Princess Louise's absence from her husband's side in Canada where he had been Governor General since 1878. The Princess had suffered a horrible sleigh accident the year before, when she was dragged by the hair for several minutes and lost one ear. To this shock the Queen attributed an aversion to her husband which had to be accepted as a sad but inescapable fact; they must try to live on friendly terms under the same roof, but the Princess could not be '*forced*' to do so. 'That is all we can do,' she wrote to the Princess Royal in September 1884. Short of allowing a formal separation, the Queen in fact did everything in her power to ease the pressure on her daughter, while 'feeling very much for' Lord Lorne. Nevertheless, the necessity of continually seeing the Duke of Argyll (Lord Lorne's father) over the Franchise crisis produced one of those situations in which the strain of being both Queen and mother was at its greatest.

The Queen's anxious temperament often led her to worry unduly over the kind of problems which face all families. But though, like many women, she could not overlook the failings of her children, she was able to focus on the virtues of her grandchildren. Young Prince Albert Victor of Wales was perhaps 'languid' from growing so fast but such a good boy that he would never go astray; little Daisy Connaught's roaring disobedience was forgiven because she was so 'funny'.

Not a few of the third and even fourth generation were assisted into the world by their indefatigable grandmother. True, the Queen's children sometimes arranged that 'dear Mama' was not told in time. But when her granddaughter, Princess Victoria of Battenberg, arrived at Windsor for the birth of her first baby on 25 February 1885, the Queen took complete command. Despite Gladstone, Gordon and all the rest, she sat beside her motherless granddaughter from seven in the morning till the child was born at five. The accoucheur, Dr Duncan, wondered how she could do it.

The circumstances of the birth seemed to Queen Victoria 'strange & affecting'. For the child, a daughter, was born in the same bed as her mother, and the Queen held Princess Victoria's hand and rubbed her arms just as she had ministered to the baby's grandmother, Princess Alice, twenty-two years ago. The baby was christened Alice and became the mother of Prince Philip, Duke of Edinburgh. Queen Victoria would have found it even more 'strange & affecting' had she known that he was to marry her great-great-granddaughter, Queen Elizabeth II.

241

32
Home Rule
1885–86

The Queen's autumn manoeuvres started off with an alarming bang. News reached her on 19 September 1885 of a popular rising in the Balkans which had placed Prince Alexander of Battenberg at the head of an enlarged Bulgaria – an eminence from which she correctly guessed that the Tsar would have him removed as soon as possible. Some fifteen months later the exiled Sandro arrived in England to a rapturous reception from the Queen, after a series of fantastic adventures in which he and his brother, Francis Joseph, had been pitted alone against the 'Russian fiends', as the Queen chose to describe his oppressors. Meanwhile, events at home, though perhaps less romantic, were no less exciting.

In the election campaign following Gladstone's defeat in the summer, political parties seemed to be standing on their heads. Parnell, after a secret interview with the Conservative Lord Carnarvon in a shuttered Mayfair house, ordered every Irishman to vote against Gladstone. Gladstone's decision not to fight another election was again revoked; but instead of bidding for Irish support during the last weeks of Salisbury's Government, he bewildered his followers by leaving Salisbury to set the pace on Ireland and Chamberlain to make the running on the home front.

When the election results were complete it appeared that after all Salisbury could carry on his Government provided the Irish Nationalists supported him; 'but of course neither the Govt. or opposition can count upon these', as the Queen truly observed. A long-drawn crisis ensued. For several weeks unstable political groups formed and dissolved. No one was more active than the Queen who carried on her campaign to persuade the right-wing Liberal, Goschen, to form a coalition to save 'our dear great country' from falling into 'the reckless hands of Mr Gladstone'. She even opened Parliament in person for the last time on 21 January 1886 in the hope that she could be of use to the Conservatives. But her efforts were in vain. Five days later the Liberal Party, with the support of Parnell, brought down the Conservative Government.

This coup turned out to be a blow with a paper truncheon. It had been achieved only by a vote on agriculture, not on Ireland, and even so the Liberals were far from unanimous. The Queen was entitled to feel, as she wrote to Lord Salisbury the following day, that only 'a Combination of Moderate & Patriotic men of both sides could last as a Govt.' This cannot excuse her method of working for that end.

She refused at first to accept Salisbury's resignation, then tried Goschen again and was persuaded only by the combined efforts of Goschen, Ponsonby and

Salisbury himself to send for Gladstone. When Ponsonby warned her that the Liberals were sharply criticizing the delay, she answered defiantly:

The Queen does not the least care but rather wishes it shd. be known that she has the grtest possible disinclination to take this half crazy & really in many ways ridiculous old man ...

Throughout Gladstone's Ministry she kept in close and continuous contact with Salisbury, forwarding copies of all Gladstone's important letters to his Conservative opponent and often enclosing copies of her own replies. Though Salisbury was glad to be kept so thoroughly informed, the unconstitutional nature of this correspondence should not blind anyone to the innocuousness of its results. Salisbury's patent duty was to lay down his pen after the first letter, having referred the Queen sternly to her new Prime Minister. He did the next best thing: gave her temperate advice. Nor did Queen Victoria's machinations hasten Gladstone's defeat by one hour. It was brought about by Joseph Chamberlain, a member of Gladstone's own Cabinet.

In the summer of 1885 Chamberlain's efforts to satisfy Ireland with local, self-governing councils had earned him the violent hostility of Parnell's extremist followers. If Chamberlain visited Ireland they threatened to duck him in a horse-pond or bog hole. From that moment Chamberlain was through with Parnell. When in February 1886 Chamberlain temporarily subscribed to Gladstone's Irish policy – vaguely defined as an 'examination' of Home Rule – it was in the private belief that he might soon be looking for a bog hole in which to dump it.

Gladstone cared little what Chamberlain believed. He told Harcourt that he would go forward with Home Rule if need be without Hartington or Chamberlain, ' – without anybody!'

The new Ministers met on 15 February. For the next four weeks Chamberlain was left to kick his heels in deep suspicion and discontent while the aged wizard worked frantically to complete his 'examination'. There was no need for the Queen to urge Gladstone to hurry, though she did so. In the incredibly short space of just over a month Gladstone had ready his first Home Rule Bill. It contained a vast land scheme to buy out the landlords, a draft for political self-government and no coercion. The Queen was well aware that there were some disaffected members in the Cabinet, such as Rosebery, but she was startled when the Foreign Secretary told her that Chamberlain and Trevelyan would resign rather than accept Gladstone's Home Rule Bill. Trevelyan she knew disliked the Irish Nationalists for he had recently told her that he would prefer not to meet any of them 'alone in a wood'; but a fierce Radical like Chamberlain – 'how could it be?'

The decisive Cabinet meeting took place on 26 March 1886. Chamberlain came determined to be conciliatory. He asked Gladstone, among other things, whether under his Bill the Irish Members of Parliament would no longer sit at Westminster where they could at least be controlled? Without any attempt to persuade, Gladstone answered, 'Yes'.

'Then I resign.' Chamberlain and Trevelyan walked out. Let them go, thought Gladstone, convinced that he could do without them.

At first it seemed as if Gladstone was right. Queen Victoria had felt his scheme to buy out the landlords, costly as it was and harmful to England, would not satisfy the Irish. But the Nationalists cheered loudly when Gladstone introduced his Bill to Parliament on 8 April 1886 in a speech that lasted three hours and twenty minutes. Such phenomenal vigour at his age caused universal wonder. Even Gladstone himself was surprised that his voice had behaved so well.

Next day Chamberlain opened the attack on the Bill. For two months the battle raged. The Queen continued to work against Gladstone and eagerly encouraged the Tories and the Liberal rebels in their public campaign against Home Rule. She never doubted that the Bill would be killed and was already planning the future with Salisbury. He must make sure that killing was followed by a change of government. Did he think she should accept a dissolution if Gladstone requested one? How would it all fit in with her holiday at Balmoral? Salisbury advised a dissolution: it would certainly seem more fair, probably result in the return of a Conservative Government and cause no interruption to Her Majesty's summer holiday.

Meanwhile Gladstone had still not been beaten. He refused to consider dropping the Bill, a move of which the Queen had been much afraid. But he was prepared to make some concessions. An offer to redraft the Bill to satisfy Chamberlain and heal the split had been turned down, much to the Queen's satisfaction. Later she heard that huge baits were being offered to Hartington, an opponent of Home Rule from the start. Would he stand firm?

The impatient Queen waited at Windsor while the debate went on. Just before she left for Balmoral at the end of May, a monster petition against Home Rule signed by 20,000 women of Ulster arrived at Windsor. It went twice round the Corridor. As for the men of Ulster, Lord Randolph Churchill incited them with his notorious slogan: 'Ulster will fight and Ulster will be right.' Queen Victoria was shocked, though when Gladstone compared Churchill to Smith O'Brien and the revolutionaries of 1848 she was more shocked still.

At last the supreme moment came. Gladstone spoke with all the inspiration of his genius and his cause. His closing words are still remembered:

Ireland stands at your bar, expectant, hopeful, almost suppliant ... think, I beseech you, think well, think wisely, think, not for the moment, but for the years that are to come.

The division was taken at 1.15 am on 8 June 1886. A combination of Conservatives, Whigs and Radicals defeated the Bill by thirty votes. Thirty was an appropriate number in the circumstances, for the embittered Irish were soon to feel that the Radical whom they believed had betrayed them was a regular Judas. 'There goes the man who killed Home Rule', said Parnell as Chamberlain went through the 'no' lobby.

After a disturbed night the Queen awoke to hear the glad news. 'Cannot help feeling relieved, and think it is best for the interests of the country.' The restrained note in her rejoicing was perhaps due to a twinge of conscience. She knew well and had often pointed out to her foreign relatives that it was her constitutional duty to support the government of the day. For five months in 1886 she had done the opposite.

Gladstone asked for a dissolution and the Queen granted it on condition that it took place at once. She offered him an earldom. He declined: even so, it seemed impossible that this white-faced, haggard old man, with a voice that often gave him trouble, and eyesight, like her own, beginning to fail, should ever lead the Commons again.

The elections showed that the temporary revolt against Beaconsfield's imperialism was over. Europe had begun in earnest its race for Africa during Gladstone's second Ministry. Bismarck's colonial acquisitions, together with Majuba and Gordon's death, had convinced the teeming populations of English and Scottish towns that they needed a strong Tory government to obtain for Britain her share of the loot. 'Primrose Day' had been inaugurated on 19 April 1886, Disraeli's birthday, to fan imperialist ardour. At Osborne everyone was ordered to wear a primrose, even the Liberal Lady Ampthill (though with a little encouragement from Ponsonby she threw it away). Voluntarily to let Ireland go did not fit in with the country's rapacious mood.

Lord Randolph Churchill helped to annihilate Home Rule by calling it the dream of 'an old man in a hurry'. When the votes were counted Gladstone and Parnell between them controlled 276 seats and Salisbury, Hartington and Chamberlain 394. To the faithful, such a blow at the G.O.M. seemed incredible.

Gladstone tendered his resignation on 20 July 1886 and the Queen accepted it briefly. He was pale and she nervous during their final meeting on the 30th, but as Ireland was not mentioned at all it went off amicably. On 3 August the Liberal Cabinet came to give up their seals. The Queen thought they looked ashamed of themselves. The triumphant Tories came an hour later.

The rest of 1886 was dominated in her eyes by the tumultuous career of her beloved Sandro and it was a tired Queen who, on the last day of the old year, hoped that 'all present anxieties be dispelled.' Ponsonby on the same day was already absorbed in official preparations for Queen Victoria's approaching Jubilee. What should he and his wife Mary give her? She would like 'a made thing' better than 'an old thing'. Ponsonby was right. The Queen, far from moving along a traditional road, was about to break new ground.

33
The Jubilee Bonnet
1887–91

A State triumph and a family tragedy absorbed Queen Victoria during 1887. Politics she left in Lord Salisbury's able hands.

The prospect of the Jubilee seemed to the Queen uninviting. How could she welcome an orgy of 'hustle & bustle'? Rheumatism and fatigue notwithstanding, she had to go on. Rehearsals had to begin. Countless telegrams had to be read. Jubilee medals had to be dispatched and Jubilee coins examined; endless lists of visitors had to be made. If the Prince of Wales had not been 'very kind & helpful' she could not have got through. But at last on 20 June the preparations were over.

The day has come and I am alone, though surrounded by many dear children ... 50 years today since I came to the Throne! God has mercifully sustained me through many great trials and sorrows.

She had awakened at Windsor to a brilliant morning, exultingly hailed by her subjects as 'Queen's weather', though it was devoid of that snap and sparkle which she liked. Breakfast was under the trees at Frogmore; there was nowhere private to sit out of doors at the Castle. After breakfast she drove through festive crowds down the short, steep hill to Windsor station and from Paddington through the Park to luncheon with a host of royalties in Buckingham Palace. In the evening she sat among over fifty Royal and Serene Highnesses with the King of Denmark on her right, the King of Greece on her left and the King of the Belgians opposite. She described it simply as 'a large family dinner'; the gold plate, she admitted, looked splendid. 'At length, feeling very tired, I slipped away.'

Next day, 21 June, the Thanksgiving Service took place in Westminster Abbey. Everything reminded her of 1851 and the Great Exhibition. Now it was a greater exhibition, an imperial one, though her arrangements were a characteristic mixture of magnificence and simplicity. She turned down the traditional glass coach flat, but had six of the famous creams to draw her open landau with an escort of Indian cavalry. Then came the males of her great family: three sons, five sons-in-law and nine grandsons.

She had obstinately refused as usual to wear the crown and robes of State. What did it matter if Lord Halifax had said people wanted 'gilding for their money', or if Mr Chamberlain thought a Sovereign should be grand, or Lord Rosebery that the Empire should be ruled by a sceptre not a bonnet? Bonnet it

Queen Victoria on her
Golden Jubilee in 1887.

should still be. A very special bonnet, however. It gleamed with springy white
lace and diamonds. All the ladies were bonneted also according to printed instructions: 'Ladies in ... Bonnets and Long High Dresses without Mantel.' Slowly she
processed up the Abbey to the strains of a Handel march. At the altar she was able
to look around, picking out the Royalties, Household, Members of Parliament. A
merciful Providence prevented her from recognizing Gladstone, 'though he was
there'.

'I sat *alone* (oh! without my beloved husband, for whom this would have been
such a proud day!)'; but the congregation gave thanks to the music of her
husband's *Te Deum* and the choir sang his anthem, *Gotha*.

Back to the Palace where there was still much to get through. After dinner the
Indian Princes and Corps Diplomatique swam past her in a shimmering mist: 'I
was half dead with fatigue ...' At 10 o'clock rockets began to shoot up from over

The Jubilee in the East –
a contemporary allegory.

six hundred hills. Her attendants rolled her into the Chinese Room to watch the fireworks, but the golden tide was breaking out of sight, so that she had an excuse to leave. The roar of London kept her awake for a little and then lulled her to sleep.

Forty-nine years ago she had returned from her Coronation ready, not to faint, but to give her spaniel, Dash, his bath. Yet Thomas Carlyle, the biographer of strong men like Cromwell and Frederick the Great, had failed to perceive the vein of iron in Victoria's character. She was like a tiny canary, he said, gazing in terror at a thunderstorm. Queen Victoria was sometimes like a thunderstorm, never a canary.

As she drove to her Coronation she had seemed to Carlyle too young even to

248

A Jubilee genealogical tree.

choose a bonnet. Since that day she had chosen a husband; husbands for her daughters and wives for her sons; ministers, prelates, an imperial creed, a religion, a way of life; and as her sign-manual she had chosen a bonnet.

By the time Queen Victoria reached Osborne on 19 July she had a month of hot hard work to her credit. There had been drives, receptions, reviews and garden parties sufficient to daunt the hardiest, but the exhausted Queen carried on through the dust and heat. At Osborne it all began again. There was the Spithead Review; 20,000 officers and men, 26 armoured ships, 9 unarmoured, 43 torpedo vessels, 38 gunboats, 12 troopships, 1 frigate and 6 training brigs. 'I was very tired.' An elaborate farewell to the Indian Princes. 'I don't know why they take up the Indians so much', muttered Ponsonby.

Heat had become an obsession. Even on cool evenings a huge block of ice squatted in the centre of the Queen's dinner-table, radiating chill. Still she must smile and drive. 'Good Sovereign – no Change required', ran the loyal inscriptions at Cowes, 'Fifty runs not Out', 'Better lo'ed ye canna be'.

She reached Balmoral at last to give her mind to the other side, the dark side of this 'never-to-be-forgotten year'.

At the Jubilee Thanksgiving Service some of the loudest cheers had been for the Crown Prince Frederick William, a golden bearded Charlemagne clothed in white and silver with the German eagle on his helmet. But Fritz, glorious though he looked, was suffering from a terrible throat infection, said by his enemies to be cancer. Shortly before his arrival for the Jubilee, the famous English surgeon, Dr Morell Mackenzie, had overthrown the diagnosis of cancer and Fritz left England in good spirits, believing that he had been cured – without having to endure the severe operation of tracheotomy. All he needed now was a peaceful convalescence. He and his wife went to San Remo, but there was no peace. From Berlin came angry demands that the Princess Royal should bring her husband back. The old Emperor was failing. Willy dashed to San Remo and made an appalling scene. On no account must Fritz return, wrote Queen Victoria: 'The more failing the Emperor becomes the more Fritz must make sure of getting well.'

But within a few weeks he was much worse. In February the dreaded tracheotomy had to be performed. A month later to the day (9 March) the old Emperor died and the new Emperor Frederick, mortally ill, arrived in ice-bound Berlin to begin his reign of 99 days. Queen Victoria was convulsed with emotion:

My OWN dear *Empress Victoria* it does seem an impossible dream, may God bless her! You know *how* little I care for rank or Titles – but I cannot *deny* that *after all* that has been done & said, I am *thankful* & *proud* that dear Fritz & you shd have come to the Throne.

How close they were now: the one Empress-Queen, the other Queen-Empress, and both Victorias.

A few weeks later, after a delightful short holiday in Florence, the Queen announced her resolve to visit the dying Emperor Frederick at Charlottenburg on the way home.

This plan was received with universal protests. The Bismarck family raised a fictitious howl: if the Queen of England was coming to push her granddaughter's marriage with Prince Alexander of Battenberg, Bismarck would resign: besides, his son Herbert wanted to marry Princess Victoria himself. The Queen insisted that the visit was neither a political nor a matrimonial excursion and brushed all objections aside.

The formidable old lady reached Berlin on 22 April. She agreed to give Bismarck an interview. Historians have not been able to decide which charmed the other most, the Iron Chancellor or the Iron Queen. Bismarck retired from the interview

Queen Victoria's private sitting-room at Windsor Castle, filled with paintings and photographs of the Royal Family.

mopping his brow: 'That was a woman! one could do business with her!' (Afterwards he adopted a more patronizing tone: 'Grandmama behaved quite sensibly at Charlottenburg'.) The Queen herself afterwards confessed to being surprised that the horrid monster was so amiable and gentle.

She kissed the dying Emperor good-bye, accepting from him a bunch of forget-me-nots, made Prince William promise to behave better in the future and returned home. Her bold visit caught the public imagination, though some newspapers expressed doubts. 'If I can be of any further use,' she wrote to her daughter, 'only tell me, & I wd even run over, papers & all ...'

But there was little more that could be done for the Emperor. He died on 15 June 1888. Queen Victoria wired to her grandson, now Kaiser William II: 'I am broken-hearted ... Help and do all you can for your poor dear Mother ... Grandmama V.R.I.'

For the rest of this year and far into the next the Queen devoted herself to mitigating her daughter's purgatory. She never for an instant doubted that her child's calamity was far greater than her own, made so much worse by the agony of seeing the proud Willy fill his father's place in such an unfilial and unfeeling way.

The Empress Frederick's troubles seemed to the Queen an unanswerable reason for offering her a winter retreat in England. When Lord Salisbury and the Prince of Wales objected to such an awkward visitor the Queen flew at them: were they frightened of William and the Bismarcks? The Empress stayed with her mother till February 1889, after which the Queen reluctantly consented to a summer visit from the Kaiser. He telegraphed his unbounded joy at being allowed to enter that 'dear old home at Osborne'. It was thought judicious to allow him to enter it in the uniform of a British admiral, an honour which he acknowledged with ebullient charm. 'Fancy wearing the same uniform as St Vincent and Nelson; it is enough to make one quite giddy.'

The Kaiser's charm was to overcome the Queen's reluctance to welcome him. The tenderness she had always felt for Prince Albert's first grandchild reasserted itself. She forgot her promises to the Empress Frederick not to address a word to 'those horrid people', Willy's suite, or only just 'Good Mng'. The chief of the suite turned out to be both 'pleasing' and 'straightforward'.

When the Jubilee was over the Queen did not return to her old seclusion, despite a worsening of her health. Indeed she now fought hard to conceal any deterioration. From 1889 onwards her sight began to fail: indignantly she wrote that there had never been such murky weather at Windsor, necessitating candles on the luncheon table. A rumour from New York that she was dangerously ill made her savage; Ponsonby put it down to wicked stock-jobbers hoping to profit from a subsequent rise.

Having renounced matchmaking, Queen Victoria was inexorably drawn into a fresh round on behalf of her grandchildren. Princess Victoria of Prussia presented the saddest problem. When the Queen heard that Sandro had now consoled himself with an Austrian singer she at once invited 'young Vicky' to be her companion while Princess Beatrice was abroad. The Queen helped to wipe away many bitter tears, while Princess Victoria's letters home shed some sharp light on Grandmama's habits. English royal nurseries were incomparably sweet and clean; the robes of Grandmama's Indian attendants were incomparably white; but Grandmama at night, on the royal train, was an incomparable fidget.

With mingled relief and trepidation the Queen learnt in 1890 that 'young Vicky' was to console herself with a German princeling: 'there is nothing so horrid as a daughter's engagement & marriage', she wrote to the Empress Frederick. 'One never knows how it will turn out...' It turned out badly.

The marriage prospects of the Wales Princes also occupied the Queen. A series of misfortunes blighted the love affairs of Prince Albert Victor ('Eddy'). His dazzlingly beautiful cousin, Princess Alix ('Alicky') of Hesse would not have him. His next choice was a Catholic Princess who would not change her religion. Lord Salisbury convinced the Queen that the affair must lapse. At last the Prince became engaged to nice, quiet, pretty Princess May of Teck during a ball at Luton Hoo, to the 'satisfaction' of both Queen and nation.

Politics too was behaving to the 'satisfaction' of the Queen. The Liberal Party appeared to be weaker than ever, since the Irish Nationalists had broken in two after Parnell had been named co-respondent in an undefended divorce suit. The Nonconformist conscience promptly dissociated Liberalism from a party led by an adulterer. The Queen watched from a distance, occasionally giving vent to a 'dreadful!' or a 'horrid!' Up and down Ireland Parnell fought with tragic desperation to maintain his position until he died on 6 October 1891. The Queen felt safe. She could not get on without Lord Salisbury and it seemed that she would not have to. She ignored Lord Rowton's warning that the Tories expected to be beaten at next year's election. In any case she would not send for Gladstone. Ponsonby let her have her say: 'No object in beginning the troubles now.'

But for the fourth time in the reign, 'the abominable old G. Man', who needed, she quaintly said, someone to 'take the sails out of' him, prepared to run in under the Queen's guns.

34
'Still Endure'
1892–95

Queen Victoria began the new year of 1892 with her accustomed survey of last year's profit and loss. On the credit side were the safe birth of another son to Princess Beatrice, Prince George's recovery from typhoid, her own good health, peace at home and abroad and Prince Albert Victor's engagement to Princess May. The wedding was fixed for 27 February.

After a festive Twelfth Night a telegram arrived on 9 January from Sandringham saying that Eddy had caught influenza but was going on 'all right'. Next day the Queen was startled to hear that Prince Albert Victor had developed pneumonia and on the 13th (a date always associated with her first suspicion that the Prince Consort might die) the report was 'as bad as possible'. She longed to 'fly' to Sandringham but was afraid of being in the way. When morning broke Princess Christian brought a telegram from the Prince of Wales: 'Our darling Eddy has been taken from us…' It was the fourteenth of the month. 'Poor, poor parents: poor May,' the Queen lamented, 'to have her whole bright future to be merely a dream! poor me, in my old age, to see this young promising life cut short!'

There was more sorrow to come. Her son-in-law Louis, Grand Duke of Hesse, died on 13 March; 'it is too dreadful to have to lose him too! … Again so near that terrible number fourteen!' She held a service for him at Windsor and for the second time that year listened to the organ playing *Now the labourer's task is o'er*. So many labourers had finished their tasks but one labourer still had to struggle on. 'Still Endure'.

Rumours were soon circulating that Prince George, the Prince of Wales's second son, would marry his dead brother's fiancée, May of Teck. They were given more credence by the fact that George had failed in his suit for his cousin, Marie of Edinburgh, who had recently become engaged to the heir of the Roumanian throne.

On 26 May, the birthday of Princess May of Teck, Queen Victoria wrote significantly in her Journal, 'may she yet be happy'. It was followed a few weeks later by the entry: 'George came to have a little talk with me'. There is no doubt what the little talk was about. The royal line must go on, and it would not be denied that Prince George possessed qualities conspicuously lacking in his brother.

I think dear Georgie so nice, sensible & truly right-minded, & so anxious to improve himself.

Mary of Teck, great-grand-
daughter of George III,
and later Queen Mary.

Prince George of Wales. Queen Victoria thought he was 'so nice, sensible & truly right-minded'.

Gladstone as an old man.

On the great battle-ground of self-improvement it was wonderful to find at last a future heir to the Throne standing squarely at her side as she settled down again to politics. Salisbury had asked for a dissolution in June and the country was once again preparing for an election.

'The poor but really wicked old G.O.M. has made two dreadful Speeches', the Queen wrote to her eldest daughter on 6 July 1892. The election campaign was drawing to a close and the first results beginning to come in. Not unprepared for a Home Rule majority, the actual figure of 45 did not surprise her. What shocked and horrified was that a mere majority, of whatever size, should be the deciding factor in a matter so important as the country's future.

For the third time in twelve years her burning vow not to send for Gladstone was extinguished by the necessities of 'the much famed Constitution'. She confided her anxieties to her friends. The Marquess of Lansdowne was told how much she dreaded entrusting the Empire 'to the shaking hand of an old, wild incomprehensible man of eighty-two and a half', her only consolation being that 'the country is sound and it cannot last'.

Opposite Queen Victoria's private railway salon, built in 1869.

Gladstone's appearance at his first audience (15 August) only confirmed the Queen's fears. They were both leaning upon sticks. 'You and I, Mr Gladstone, are lamer than we used to be!' After this human start she relapsed into cold distaste.

I thought him greatly altered & changed, not only much aged, walking rather bent, with a stick, but altogether; his face shrunk, deadly pale, with a weird look in his eye, a feeble expression about the mouth, & the voice altered.

Queen Victoria's opinion of the rest of the Liberal Cabinet was not much higher than of their leader. When they arrived at Osborne for their first Council on 18 August the Queen gave a horrified gasp: 'A motley crew to behold.' Sir William Harcourt (whom she described elsewhere as having grown 'rather awful looking now, like an elephant') assured her how anxious they all were to please her. 'I merely bowed.' The bulk of the 'crew' had to be sworn in together and instead of rising afterwards to kiss her hand they all crawled forward on their knees. This struck her as ludicrous rather than loyal.

The plaintive language with which Queen Victoria chose to begin her Journal on 24 May 1893 – 'My poor old birthday, my seventy-fourth' – was a familiar formula, nothing more. In reality she felt distinctly pleased with her recent record, as she proved by her very next words: 'I wish now it was instead sixty-fourth.' Besides the satisfaction of seeing Egypt strongly garrisoned and expecting to see Home Rule beaten, she observed that all branches of her family were moving harmoniously forward along the lines she had chosen for them.

First and foremost came the engagment on 3 May of Prince George, now Duke of York, and Princess May of Teck. 'The Country are delighted,' only 'poor dear Alex', the bereaved mother of Prince Albert Victor, was 'very tried' by the rejoicings but 'knows it must be' – an attitude which to Queen Victoria seemed impeccable. The wedding took place on 6 July 1893 in overpowering heat and a bath of tears, most of them cheerful ones.

That August when the Queen was going into ecstasies over 'the dear young *ménage*' of the Yorks, the scandalous old *ménage* of her brother-in-law, Duke Ernest II of Saxe-Coburg, at last came to an end. The Queen's final judgement on the departed sinner adroitly killed two wicked old birds with one stone. In one respect, she told her daughter Vicky, he was like Gladstone, for 'he persuaded himself that things were right which were wrong'.

Gladstone's second attempt to pass a Home Rule Bill for Ireland seemed to Queen Victoria a case in point. The right course was surely to introduce 'gradual self-government'; it could only be wrong to rouse the kind of storms which rocked Parliament during this summer of 1893. A climax was reached on 27 July when an attempt by Chamberlain to liken Gladstone to King Herod was violently interrupted by Irish shrieks of 'Judas! Judas!' Fisticuffs broke out on the floor of the chamber and hissing in the gallery; despair swept over Gladstone at what he called 'a black day'. Nevertheless it ended satisfactorily for him with a majority of 30 for the preamble of his Bill.

The annihilation of Home Rule for ever, so far as Queen Victoria was concerned, came in September 1893. The Bill passed its third reading in the early morning of the 2nd, by the slender majority of 34; the Queen heard that it would have been even less if many Liberals had not relied on the House of Lords killing the Bill. They did not rely in vain. An almost indecent vote of 419 to 41 against the Bill showed what these 'ancient monuments' could do and dare, when not in fear of demolition. But 'the Mob' also, as Queen Victoria noted, cheered Lord Salisbury after the debate and sang 'Rule Britannia'. Indeed the country as a whole was no longer on the side of small nations; if people had to choose between Home Rule and Rule Britannia they would choose Britannia.

Gladstone's days were numbered, for a crisis over national defence was beginning to open a fatal rift between him and his Cabinet colleagues. Popular alarm at the weakness of Britain's navy had been brought to a head by a sensational naval disaster in June 1893. Admiral Tryon made an error in turning his flagship, HMS *Victoria*, collided with HMS *Camperdown* and sank to the bottom of the Mediterranean taking with him more than half of the *Victoria's* officers and men. 'Too awful!' wrote the Queen: 'Too dreadful to contemplate!' She immediately cancelled a Court ball, sent one of her famous letters of condolence to Lady Tryon ('forgive my intrusion on your terrible grief'), made some remarks in her Journal about the unwieldiness of 'these ironclads' and found a crumb of comfort in the nobility of Tryon's last words: 'It was all my fault.' But she could not forget two grim facts: Britain was yet another ship short, and Gladstone refused to replace it.

Criticism of Gladstone's attitude towards proposals for a more powerful navy became widespread during the autumn and winter. He took no notice. Gladstone thought the Admiralty was 'mad! mad! mad!' and Rosebery recalled Palmerston's prophecy (a favourite one of the Queen's) that Gladstone would die in a madhouse.

On 29 December 1893 the G.O.M., still in the saddle but only just, reached the impressive age of eighty-four. The Queen could hardly endure to enter a new year in the hands of 'a deluded old fanatic'.

For two months of the new year, but no longer, Queen Victoria was required to remain in those 'deluded' hands. At the beginning of February the amazing old fighter, who was on holiday in Biarritz, sprang on his Cabinet a proposal for a snap election on the issue of the House of Lords. One of them called him 'preposterous', another 'absolutely insane' and all put their names to a decisive telegram: 'Your suggestion is impossible.' Gladstone, still at Biarritz, looked southwards towards Gibraltar, compared himself to the Rock and dismissed his colleagues as criminals. Everyone knew he must resign but having arrived back in Downing Street he kept the Cabinet in suspense for another fortnight.

Characteristically, Gladstone broke to the Queen his intention of resigning by stages, cloaking his first intimations that some news was on the way in so much mystery that the Queen was bewildered and alarmed. So many hints and innuendoes followed in the next few days that Gladstone's final, formal resignation was to be a humiliating anti-climax.

On 1 March he at last informed the Cabinet of his decision to retire. The reaction of his colleagues he later caustically described as 'that blubbering Cabinet' – though at the time he referred to it as 'a really moving scene'.

Next day Queen Victoria invited the Gladstones to dine with her at Windsor and stay the night. The following afternoon Gladstone solemnly entered upon the last lap of his devious road to retirement. He wrote out a formal resignation, placed it in a dispatch box and carried it to the Queen. This should have been the moment for a grand finale. Unfortunately the Queen dealt with him as casually as he himself had dealt with his blubbering colleagues. They had another desultory conversation which, in Gladstone's words, was 'neither here nor there'. He then kissed her hand and left. She had neither asked his advice about a successor nor offered him a word of thanks.

One good reason for the Queen's failure to realize that this at last was 'Resignation Day' was the fact that she did not open the box until he had gone. Queen Victoria and Gladstone were incapable of conversing together seriously and naturally during their later years, and the Queen was quite unaware of the significance of this audience. Having read his formal resignation she sat down at once and drafted what seemed to her an appropriate reply. After going over the old ground for the very last time – his age, his eyes and his 'arduous labours', now happily concluded – and wishing him a peaceful future with his excellent wife, she brought her letter somewhat abruptly to an end: 'The Queen would gladly have conferred a peerage on Mr Gladstone, but she knows that he would not accept it'.

To Gladstone the letter was an insult. It confirmed his bitter suspicion that he meant nothing to her. Their separation reminded him of a day sixty-three years ago when he parted without a pang at the end of a Sicilian holiday from his mule:

I had been on the back of the beast for many scores of hours. It had done me no wrong. It had rendered me much valuable service. But ... I could not get up the smallest shred of feeling for the brute. I could neither love it nor like it.

Gladstone's famous analogy of the Sicilian mule further illustrates both his brilliance and his blindness. To compare himself to a mule was a stroke of genius for his mulish obstinacy undoubtedly caused enormous offence; but to suggest that she felt he had done 'much valuable service' and 'no wrong', like his Sicilian mule, was a sad fantasy. Far from entertaining no feelings whatsoever, 'not the smallest shred' for the brute, she disliked him intensely.

She disliked his appearance, his long-windedness and his interminable tricks. She shivered at his 'cold loyalty' and compared it with the 'warm devotion' of others. She was also profoundly jealous of him in a way that only women already in positions of power are jealous of men. The 'People's William' competed with the 'People's Victoria'. Pointedly she dubbed his campaigns 'Royal Progresses', his press reports 'Court Circulars'. As his influence over the country grew, he seemed to curtail hers. Constitution, Army, Church, Ireland, Europe, Africa wherever she looked, he had done his best to diminish her prerogative and power. He would neither listen to what she told him nor tell her what her Ministers were saying. When one of them declined to pass on information witheld by Gladstone, she remarked bitterly that his first 'allegiance' should have been to his Sovereign.

After Gladstone's retirement the Liberal succession was expeditiously decided by the Queen without consulting the Grand Old Man. She chose Lord Rosebery. He

Lord Rosebery; like Queen Victoria he suffered from 'nerves' and chronic shyness.

was something of a kindred spirit, suffering from 'nerves' and chronic shyness like herself. When as a widower he broke his morbid seclusion to become Foreign Secretary again she promised to help, assuring him that work would do him good. In Imperial affairs he shared the Queen-Empress's 'large ideas'. A final reason for making her choice swiftly and choosing Rosebery was that she had planned to go abroad almost at once for her indispensable spring holiday and another wedding of grandchildren. It was therefore necessary to find someone who would carry on the Gladstone Government without a break.

She was somewhat alarmed to understand that Rosebery intended to go on with most of Gladstone's proposed legislation, with the important exception of Home Rule. But by the middle of April Florence had soothed away her irascibility, and she could endure to read Rosebery's unanswerable plea that a House of Lords which went to sleep during a Conservative administration but roused itself to veto every Liberal measure, must be reformed. She finally agreed that the Lords ought to be 'reconstructed' but not in response to agitation. Nor as a result of Rosebery's sallies. She ordered him in June to 'take a more serious tone and be, if she may say so, less jocular, which is hardly befitting a Prime Minister.'

Meanwhile Queen Victoria had moved from Florence to Darmstadt for the wedding of her grandchildren, Alice's son Ernest and Alfred's daughter 'Ducky'. The day after the wedding she heard that the groom's sister was to make an even more remarkable match. The Queen's loveliest granddaughter, Princess Alix of Hesse, had at last accepted the Tsarevitch Nicholas. It was in fact the Kaiser, Queen Victoria's rival matchmaker, who had persuaded his cousin to swallow her scruples about joining the Russian Church and marry the man she loved. The Tsar of Russia died suddenly in October, so that Princess Alix became an Empress as well as a wife in the space of three weeks. The Queen was not altogether happy about this most splendid of her grandchildren's marriages. She noted that 'the position is an anxiety' and, as if with prescience, wrote on the eve of her grand-daughter's coronation: 'Alicky's fate will be sealed tomorrow morning.' A quarter of a century later the Russian Revolution ground her into the dust.

An event which brought almost universal joy occurred on 26 June 1894 – the birth of a son to the Duke and Duchess of York. Queen Victoria's relief was tempered by a touch of impatience at the public excitement generated by this achievement. After one newspaper had suggested that it was the crowning glory of her reign, she wrote to the Empress Frederick:

It is a great pleasure & satisfaction, but not such a marvel, for if Alicky had not refused Eddy in '89 – I might have had a gt-gd Child 4 years ago already. As it is, however, it seems that it has never happened in this Country that there shld be three direct Heirs as well as the Sovereign alive.

As the second generation of the Royal Family married and multiplied, the older generation of the Queen's Household began to die off. On 7 January 1895 Sir Henry Ponsonby, who had been wilting for some time, suffered a severe stroke. The Queen was deeply distressed. In the following November he died. 'Too sad, too sad!' The inevitable hymn, *Now the labourer's task is o'er*, struck her as being 'particularly applicable' to 'dear Sir Henry'. Within days she was commemorating him with the inevitable bust.

While Ponsonby had lain paralysed at Osborne, the last Liberal Government of Queen Victoria's reign battered itself to death. Suitably enough the final blow came when the Government was blown sky-high in a snap decision on the War Office's supply of cordite. The Government at once resigned. It had been the most uncomfortable Cabinet in British history. Rosebery was not on speaking terms with Harcourt and also had to endure his old enemy, insomnia. To the Queen he confided that 'quite dreadful' scenes had regularly disgraced the Cabinet. 'His only regret was to leave me'. None of the Cabinet was sorry to resign.

Queen Victoria, however, with her talent for the *volte face* which makes her such a fascinating character, would gladly have kept them longer. The change of Government, she wrote on 1 July to the Empress Frederick, was 'not such a source of satisfaction as it might have been for I am losing some people who cannot be replaced.' She concluded a list of sad losses with this unique admission:

And personally I am vy fond of Ld Rosebery & prefer him (not his Politics) to Ld S. – he is so much attached to me personally.

She admired Salisbury because he was supremely adult; Rosebery, even at his worst, was in her eyes that far more fetching character, a prodigal son.

It looked as though, with the passing of Gladstone, Queen Victoria might have settled down happily with moderate Liberal Ministers. But the opportunity, if there really was one, had come too late. The general election of 1895 resulted in a huge majority for the Tories. 'If only the Lords are prudent,' she wrote, 'it ought to last a long time.'

It outlasted Queen Victoria.

35
The Labourer's Task
1892–1900

The Golden Jubilee had seen the fulfilment of one of Queen Victoria's long-felt ambitions. She had become the proud possessor of two Indian servants. This was among other things her way of stating her abhorrence of racial prejudice, but it was also to enable her to acquire what she considered sufficient knowledge of her Indian Empire to teach her Indian civil servants how to do their jobs.

The most influential of the Queen's Indian servants was Abdul Karim, a slim and clever twenty-four-year-old when he first entered the Queen's service. Like John Brown before him his duties were manifold and, as his influence on the Queen grew, his promotion was rapid. He cooked her curries and taught her Hindustani; soon he was giving her instruction in Mohammedanism and Indian sociology as well. In 1889 he complained of the indignity of his serving at table. 'He was a clerk, a Munshi, not a menial'. (This was technically true, for he had been a vernacular clerk in Agra gaol where his father was the prison doctor). The Queen, sensitive to a situation where human dignity seemed to be involved, created him the Queen's Munshi and, like the young Prince Albert, he rapidly graduated from blotting the Queen's letters to assisting in their composition.

It was not long before the advance of the Munshi kindled the same kind of jealousies that had previously been reserved for the Queen's Highland Servant. But this time the antagonism was magnified by racial prejudice. Despite such antagonisms, the Munshi, always a pusher, climbed steadily. Cottages were built for him; his wife, nephew and 'aunts' were brought from India and every time Mrs Abdul Karim fell ill, reported Dr Reid, a different tongue was put out for him to examine.

At length the news of yet another promotion for the Munshi in 1894 inspired four of the younger courtiers, led by Colonel Bigge (assistant secretary) and Dr Reid, to act. Abdul was to be formally designated the Queen's 'Indian Secretary' with an office, clerks under him and the appropriate title of 'Hafiz'; all early photographs which showed him waiting at table were to be destroyed. The dauntless four sent a report to the Queen purposely obtained from India, casting doubt on Abdul's social origins. Shocked and offended, she dashed off a hasty defence of her favourite to Sir Henry, following it up on 10 April with a powerful counter-attack:

> ... to make out that the poor good Munshi is so *low* is really *outrageous* & in a country like England quite out of place ... She has known 2 Archbishops who were the sons respectively of a Butcher & a Grocer ...

Sir Henry duly recorded in a memorandum dated 11 June 1894 that the Munshi was now 'Hafiz'. But rumbles over his social status did not diminish. Seven months later came Sir Henry's stroke. His place was filled by Sir Fleetwood Edwards as Keeper of the Privy Purse and as Private Secretary, the vigorous Colonel Bigge. Queen Victoria's first words to Sir Henry's successors on their formal appointment in May 1895 were significant:

The Queen is sure that they will follow in his footsteps, and be as kind to all of all ranks, as he always was.

There were no signs at present, however, that Sir Henry's kindness (or rather, grudging tolerance) towards 'these Injuns', as he called the Munshi and his colleagues, would be practised by the new generation.

Throughout the next two years there was a running battle between Queen Victoria and her advisers, the Queen determined to 'keep up' the Munshi, and the rest to pull him down. Her greatest triumph was in squeezing a high honour for the Munshi out of Lord Rosebery and Sir Henry Fowler – the C.I.E. – after having failed to make the Viceroy acknowledge a sentimental Christmas card ('*A wish* of my heart be yours to-day') sent to him by her protégé. The Governors of Bombay and Madras had returned similar cards to sender.

The truth was that successive Ministers, Liberal and Conservative alike, found the Munshi a 'bore' rather than a danger. They knew the Munshi bought plots of Government land 'at his own price'; they understood that the Queen showed their letters to him and they must therefore write 'accordingly'; they were even willing to have him watched though not 'shadowed'; but nothing would induce them to get mixed up in what Lord George Hamilton, Indian Secretary in Lord Salisbury's Ministry, called 'the Court's mud pies'.

In 1897 the whole affair finally exploded. On Queen Victoria's spring holiday abroad she proposed to take Abdul with her, which meant that he would have to eat with the Household. At this they 'put their feet down', deputing Harriet Phipps, the Queen's personal secretary, to deliver an ultimatum – no Munshi or no Household. The Queen flew into one of her now rare rages, sweeping everything off the top of her desk on to the floor. In the end Lord Salisbury himself had to be summoned and ingeniously persuaded her that the French were too 'odd' to understand the Munshi's position and might be rude. Abdul, therefore, did not join the huge royal caravanserai on its semi-public progress to Cimiez. But he turned up soon afterwards, as Princess May wrote to Prince George, 'to the despair of the poor gentlemen' and what's more invited Rafiuddin Ahmed, a protégé of his who was politically suspect, to come too. This was going too far. At forty-eight hours' notice Rafiuddin Ahmed, protesting loudly to the Munshi who had been forced to act as go-between, was sent packing, and confidential requests were flashed in cypher all over India for fresh information on the Munshi's birth, parentage, history, 'wife or wives'.

Although no new information was forthcoming, this storm led to a decline in the influence of the Munshi. The Queen was persuaded by the concerted pressure of 'old Indian officers in her Court' and her secretary, Colonel Bigge, to put the Munshi more into his proper place.

Even after this crisis the Queen continued to labour for Abdul and Ahmed. Lord Salisbury was kept busy answering a stream of royal letters concerned with such matters as clearing their names of the accusations of the Court or getting them jobs and privileges. Salisbury showed remarkable patience and tact in stalling some of the more outrageous of her demands. But no one could persuade her to get rid of the Munshi. As Lord George Hamilton said, it was no use arguing with an old person about a servant.

What is to be the verdict on Queen Victoria's last exotic friendship? The Queen's worst fault was in allowing the Munshi to bias her in favour of Mohammedans: during a period of increasingly serious Hindu-Moslem riots, this was dangerous. She was also indefensibly violent about her Court during the 1897 crisis, contrasting their 'shameful' behaviour with Salisbury's 'kind good advice'. She seems to have recognized afterwards the weight of their responsibility for her personal contacts. '*All* is quiet & satisfactory now', she wrote to Lord Salisbury on 27 December 1898, 'excepting that the injured individual [the Munshi] cannot get over it.' It was upon the 'red-tapist' India Office and a 'jealous' Parsee MP that she ultimately laid the blame for what had happened.

The wind of change which she had hoped to see blowing through the Foreign Office and India Office was quietly allowed to drop after her death. A bonfire of the Munshi's papers was made by order of King Edward VII at Frogmore Cottage, one of the Munshi's homes. Solemnly watching the flames stood a silent circle: Abdul himself, his nephew, Queen Alexandra representing the King, and Princess Beatrice representing Abdul's late protectress. He lived on at Karim Lodge, Agra, until his death in 1909, when King Edward ordered a second holocaust of papers. Lord Minto, the Viceroy, begged that old Mrs Karim might be allowed to keep a few letters in Queen Victoria's handwriting. 'It will do good'. Permission was granted.

Sad personal news arrived from Africa. Early in December 1895 Prince Henry of Battenberg, the indispensable support of her old age, had joined the Ashanti expedition. The Prince was bored with the eternal round of Court life, and the Queen's conviction that he would succumb to fever had been overridden. Unhappily, her fears were on this occasion justified. Poor Liko, after appearing to recover from a 'slight' fever, died in Madeira in January. Liko, 'our help, the bright sunshine of our home', was dead. It seemed as if the dreadful years of Prince Albert's and Prince Leopold's deaths had come back, though the Queen noticed how much more patiently Beatrice bore her tragedy than she herself had done.

The Court moved from Windsor to Osborne, from Osborne to Balmoral; but the light had gone out of the house. The Journal speaks of an awful blank, stillness everywhere, weather 'very dreary, as dreary as our hearts', Hindustani lessons not going well. Throughout the summer her political comments are noticeably less vivid than during the previous year. 'Saw Ld Salisbury under the trees & talked to him about everything', is a typically lifeless entry.

But life was not yet over. Her spirits were lifted by the news that an expedition was at last to be sent to recover the Sudan. And as an attempt to sweeten the increasingly adverse opinion in Europe towards British exertions in Africa, Lord Salisbury persuaded the Queen to invite the young Tsar and Tsarina to Balmoral. Politically, the Tsar's visit was a failure. But emotionally it was a great success; 'It seemed quite like a dream', sighed the Queen in ecstasies, 'having dear Alicky and Nicky here'. Church bells rang, pipes played, Alicky looked charming in white serge, mountains of luggage perfumed the passages with sweet Russia leather and every bush and ditch concealed a detective.

Queen Victoria awoke on 23 September 1896 to an avalanche of congratulatory messages. 'Today is the day on which I have reigned longer, by a day, than any English sovereign'. Her grandfather, George III, had hitherto held the palm but for many of his long years the record had been an unhappy one – the King supposedly mad and the Regent certainly bad – whereas the old Queen seemed to be increasing in sense and virtue with every year that she reigned.

The labourer's task was still not o'er. On 1 January 1897 Queen Victoria prayed as usual to be of use to her country. The country decided that she could be put to the highest possible use by a spectacular celebration of her Diamond Jubilee.

Sixty years a Queen! It was a thought to evoke the quintessence of loyalty – imperial glory radiating from a little 'Lady Ruler' (as Alfred Harmsworth, founder of modern popular journalism, delicately called her) touched with many sorrows and the magic of old age. The Golden Jubilee, as we have seen, had inflamed the people's imagination with imperial dreams. Ten years later those dreams were recognized to be national policy. The Colonial Minister, Joseph Chamberlain, was the first to think of turning the Diamond Jubilee into a festival of Colonial Premiers rather than Crowned Heads. Queen Victoria adopted the imperial idea with alacrity. Apart from its intrinsic appeal, it would have been more than she could bear at her age to cram Buckingham Palace and Windsor yet again with kings, emperors and their suites. One emperor in particular would have been entirely unacceptable. The Kaiser, who had inflamed British opinion by congratulating President Kruger on the preservation of his 'independence' after the Jameson Raid and had then insulted the Prince of Wales, was far too unpopular to parade in the London streets.

Her own parade on 22 June was to carry her subjects to a climax of loyalty. As if to put a seal on the legend of 'Queen's Weather', the sun came out from a dull sky just as the first guns in Hyde Park announced that she had left the Palace, having previously touched an electric button which telegraphed her Jubilee Message round the Empire:

'From my heart I thank my beloved people. May God bless them!' Queen Victoria's account of her reception by London was by no means exaggerated.

None ever, I believe, has met with such an ovation as was given to me, passing through those six miles of streets … the crowds were quite indescribable, and their enthusiasm truly marvellous and deeply touching. The cheering was quite deafening, and every face seemed to be filled with real joy.

London's sense of its own greatness, as the metropolis of a far-flung Empire, vied with a poignantly personal affection for the venerable figure who was both a living and a symbolic mother. 'Our Hearts Thy Throne', declared a triumphal arch at Paddington; the Bank of England declaimed: 'She Wrought Her People Lasting Good'. 'Go it, old girl!' called an ecstatic voice from the crowd as she appeared on the Palace balcony in her wheeled chair.

Jubilee summer blazed and cheered itself to a standstill. For the first time in her life she was pelted with confetti as she drove through Windsor on 24 June after a long thundery day. Smiling gaily, she swung her little parasol from side to side to

A Jubilee plate, one of the many souvenirs made to commemorate the longest reign in English history.

ward off this strange manifestation of joy. Soldiers, ships, fire brigades and public schoolboys were all reviewed. At a march past of Volunteers from thirty public schools, Her Majesty felt that Eton and Harrow were 'perhaps' the best. It was 'very thrilling' to hear the frantic cheers from the throats of 4,000 'young fellows' though sad that owing to the heat 40 of them had to be laid out under the trees. On a Jubilee mug 'a few' of the Queen's 'Notable Achievements in Peace and War' were listed – from 'Railways 1837' to 'Imperial Institute 1897' – while beneath a triple portrait of Her Majesty draped in laurels and supported by the Bible was inscribed the remarkable line:

The Centre of a World's Desire

Nevertheless, it was not entirely bombast. She was incomparably the best Queen the world had got, and more than one foreign nation, still struggling under a rule of tyranny, self-indulgence or fatuity, wished she were theirs.

268

One man who perhaps knew her better thought otherwise. Mr Gladstone hoped that Queen Victoria would celebrate her Diamond Jubilee by abdicating. Just under a year later the Grand Old Man died. The Queen found it impossible to be complimentary to him even in death. A cold letter of thanks for her husband's loyalty was sent to Gladstone's widow, but no expression of royal regret appeared in the *Court Circular*. A letter to the Empress Frederick expressed the Queen's final judgment:

The Marquess of Salisbury, Conservative Prime Minister.

I cannot say that I think he was a 'great Englishman'. He was a clever man, full of talents, but he never tried to keep up the honour and prestige of Gt Britain. He gave away the Transvaal & he abandoned Gordon, he destroyed the Irish church & tried to separate England from Ireland & he set class against class. The harm he did cannot be easily undone.

Then she recollected herself. 'But he was a good & vy religious man'.

'He gave away the Transvaal'. Gladstone's error must be rectified. Britain must recover the Transvaal and revenge the disaster of Majuba Hill. Such was the Queen's view of the Boer War which broke out on 11 October 1899. She was by no means a warmonger, but she was always prepared for the country to fight for what it had once possessed and lost.

For the first few weeks of the war the Queen busied herself in wishing God speed to departing troops – 'quite a lump in my throat' – and looking after the interests of the weak. Lord Salisbury was urged to prevent war taxation from falling on the working classes and Lord Wolseley to arrange a comfortable voyage for the horses – both in vain; but a year-long battle to get commissions for Army bandmasters was won. By the end of October, however, events had moved too fast and unfavourably for the Queen to draw pleasure from her small works of mercy. Crack British armies were besieged in Ladysmith, Kimberley and Mafeking. The entries in her Journal are short and depressed. 'No news today only lists of casualties'.

When news did arrive it was always of more reverses. There were no gillies' balls at Balmoral, no games at Braemar. By a strange fatality, Mausoleum Day fell in 'Black Week'. Three Generals were defeated in a row: Gatacre on 10 December, Methuen on the 11th and Sir Redvers Buller at Colenso on the 15th. The Queen's blindness had caused her on one of these candle-lit mornings to mis-read defeat as victory. She arrived, a radiant figure, for breakfast only to learn the truth from Princess Beatrice. After a moment's silence she said: 'Now perhaps they will take my advice, and send out Lord Roberts and Lord Kitchener, as I urged them to do from the first'.

But the Queen did not just sit back during this crisis in national morale. This surely was the climax of her vocation to 'be of use'. She was flying about reviewing troops and visiting hospitals as if she were young again. Parcels of knitting were dispatched to her 'dear brave soldiers' and when it transpired that the dear brave officer-class had accidentally got them all, she ordered 100,000 tins of chocolate for the men. One of the tins, she afterwards heard, had stopped a bullet, while

By the end of the century
women were beginning to
react against the ideal
of propriety and
submissiveness of the
mid-Victorian era.

Cheltenham Ladies College,
one of the earliest public
schools for girls received
a visit from Vicky during
her visit to England in 1897.
Miss Beale, one of the
founders, is far right.

Bicycling was an activity
eagerly taken up by the
'new women' of the
eighteen-nineties.

Queen Victoria had relaxed
her earlier attitude to
smoking but she never
approved of women
smoking in public.

another had compensated for the wound it could not avert. 'I would rather lose a limb than not get that!' declared a legless hero to whom she offered a tin.

In February 1900 the tide turned. Ladysmith was relieved on the 28th. Queen Victoria repaired at once to the Mausoleum. A week later she made two triumphal drives through London, at which her welcome outshone in spontaneity both the Jubilees. No police, no soldiers. Lord Esher spoke of 'a domestic nation on a gigantic scale'. Throughout and ever since Black Week she had been a model of vigorous courage – no complaints, no self pity. 'Please understand that there is no one depressed in this house,' she told Balfour at Windsor during the crisis; 'we are not interested in the possibilities of defeat; they do not exist'. Now, with the spring, came the moment for her last sacrifice. French press attacks on Britain had increased and it was decided that she must not risk a holiday in Cimiez, though the journey to Italy might possibly be undertaken. In March she informed the Empress Frederick that even this was not to be. Vicky would be startled to hear that despite her pining for 'the sunny flowery south', she was going next month to visit Ireland.

And so, for just over three weeks (4 to 26 April) Queen Victoria visited a part of her dominions which she had not set foot in for thirty-nine years. Gratitude to the gallantry of Irish soldiers in South Africa had chiefly influenced her decision; she was suddenly consumed with longing to be loved by Ireland. In furtherance of her desire, she decreed the wearing of shamrock by Irish soldiers on St Patrick's Day and created a new regiment of Irish Guards. Even so, there were few flags in the back streets of Dublin where she did not drive, and these few caused scuffles. The Queen heard only the cheers of the loyalists, which were 'almost screams', just as she remembered them in 1843 though a thousand times louder. How touched she was by 'this warm hearted sympathetic people', who burst into 'God Save the Queen' every time they caught sight of her, a small, rotund, black figure drawn by a white donkey round and round the grounds of Viceregal Lodge.

Five days before her eighty-first birthday Mafeking was liberated. Queen Victoria happened to be visiting Wellington College and was hailed on a streamer as 'Queen of Mafeking'; people were 'quite mad with delight', she recorded in her Journal and the goings-on in London 'indescribable'. The word 'mafficking' was coined to describe them.

She held the last of her many birthday celebrations on 24 May 1900 with mixed feelings:

Again my old birthday returns, my 81st! God has been very merciful and supported me, but my trials and anxieties have been manifold and I feel tired and upset by all I have gone through this winter and spring.

Six extra men had to be rushed to Balmoral to help with the torrent of nearly four thousand congratulatory telegrams. It seemed impossible that this living symbol of an era and an Empire should not be eternal.

36

'Mother's Come Home'

1900–1901

The Queen's prayer for the new century was at once an indication that she knew that she was not eternal and a sign of her continued spirit. She prayed to be spared 'yet a short while' with all her faculties and just a little of her eyesight to serve her family and country. Once again her spirit was to be undermined by family tragedies.

At the end of July a telegram announced that 'poor dear Affie's state of health' was despaired of: he had an incurable disease of the throat – 'alas! one can only too well guess at its nature!' Within a week he was dead. 'Oh, God! my poor darling Affie gone too... It is hard at eighty-one!' The Queen, suffering from shock, felt that 'they' should not have kept the truth from her as long as they did.

The duplication of sorrows, so constant a pattern in Queen Victoria's life, pursued her to the end, for her soldier grandson, Prince Christian Victor of Schleswig-Holstein, died in October at Pretoria of enteric fever. Shaken to the core, she could not sleep and an unconquerable disgust for food prevented her from taking anything but arrowroot and milk. All through this 'horrible year', moreover, she had been without the comfort of a visit from the Empress Frederick who was desperately sick at Kronberg.

'It was wretchedly gloomy & dark', she wrote in her Journal on 6 November. In this weather and mood she left Balmoral for the last time. At Windsor her insomnia and general wretchedness increased until she was, in the words of her grandson Prince George, 'very seedy'.

The Queen struggled into December. 'Did not feel well', she wrote on the 9th, 'though they say I am getting better'. There was a kindly conspiracy to blame her blindness on the weather – 'No one ever remembered such cloudy days' – and to conceal from her the effect of the Boer War on her popularity abroad. German attacks, they told her, were due to jealousy, French to a few agitators, Austrian to the middle classes and Russian to Heaven knows what. The old Queen was not deceived.

The 'horrible year' blew itself out in a wail of wind and rain. Even the magic of Osborne now failed her as she fell into an erratic routine brought about by insomnia at night, followed by drugged slumber in the morning and invincible drowsiness in the afternoon. For the first time the Queen allowed a new year to crawl in without a good resolution. 'Another year begun & I am feeling so weak and unwell that I enter upon it sadly'.

The monstrous procession of nights and days dragged on, but there was little sign of improvement. On 14 January – the fatal fourteenth – there was a blank in

The towns and cities of late Victorian Britian were expanding rapidly and thousands of new suburban homes like these were being built.

her Journal for the first time in sixty-nine years. She never wrote in it again.

On the 17th there was difficulty with speech and mental confusion. A heart specialist was summoned and on the 18th her children; the Duke of Connaught happened to be staying in Berlin so that the Kaiser heard the news and included himself in the invitation. The Prince of Wales arrived on Saturday the 19th and the first bulletin went out. 'The Queen has not lately been in her usual health', it began, going on to describe the 'great strain upon her powers' during the past year. Randall Davidson, now Bishop of Winchester, crossed to the Island in a gale, to provide spiritual comfort during her last days.

'Nothing else but the Queen's illness is spoken or thought of', reported *The Times* foreign correspondents: in Vienna 'keenest anxiety', in Brussels 'painful

suspense', abstentions *en masse* in Athens from the Parnassus ball; a chivalrous wish from President Kruger for 'prompt recovery'. On 22 January *The Times* still hoped that her 'extraordinary fund of vitality' might yet pull her through.

At Osborne House the Kaiser waited, tactfully out of sight, and the Prince of Wales returned to his mother's room. She opened her arms whispering her last word, 'Bertie'. After luncheon the family were assembled, including the Kaiser whose dignified sorrow earned the admiration even of his cousins. He only wanted to see Grandmama before she died, he told them, but if that was impossible he would quite understand. He won his place at the death-bed.

Kneeling at the back of the bed and helping to support her was a nurse from the Cottage Hospital. (A later report said she was an Army Sister.) There were three

doctors present, Sir James Reid, Sir R. Douglas Powell and Sir Thomas Barlow. A few days afterwards Barlow described the bed itself, on which the Queen died, as 'a simple, narrow mahogany bedstead with a quite small chocolate coloured canopy at the head'. A bed answering to this description is still at Osborne House and it is improbable that she actually died in the double bed now in her room; it would have been most awkward for nursing, and taken up precious space needed by the assembled relatives. Barlow noted that once when her dressers had been doing something for her, she looked up and said with infinite tenderness, 'My poor girls', as if sorry for their trying task.

At intervals Davidson and the Vicar of Whippingham prayed aloud. There was no response from the figure on the bed, until the former happened to recite the last verse of her favourite hymn, *Lead Kindly Light*. Then he noticed that she was listening.

> *And with the morn those angel faces smile*
> *Which we have loved long since and lost awhile.*

Queen Victoria with Princess Beatrice of Battenberg, Princess Victoria of Hesse and Princess Alice (mother of Prince Philip).

She had waited forty years for the 'morn' and now at last it was coming.

As the frosty darkness began to fall about four o'clock another bulletin was issued: 'The Queen is slowly sinking'. Her chief doctor, Reid, assisted by the Kaiser, supported her on her pillow, one on each side. Not until she died two-and-a-half hours later did the Kaiser withdraw his arm; nor could he ease the strain by changing sides with Reid, for his left arm was withered. His Grandmama deserved every sacrifice.

Around her bed stood her children and grandchildren. She spoke to each of them and each kissed her hand in farewell, but as she drifted further and further from them they took to calling out their names, as if to bring her back. As the end drew near the appealing voices fell silent. 'Then came a great change of look', Davidson noticed, 'and complete calmness'. She died just after half-past six.

Her two young grandsons, Prince Alexander and Prince Leopold of Battenberg, ran downstairs to give the news to their tutor. 'It is all over', said the elder dramatically. 'We saw her die'. He spoke as if he had seen the end of the world.

Immediately the house was surrounded by police to prevent the news from spreading before the Prime Minister had been informed. Ten minutes later a message was read to the crowd at the gate:

Her Majesty the Queen breathed her last at 6.30 p.m., surrounded by her children and grandchildren.

Pandemonium broke loose. A yelling stampede of journalists on bicycles hurtled down the hill to Cowes to be first with the telephones, bawling as they went, 'Queen dead!' The famous 'hush' which had always surrounded 'The Widow at Windsor' was shattered at a blow. A new age had begun.

The Queen always drew a sharp distinction between personal mourning, of which she approved, and a black funeral. Having once seen the local hearse at Balmoral,

Queen Victoria in a pony cart surrounded by great-grandchildren

Queen Victoria's funeral
procession on its way
from the Albert Memorial
Chapel to the Mausoleum
at Frogmore.

complete with plumed horses, she never allowed it to appear again. Her own funeral should be military and white.

Faithfully her minute instructions were carried out. As Ponsonby once said, there was nothing the Queen liked more than arranging a funeral. Undertakers having been expressly forbidden, the Kaiser measured her for her coffin and would have lifted her in had not the Prince of Wales and Prince Arthur fiercely asserted that this was the right of her sons. With amazement Prince Arthur found that his awe-inspiring mother had dwindled to a featherweight. Her little silver crucifix from above her bed was put into her hands; spring flowers were scattered on her white dress; her lace wedding-veil covered her face and her white widow's cap her hair. Her robes and the diamonds of her Imperial Crown, placed upon the coffin, matched the brilliance of the four Grenadiers who stood on guard. At the Kaiser's suggestion a Union Jack was hung in the room, which he afterwards begged as a memento.

After all the darkness and storm, it was 'a midsummer day transplanted into winter' on 1 February, when the coffin, covered with a white and golden pall embroidered with a cross and the Royal Arms, was carried to the smallest of the royal yachts, *Alberta*, placed on a crimson dais and transported between many miles of warships to the mainland. Next morning Lady Lytton travelled on a special train, blinds drawn, with the coffin to Victoria station. People knelt in the fields as the train sped by. Black hangings were banished from the London streets and purple cashmere with white satin bows was used instead; the ominous drum-roll of Handel's 'Funeral March' was replaced, according to instructions, by Chopin, Beethoven and Highland laments. The Royal Standard, 'thrown partially over the pall' as the Queen had commanded, blazed upon the summit of the gun-carriage which bore her to Paddington station.

The crowds at Windsor lining the long route expected to see the Royal Artillery drawing the gun-carriage home. But after waiting in the icy cold one of the horses shied and snapped the traces. There was a moment of panic. Dared they continue the procession or must the Queen be hurried up the short cut to the Castle? 'I would wish just to say that as a gun carriage is very rough jolting and noisy', she had written in her will, 'one ought to be properly arranged...' With great presence of mind Prince Louis of Battenberg ordered a Naval Guard to drag the gun-carriage the long way round, using the train's communication cord and horses' harness. There was a salute of 81 guns, one for each year of her life, in the Long Walk. After a short service in St George's – the most that Queen Victoria could endure in that uncongenial place – she lay until 4 February in the Albert Memorial Chapel. Then the family alone took her to the 'dear Mausoleum'. There under its Victorian *cinquecento* domes, shining with gold and mosaics, she joined her husband at last.

After the funeral was over and the family had streamed out on to the winter grass dotted with snowdrops, sleet began to fall. Inside the Mausoleum the gas lamps were left burning quietly. The sleet soon changed to snow and the doors of the Mausoleum closed softly upon a white world. The Queen had had her white funeral.

INDEX

Abbreviations: V for Queen Victoria, A for Prince Albert

Abercromby, James, Speaker, 35

Aberdeen, Lord, 68; Foreign Secretary (1841), 103, 106; Prime Minister (1852), 133, 135, 136, 138

Adelaide of Saxe-Meiningen: as Duchess of Clarence, 14; as Queen, 24, 33, 46, 83, 91

Adolphus, Prince, Duke of Cambridge, 13, 14, 83

Afghan War, 220, 224

Ahmed, Rafiuddin, 264

Albert of Saxe-Coburg-Gotha, Prince, 15, 80, 87; visits England, 32, 33; marriage with V, 76–85; Parliament and, 81, 82; and Lehzen, 87, 93, 96–7; appointed as possible Regent, and name included in Liturgy, 89; Melbourne advises V to be guided by, 93; reforms household, 98, 100; visits House of Commons, 105; and foreign affairs, 112, 115, 118, 119, 157; and 1851 Exhibition, 127, 131; calumnies on, 136, 138; and French royalties, 137, 141; and Princess Royal, 145–7, 150, 152; created Prince Consort, 147; and Prince of Wales, 153–4; in carriage accident, 158; averts crisis with USA, 164; illness and death, 159, 162–4, 166–8

Albert Victor, Prince ('Eddy'), Duke of Clarence, 172, 201, 241, 252; death, 253

Alexander of Battenberg ('Drino'), 277

Alexander of Battenberg ('Sandro'), 239, 242, 245, 250, 252

Alexander, Prince of Orange, 33

Alexander I, Tsar of Russia, 17

Alexander, Tsarevitch, 74

Alexander of Württemberg, 28

Alexandra of Denmark ('Alix'), 158, 175; as Princess of Wales, 176, 177, 197, 257; as Queen, 265

Alfred, Prince ('Affie'), Duke of Edinburgh, 100, 153, 200; marriage, 208, 211; death, 273

Alice, Princess, 100, 135; engagement, 158; at death of A, 167, 168, 171; marriage, 178; V and, 177, 178, 190, 197, 199–200; death, 219–20

Alice of Battenberg, 241

Alix of Hesse ('Alicky'), 252, 260; as Tsarina, 265

Amberley, Lady, suffragist, 208

Ampthill, Lady, 245

Anson, George, 92

Arabi Pasha, 228

Argyll, George Douglas Campbell, 8th Duke of, 199, 223, 227, 241

Arthur, Prince, Duke of Connaught, 126, 153, 166, 221; V and, 201, 229; at V's death, 274, 280

Ashanti War, 216, 220

Augusta of Cambridge, Princess, 57

Augusta, Crown Princess of Prussia, 131

Augusta of Hesse-Cassel, Duchess of Cambridge, 13

Augustus of Saxe-Coburg-Kohary, 28, 32

Augustus, Prince, Duke of Sussex, 13, 28, 83

Baly, Dr William, 159

Baring, Sir Evelyn, 235

Barlow, Sir Thomas, 277

Barrett, Elizabeth, quoted, 37

Bauer, Caroline, actress, 23

Bauer, Fräulein, governess, 204

Beatrice, Princess ('Baby'), 135, 147, 158, 163, 166; V and, 27, 176, 200, 216; marriage, 239, 253, 265

Bedford, Duchess of, 92; as Lady Tavistock, 62, 63

Beechey, Sir William, portrait of V by, 18–19

Bentinck, General Sir Henry, 138

Berlin, Congress of (1878), 215

Bigge, Sir Arthur, 71, 262, 263, 264

Bismarck, Count Otto von, 150, 177, 190, 215, 239, 245, 250–1

Bismarck, Herbert von, 250

Blunt, Wilfred Scawen, 211, 229

Boer War, 269, 272

Boudin, Mme, dancing mistress, 28

Boycott, Capt., 226

Bradlaugh, Charles, 223

Bright, John, 154, 224, 229

Brock, Mrs, nurse, 20, 28

Brown, John, 51, 126, 135, 158, 178–83, 192; death, 230–3

Bruce, Lady Augusta, 159

Bruce, Col., Governor to Prince of Wales, 166, 167

Buccleugh, Walter Francis Scott, 5th Duke of, 104

Buggin, Lady Cecilia, 13

Buller, General Sir Redvers, 269

Burghersh, Lord, 137

Burke, T.H., Under-Secretary for Ireland, 228

Canrobert, General, 143
Carlyle, Thomas, 37, 56, 248
Carnarvon, Lord, 214, 215, 242
Cavendish, Lord Frederick, 228
Cetewayo, Zulu king, 223
Chamberlain, Joseph, 224, 242, 246; and Ireland, 238, 243, 244, 257; Colonial Minister, 266
Charles of Leiningen, 11, 34, 35, 58
Charlotte, Princess of Wales, 11, 17
Chelmsford, Lord, 223
chloroform, 134
Christian of Schleswig-Holstein, 182, 199
Christian Victor of Schleswig Holstein, 273
Churchill, Lady, 158
Churchill, Lord Randolph, 224, 244, 245
Clarendon, Lord, 139, 186, 190
Clark, Dr (later Sir) James, 32, 40, 96, 101, 154, 197; and Lady F. Hastings, 62, 63-4, 75; at A's death, 159, 164, 166, 168
Clarke, Sir Charles, 64
Cobden, Richard, 103
Conroy, Sir John, 18, 22, 23-6, 28, 29; tries to make V take him as secretary, 32, 34, 35; at and after V's accession, 41, 44, 57; and Lady F. Hastings, 62; resigns, 74-5
Conyngham, Lady, 19, 20
Conyngham, Lord, Lord Chamberlain, 35-6, 47
Corn Laws, 103, 104, 105
Creevey, Thomas, diarist, 50
Crimean War, 136, 137-41, 143-4

Davidson, Randall: Dean of Windsor, 231-2; Bishop of Winchester, 274, 277
Davys, Rev. George, teaches V, 21
Derby, Lord (14th Earl): as Lord Stanley, 104, 105; Prime Minister (1852), 132, 133, (1858) 156-7, (1860) 190, 192; mentioned, 139, 186, 187
Derby, Lord (15th Earl): Foreign Secretary (1874), 214, 215; Colonial Secretary (1882), 229
Dilke, Sir Charles, 204, 206, 229, 238
Dillon, Miss, maid of honour, 50
Disraeli, Benjamin (later Lord Beaconsfield), 53, 103, 139, 176, 217; Chancellor of the Exchequer, (1852) 132, (1858) 190, 192; Prime Minister (1868), 192-4, 202; in opposition, 206; Prime Minister (1874), 208, 209-15, 220-1, 222; corresponds with V, 224; death, 225
Disraeli, Mrs, 132, 192
Duncan, Dr, 241

Edward, Prince, Duke of Kent: marriage, 11, 13-14; death, 14, 18; V pays debts of, 47, 57
(Albert) Edward, Prince of Wales (later Edward VII: 'Bertie'), 100, 123, 126, 153-4, 162, 163, 172; at A's death, 167, 168; travels, 175, 211; marriage, 176, 177; V and, 197-8,

203, 218, 222, 246; ill with typhoid, 206; at V's death, 274, 275, 280; as King, 265
Edward of Wales, Prince (Edward VIII), 260
Edwards, Sir Fleetwood, 263
Elizabeth II, 241
Elizabeth ('Ella') of Hesse, 201
Ernest, Prince, Duke of Cumberland, 13, 23-4, 38
Ernest of Hesse, 260
Ernest I of Saxe-Coburg Gotha, 66, 80
Ernest of Saxe-Coburg-Gotha, 32, 33, 76, 78, 80, 81; as Ernest II, 123, 158; death, 257
Ernest of Württemberg, 28
Esher, Lord, 272
Eugénie, Empress, 137, 141, 143, 155

Feodore of Leiningen, 11, 15, 25
Ferdinand of Portugal, 162
Ferdinand of Saxe-Coburg-Kohary, 28, 32
Fitzgerald, Hamilton, 64, 65
Fitzroy, Lord Charles, 188
Florschütz, Herr, tutor to Albert, 80
Forster, W.E., 228
Fowler, Sir Henry, 264
Fowler, William, portrait painter, 23
Francis Joseph, Emperor of Austria, 118
Francis Joseph of Battenberg, 242
Franco-Prussian War, 203-4
Frederick, Prince, Duke of York, 13
Frederick William, Crown Prince of Prussia ('Fritz'), 131, 204, 239; marriage to Princess Royal, 145-7, 150; death, 250

Gatacre, General Sir William, 269
George III, 13, 18, 60, 266
George IV: as Prince Regent, 13, 17; as King, 18, 51; and V, 19-20; death, 22
George, Prince, Duke of York (later George V), 201, 232, 253; marriage, 257, 261
George of Cambridge, 28, 33, 57; as 2nd Duke of Cambridge, 155, 211
George of Cumberland, Prince (later King of Hanover), 14, 33
Gibbs, F.W., tutor to Prince of Wales, 153
Gladstone, W.E., 133, 217; Chancellor of the Exchequer (1865), 185, 193; Prime Minister (1868), 194, 196; and V, 204-5, 206, 208; in opposition, denounces Turks, 211, 212, 213, and attacks Disraeli's foreign policy, 226-7; Prime Minister (1880), 222, 223, 228, 230, 234; and Ireland, 226-8, 238, 243-4, 257; and Gordon, 237, 238; Prime Minister, (1886) 243, 245, (1892) 256-7; resigns, 258-9; death, 269
Gladstone, Willie, 194
Gordon, General C.G., 235-8
Gortchakoff, Prince Alexander, 215
Goschen, G.J., 230, 242
Graham, Sir James, 68
Grant, John, ghillie, 123, 126, 131, 158, 179
Granville, Lord: Foreign Secretary, (1851-2)

118, 132, (1880) 224, 238, 239; Liberal leader, 221, 222

Great Exhibition (1851), 127, 131

Greville, Charles, diarist, 17, 60, 74, 83, 107, 138, 144; Clerk of the Privy Council, 38, 40, 47, 81

Grey, Lord (2nd Earl), 22

Grey, General Sir Charles, 158, 174, 204

haemophilia, 135

Halifax, Lord, 246

Hamilton, Lord George, 264

Harcourt, Sir William, 224, 230, 257, 261

Hartington, Lord (later 8th Duke of Devonshire), 221, 222; Secretary for India (1882), 224; Secretary for War (1882–5), 229, 235, 238, 239; and Ireland, 243, 244

Hastings, Lady Flora, 28, 58; illness of, 62–4, 65, 68, 70; death, 75

Hastings, Marquess of, 64, 65

Haynau, General, 117

Helen of Waldeck, 228

Helena, Princess ('Lenchen'), 105, 168; marriage, 190, 199, 200

Helps, Sir Arthur, Clerk to Privy Council, 175

Henry of Battenberg ('Liko'), 239, 240, 241; death, 265

Henry of Prussia, 201, 241

Heytesbury, Lord, 109

Hicks Pasha, 235

Hobhouse, Sir John, 47

Holland, Lady, 51, 60

Home, Col, 229

Howley, William, Archbishop of Canterbury, 29, 35–6, 40, 53, 56

income tax, 93, 208

Indian Mutiny, 155–6

Ireland: famine, 103, 109; disestablishment of Church, 194, 196; Gladstone and, 226–8, 238, 243–4, 257

Jenner, Dr (later Sir) William, 179, 185, 190, 205, 230; at A's death, 159, 164, 166, 167, 168

Jerome of Westphalia, 143

Kalomine, Alexandrina, 239

Karim, Abdul (the Munshi), 262–5

Kitchener, General Lord, 269

Kossuth, Lajos, 117, 118

Kruger, President, 266, 275

Landseer, Sir Edwin, 217

Lansdowne, Lord, 228, 256

Lees, Dr Cameron, 231, 232

Lehzen, Baroness Louise, 15; in V's girlhood, 20–1, 24, 25, 31, 36; Conroy and, 25, 34, 35; appointed Lady Attendant to V, 40, 47, 58, 60, 61; at Coronation, 56; and Lady F. Hastings, 62, 63, 65, 71, 75; after V's

marriage, 83; departure of, 93, 96, 97

Leopold, Prince, Duke of Albany, 134, 135, 158; V and, 200, 218–19, 225, 230; marriage, 228; death, 233

Leopold of Battenberg, 277

Leopold of Saxe-Coburg-Saalfeld: husband of Princess Charlotte, 11; King of the Belgians, 23, 29, 107; and V, 18, 22, 28, 29–31, 32, 33, 34, 40, 47, 177; and V's marriage, 66, 74, 76, 78; on birth of Princess Royal, 91; at A's death, 171; death, 178, 185, 193

Lieven, Princess, 17, 28, 67

Lilly, Mrs, midwife, 89, 106

Lister, Dr Joseph, 205

Liverpool, Lord, 35

Locock, Dr (later Sir) Charles, 88, 89

Löhlein, valet to A, 166

Longford, Lady, 97

Lorne, Marquess of (later 9th Duke of Argyll), 198–9, 241

Louis of Battenberg, 239, 280

Louis of Hesse-Darmstadt, 158, 239; death, 253

Louis Philippe of France, 101, 111

Louise, Princess, 112, 190; marriage, 198–9, 241

Louise of Orleans, Queen of the Belgians, 29, 31, 47

Louise of Saxe-Gotha-Altenburg, 80

Lyndhurst, Lord, 68

Lyttelton, Lady, 100

Lytton, Lady, 280

Macaulay, T.B., 97

Macdonald, Annie, wardrobe maid, 182

Mackenzie, Dr Morell, 250

Mahdi, the, 235, 236, 237; death, 238

Margaret of Connaught, Princess ('Daisy'), 241

Marie of Edinburgh, Princess, 253

Marie of Leiningen, 187

Marie Alexandrovna of Russia, Duchess of Edinburgh, 208

'Marlborough House set', 197

Martin, Sir Theodore, 185, 208, 211, 225

Martineau, Harriet, 57

Mary, Princess, Duchess of Gloucester, 20

May of Teck, Princess: engaged to Prince Albert Victor, 252, 253; marriage to Prince George, 257, 261, 264

Melbourne, Lord: Prime Minister (1835–41), 35, 37, 39, 40; and V, 32, 44–5, 47, 50–1, 58–60, 61; Duchess of Kent and, 44, 57–8; at Coronation, 53, 56; and Lady F. Hastings, 62, 64, 65, 68, 75; and V's marriage, 78–9, 81–2, 83, 86; and Ladies of Bedchamber, 67–8, 69, 70, 71, 74; and appointment of Regent, 89; out of office; continues to advise V, 92–3; death, 127

Mendelssohn, Felix, 150

Methuen, General Lord, 269
Mordaunt, Sir Charles, 211

Napoleon III of France, 118, 132, 150, 157, 204; visit of A to, 137; visits England, 141, 143, 155; Prince of Wales and, 153
Napoleon, Prince, 143
Nautet, Mme Charlotte, masseuse, 231, 233
Newcastle, Henry Pelham, 5th Duke of, 138
Nicholas I, Tsar of Russia, 118, 141
Nicholas, Tsarevitch, 260, 265
Nightingale, Florence, 139, 229
Normanby, Lady, 92
Northcote, Sir Stafford, 223
Northumberland, Duchess of, 22, 27

O'Connor, Feargus, 113
Orsini, Felice, 156
Otho, King of Greece, 116

Pacifico, Don David, 116
Paget, Lord Alfred, 168
Palmerston, Lord, 28, 39, 47; Foreign Secretary (1830), 104, 106, 107, 109, 115–18; dismissed, 118, 132; Home Secretary (1852), 133–4, 135; resigns, 136, 137, 138; Prime Minister (1856), 139, 154, 156, 167, 174, 176, 177; death, 178
Panmure, Lord, 140
Parnell, Charles Stewart, 224, 226, 228, 242, 243, 244; death, 252
Paxton, Joseph, 127
Pedro V, King of Portugal, 162, 164
Peel, Sir Robert, 28, 39, 67; and Ladies of Bedchamber, 67, 68, 69–71, 74, 92; Prime Minister (1841–6), 44, 92–3, 101, 103, 104, 105, 106; in opposition, 116; death, 127
Philip, Prince, Duke of Edinburgh, 241
Phipps, Sir Charles, 167, 179
Phipps, Harriet, 264
Ponsonby, Arthur, 232
Ponsonby, Sir Henry, 178, 204, 205, 206, 209, 213, 242–3, 252; and John Brown, 231, 233; and Jubilee, 244, 250; death, 260, 261, 263
Portman, Lady, 63, 64
Powell, Sir R. Douglas, 277
Primrose Day, 245

Reid, Dr (later Sir) James, 230, 262, 277
Richmond, George, portrait painter, 217
Roberts, General Lord, 269
Roebuck, John Arthur, 138
Rolle, Lord, at Coronation, 56
Rosebery, Lord, 221, 243, 246; Prime Minister (1894), 259–60, 261, 264
Rowton, Lord, 224, 225, 230, 252
Russell, Lord John, 67, 136, 138; fails to form government (1845), 104, 105; Prime Minister (1846), 107, 109, 111, 114, 115, 117, 119, 132; resigns from Aberdeen's government (1855), 138; as Earl Russell, Prime

Minister (1865), 174, 177, 185, 186, 187, 190
Russo-Turkish War (1877–8), 213–15

Sahl, Hermann, librarian, 204
St Laurent, Julie de, 11
Salisbury, Lord: Foreign Secretary (1875), 215; in opposition, 237; Prime Minister (1885–6), 242; after resignation, V continues to correspond with, 93, 243, 244; Prime Minister (1886), 251, 256, 258, 261, 265, 269
Schouvaloff, Count Peter, 215
Scott, Sir Walter, 21, 101
Seymour, Francis, 168
Shaftesbury, Lord, 213; as Lord Ashley, 69
Siebold, Fräulein, midwife, 15
Sigismund ('Siggie') of Prussia, 190
Smiles, Samuel, 127
Snow, Dr John, 134
Sophia, Princess, 25
Southey, Mrs, 90
Späth, Baron and Baroness, 25
spiritualism, 155, 182–3t
Stephenson, Sir Benjamin, 35
Stockmar, Baron, 35, 37, 40, 41, 44; and V, 45, 58, 71, 93, 96, 106; draws up memorandum to Palmerston, 116–17; and A, 158, 162; death, 172
Stopford, Horatia, 224
Stopford, Lady Mary, 58
Suez Canal, 211–12
Sutherland, Duchess of, 46, 59, 92, 171

Tait, Archibald, Archbishop of Canterbury, 210
Tennyson, Alfred, 231
Torrington, Lord, 82, 162
Transvaal, 226, 269
Trevelyan, Sir G.O., 243
Tryon, Admiral Sir George, 258

Victor Emmanuel II of Italy, 144, 153
Victoria, Queen: birth, 14; childhood, 15, 17, 19–21; collection of dolls, 21, 25; education, 21, 22, 27–8, 97; tours, 26–7, 29; her diary, 27, 29, 37, 40; her dog Dash, 28, 33, 47, 56, 91; possible husbands, 28, 32–3; meets Leopold and Louise of Belgium, 29–31; has typhoid, 31; refuses to take Conroy as her secretary, 32, 34, 35; accession, 35–41; chooses household, 46; her finances, 47; coronation, 50–6; her hot temper, 20, 51, 60, 87, 96, 97; disenchantment sets in, 57–61; and prospect of marriage, 66, 74; and Lady F. Hastings, 62, 64, 65, 75; and Ladies of the Bedchamber, 67–71, 74; engagement, 76–82; wedding, 82–5; early days of marriage, 86–8; attempts on her life, 88–9, 114; birth of Princess Royal, 89–91, and of other children, 100, 105, 112,

127, 134–5, 147; and departure of Lehzen, 93, 96, 97; 'in a safe haven', 98, 100–6; at Osborne, 101, 113, 120, 123, 126; at Balmoral, 115, 123, 126; Princess Royal's marriage, 145–7, 150; letters to Princess Royal, 150–2, 201, 219; and death of her mother, 159, 161–2; and illness and death of A, 162–4, 166–8, 172; memorials to A, 171–2, 193; mourning for A, 172, 174, 175; marriages of her children, 176, 178, 198–9, 208, 228; her relations with her children, 197–201; and John Brown, 178–83, 231–3; *Leaves from the Journal*, 201–2, 211; illness, 205–6; Prince of Wales's illness, 206; *More Leaves*, 231, 233; Jubilee, 246–50; longest reign, 266; Diamond Jubilee, 266–7, 269; illness and death, 273–7; funeral, 277, 280;

her relation with her ministers: Melbourne, 44–5, 47, 50–1, 58, 92–3; Palmerston, 107, 115–19, 133–4; Russell, 107, 185; Granville, 132; Derby, 132, 133; Disraeli, 132, 191, 192–4, 196, 209–15, 225; Gladstone, 194, 196, 222, 223–4, 234, 242–4, 256–9;

and home affairs; social questions, 45, 103, 109, 113–14, 234; 1851 Exhibition, 127, 131; consents to open Parliament again, (1866) 185, (1877) 213, (1886) 242; republican feeling, 204–5; women's rights, 208; Public Worship Bill, 210;

and overseas affairs: Egypt, 107, 214, 228–9, 235, 238; Ireland, 109, 194, 196, 226, 237, 242–4; 1848 revolutions, 111–12; Sicily and Greece, 116; France, 118, 132, 142–3, 155, 156; Russia and Turkey, 135–41, 211, 202–14; India, 155–7, 210–11; Prussia, 176–7, 187, 190, 203–4; South Africa, 214, 216, 226, 269, 272, 273

Victoria, Princess Royal ('Vicky'), 89–90, 91, 93, 126, 135; marriage, 145–7, 150; V's letters to, 150–2, 201, 219; V and, 158, 174, 176, 190, 194, 198, 200, 214; as Empress Frederick, 250, 251, 273

Victoria of Prussia ('Moretta'), 239, 252

Victoria of Hesse, 201, 239, 241

Victoria of Saxe-Coburg, Princess of Leiningen, Duchess of Kent, 13–14, 17, 19; question of Regency for, 22, 34; and Conroy, 24, 33, 46, 57; and V, 24, 25, 26, 28, 29; at accession of V, 36, 40, 41; relations with V, 46, 51, 57–8, 66, 75; at Coronation, 53; and Lady F. Hastings, 64, 65; and V's marriage, 78, 79, 82, 83, 91; at Windsor, 158; death 159

Victoria Melita of Edinburgh, Princess ('Ducky'), 260

Victoire of Saxe-Coburg-Kohary, Duchess of Nemours, 111

Ward, Lord, at Coronation, 53, 56

Watson, Dr, and A's illness, 167, 168

Wellesley, G. V., Dean of Windsor, 168

Wellington, Arthur Wellesley, Duke of, 35, 39, 67, 105; and Duchess of Kent, 22, 24; and Lady F. Hastings, 65; and Ladies of Bedchamber, 68, 69, 71; and Conroy, 74; death, 133

Westminster, Lady, 176

William IV: as Duke of Clarence, 13; and Conroy, 23; illegitimate children of, 25; and V, 29, 32, 33, 35; death, 35

William, Crown Prince of Prussia, 101, 127; King and Emperor, 204, 211

William of Prussia, 152, 176, 201, 219, 241; as Emperor William II, 251, 260, 266; at V's death, 274, 275, 280

William Frederick, Prince, Duke of Gloucester ('Silly Billy'), 25

Wolseley, General Sir Garnet, 229, 237, 269

Zulu War, 220, 223